MW00355853

Malte Liesner
Latin Historical Phonology Workbook

Reichert Verlag Wiesbaden 2014

Latin Historical Phonology Workbook

Malte Liesner

Reichert Verlag Wiesbaden 2014

Bibliografische Information der Deutschen Nationalbibliothek

Die Deutsche Nationalbibliothek verzeichnet diese Publikation in der Deutschen Nationalbibliografie; detaillierte bibliografische Daten sind im Internet über http://dnb.dnb.de abrufbar.

© 2014 Dr. Ludwig Reichert Verlag Wiesbaden
ISBN: 978-3-95490-022-0
www.reichert-verlag.de
Das Werk einschließlich aller seiner Teile ist urheberrechtlich geschützt.
Jede Verwertung außerhalb der engen Grenzen des Urheberrechtsgesetzes
ist ohne Zustimmung des Verlages unzulässig und strafbar.
Das gilt insbesondere für Vervielfältigungen, Übersetzungen, Mikroverfilmungen
und die Speicherung und Verarbeitung in elektronischen Systemen.
Printed in Germany

Preface

When I was younger, I always wanted to be a poet. During my time at the university in Würzburg and Cologne, I wrote a lot of poems, many of which were published in magazines and anthologies. Poems express something that is beyond words, something that cannot be said but only felt and imagined. Now, I am writing books about historical phonology, and in some way this science has become my poetry. To me, the chains of derivations, which lead from unattested reconstructed word forms to the oldest languages of the world, express more than just language change.

> Language is a ford through the river of time
> It leads us to the dwelling of those gone ahead
> But he does not arrive there
> Who is afraid of deep water
> *Wladislaw Markowitsch Illitsch-Switytsch* (1934–1966)

I am deeply thankful to Gwain Hamilton (Montreal) who proofread parts of the English version amidst a busy work and family life and helped me with any questions I had concerning style and grammar. Thank you, Gwain! I know what it's like to raise children and support a family these days. Furthermore, the comments from Michiel de Vaan (Leiden) and Tiziana Quadrio (Würzburg), who both read the German version after its publication, helped a lot to improve the text. In this English edition, I have also corrected all the errors mentioned in the reviews by Todd Clary (Montreal), Matthew Scarborough (Cambridge), Harald Bichlmeier (Jena) and Nicholas Zair (Cambridge), who also helped me with questions regarding chapter 38. Finally, Michael Weiss (Cornell) kindly answered all my questions about the translation of technical terms.

One of my teachers at the university in Würzburg once said that Indo-European linguistics has already seen its greatest days. All of the major sound laws have been found and what is left is to refine them. I strongly believe that the greatest days of Indo-European linguistics are still to come. When data from all the word's languages will have been unified enough to prove the existence of macrofamilies, it will be crystal clear that we all come from a common source, that we all have a common origin, and that we humans are one and share the same past as we will share our future on this planet together.

Königsberg, Germany. January 2014   Malte Liesner

Contents

Developments of Latin Consonants

1   Latin in Space and Time

Latin belongs to the Italic branch of the Indo-European (IE) language family, which is one of the world's major language families and consists of several hundred languages and dialects. At first, the spread of Latin was limited to Rome and the rural areas surrounding Rome. It was not until the political rise of the city of Rome in the first and second centuries AD that Latin spread over vast parts of Europe, within which even today the Romance languages "the direct descendants of Latin" are spoken. Two other representatives of the Italic language branch were Oscan, spoken in southern Italy, and Umbrian, spoken in northern Italy. Appendix 5 presents an overview of the Indo-European, Italic and Romance languages. The IE languages exhibit systematic correspondences in grammar and vocabulary which enable to reconstruct a common proto-language out of which the individual IE language branches evolved. This proto-language, known as Proto-Indo-European (PIE), is not attested in writing but only reconstructed by the systematic comparison of correspondences within the Indo-European languages.

● Synchronic and diachronic approach to language study

A study of texts of a certain era, such as Classical Latin, invariably includes an analysis of the synchronic stage of the language system. It is likewise possible to study the linguistic changes that have led to a certain language system or developed it further. The study of these changes in words and categories is known as the diachronic approach. The structure of Latin around 700 BC differed from its structure in 100 BC even as it differs from today's Romance languages because languages are subject to constant change. These developments can be modeled systematically and regularly up to a certain point. This book deals with the developments from PIE to Latin as well as developments within Latin itself. Firstly, those changes will be examined which can be deduced from Latin itself before dealing with the undocumented prehistory, which can only be deduced by comparing Latin with other IE languages.

● Diachronic periodization of Latin language history

The history of Latin is traditionally divided into the following stages, which exhibit characteristic phonological features that are summarized in appendix 4.

Early Latin (EL)	ca. 700 BC – ca. 240 BC	Start of inscriptional attestation
Old Latin (OL)	ca. 240 BC – ca. 100 BC	Start of literary attestation
Classical Latin (CL)	ca. 100 BC – ca. 14 AD	Standardization of Latin grammar
Post-classical Latin	ca. 14 AD – ca. 200 AD	First deviations from the standard

Early Latin (EL) is the oldest language stage attested by inscriptions that often differ considerably from Classical Latin (CL). This can be illustrated by the two EL forms *dᵤenos* and *ioᵤksmenta*, which developed to CL *bonus* 'good' and *iūmenta* 'draft animals'. The amount of significant linguistic data that we possess for this preliterary language stage is, however, so scant that we can reconstruct only the barest of pictures of the language system extant at that time.

The onset of the literary activity of Livius Andronicus, a Greek who wrote in Latin, can be regarded as the starting point of the next language stage, known as Old Latin (OL). Other representatives of that time include Plautus, Ennius and Cato. Already the works of the comedy playwright Plautus exhibit many features of the common speech known as Vulgar Latin, e.g. the use of intensive and diminutive forms, the use of the negated command with *nē*, and indirect questions employing the indicative instead of the subjunctive, all of which were not permitted in CL. The next language stage, that of Classical Latin, was strongly influenced by the language of Cicero, Vergil and Horace and started around 100 BC. One of its main features was a heavy standardization in opposition to Old

Latin and Vulgar Latin. Word choice, sentence structure and pronunciation of CL differed greatly from the common speech. From the time of Augustus's death at around the year 14 AD until around 200 AD, one speaks of post-classical Latin, the most known representatives of which include Seneca, Pliny and Tacitus.

- ## Language is a multi-layer system of different registers

A language is not a uniform structure but consists rather of numerous heterogeneous groups of speakers speaking different variant forms of the same language. The Latin spoken in Rome was known as *sermo urbanus*, in contrast to rural Latin, which was called *sermo rusticus* and employed such forms as *Clōdius* and *prēndō* for the standard *Claudius* and *prehendō*. This variation among the speakers of one language is known as a **dialect** or **diatopic difference**. A community of speakers can be further divided into subgroups sharing similar occupations or age. The characteristic use of language of such a subgroup is known as a **sociolect** or **diastratic difference**. Examples include the language of soldiers, known as *sermo militaris*, or the language of lower social status, known to the upper class as *sermo plebeius* or *sermo vulgaris*. Be it consciously or unconsciously, every person adapts his or her language style to the requirements of the situation. Cicero's speeches delivered before the senate do not give an insight into the normal conversation at a market fish stand. The Latin term *sermo familiaris* designated the style of language employed when speaking to familiar persons and the term *sermo cotidianus* designated everyday language. These differences of language usage are called **diaphasic differences** (cf. Müller-Lancé 2006:52–58).

- ## Classical Latin (CL) and Vulgar Latin (VL)

The usage of diatopic, diastratic and diaphasic registers of a language may change and overlap over a period of time. In classical times, the educated speech was equated with the *sermo urbanus*, and the uneducated speech was equated with the *sermo rusticus* regardless of where the speaker came from. The diatopic contrast shifted to a diastratic contrast. When even educated speakers like the patrician Publius Claudius, by calling himself Clōdius, adapted to the everyday language of the common people, the contrast shifted from diastratic to diaphasic. The commonly spoken language of everyday life is called Vulgar Latin (VL), in contrast to the written language of Classical Latin (CL), which is mainly represented by Cicero's writings. Furthermore, in this book the term VL is phonologically defined by starting from CL because already in classical times VL showed a stronger tendency to integrate the phonological features illustrated in appendix 4 into its language system. The given sound change numbers (SCN) refer to the index of the book in which all phonological changes are enumerated.

2   Spelling and Pronunciation

In this world, numerous ways of writing down human languages are found. The graphical visualization of a human sound or a combination of sounds is called a grapheme. In English, the grapheme {c} or {C} is commonly used to denote a voiceless dorsal stop such as in *college* or *combination*, whereas this sound is represented in India by the symbol {क} and in Arabic by the symbol {ك}. Graphemes are arbitrary symbols for human language sounds and are most commonly written by linguists in <angle> brackets. In this book, however, graphemes are surrounded by {curly} brackets in order to avoid confusions with the derivational operator sign >. During the literary era of Latin, the following array of graphemes, commonly known as an alphabet, were used {A B C D E F G H I K L M N O P Q R S T V X Y Z}. For better legibility, these capital letters are rendered by their corresponding lower case characters. Furthermore, {V} is written {u}.

- ## Correlation of grapheme and represented sound

The correlation of a grapheme to the sound it represents is not always clear. The Latin sound /k/ was written by the three different graphemes {c}, {k} and {q} depending on whether the vowel following was /e/ and /i/, /a/ or /u/. On the other hand, a grapheme can be used to represent several sounds. Just as in English, the Latin grapheme {l} was used to represent either a 'light' /l/, such as in *language*, or a 'dark' [ł], such as in *milk*. The Latin grapheme {x} even symbolized the sequence /ks/, which consisted. The use of slashes and squared brackets for representing /l/, /e/, /ks/ and [ł] are explained in unit 4.

- ## Semiphonetic transcription of graphemes

This book is strict in its separation of spelling and pronuciation. To preprocess Latin words for sound change derivations in which one sign is used to represent one defined sound, one must derive the pronuciation from the spelling. As we are not aware of the actual pronunciation of Latin because we do not have any voice recordings, the analysis must necessarily be a model of Latin pronunciation. A good overview of the reconstructed Latin pronunciation is given by Allen 1978.
The following transformations must be carried out: **1.** The graphemes {c}, {x} and {qu} stand for /k/, /ks/ and /ku̯/. **2.** {i} and {u} stand for /i̯/ and /u̯/ if they do not form the nucleus of a syllable, in which case they stand for /i/ and /u/. Therefore, *u̯ertō* is transcribed instead of *verto* and *i̯am* is transcribed instead of *iam*. /u̯/ corresponds to the {v} of standard Latin texts. This transcription is necessary because /v/ is phonologically used to represent a labiodental fricative such as in the English *vase* and not the labiovelar approximant /u̯/ found in Latin and in the English *wet*. **3.** {n} before {g} or {k} must be transcribed with velar [ŋ]. **4.** {l} before the vowels /a/, /o/, /u/, before consonants and in the final position is represented by [ł]. **5.** A single {i} between vowels represents geminate /i̯i̯/.

- ## Macrons must be added to mark long vowels

Latin spelling does not indicate whether a vowel is short or long. The grapheme sequence {parere} could represent *parere* 'to generate' or *parēre* 'to appear', {legit} could stand for *legit* 'he reads' as well as for perf. *lēgit* 'he read' and {regeris} could stand for *regeris* 'you are governed' or *regēris* 'you will be governed'. Vowel length must be indicated with a macron above the vowel because the semantics of Latin words can change according to vowel length.

Exercises

E1 Transcribe /k/ for {c} in the following verbs and add macrons for long vowels.

{carpo}	*karpō*	'I pluck'		{tracto}	trakto	'I drag'
— {deleo}	dɛlẽo	'I destroy'		{rego}	rɛgo	'I govern'
{exerceo}	ɛksɛrkẽo	'I work'		{arceo}	arkẽo	'I enclose'

E2 Transcribe /u̯/ for {u} if it is the semivowel /u̯/ and not the vowel /u/.
The sequence {qu} is transcribed /ku̯/, the grapheme {x} is transcribed /ks/.

{ualide}	*u̯alidē*	'very'		{oblitus}	oblitus	'forgotten'
{uerto}	u̯ɛrto	'I turn'		{quid}	ku̯id	'what?'
{coquo}	koku̯o	'I cook'		{uiuus}	u̯iu̯us	'alive'
{quippe}	ku̯ippɛ	'of course'		{dexter}	dɛkstɛr	'right'
{obliuiscor}	obliu̯iskor	'I forget'				

E3 Transcribe the grapheme {l} as 'normal' /l/ before /i/ and as 'dark' [ɫ] in all other positions.

{exilium}	*eksilium*	'exil'	::	{exulare}	*eksuɫāre*	'to be banished'
{simul}	simuɫ	'at once'	::	{similis}	similis	'similar'
{familia}	familia	'family'	::	{famulus}	famuɫus	'servant'
{sepelio}	sɛpɛlio	'I bury'	::	{sepultus}	sɛpuɫtus	'buried'

E4 {n} is transcribed [ŋ] before {g} or {k}.

{iungo}	*iuŋgō*	'I join'		{tango}	taŋgo	I touch'
{frango}	fraŋgo	'I break'				

E5 The non-syllabic element /i̯/ and /u̯/ of diphthongs is transcribed with a semicircle beneath.

OL {sibei} *sibei̯* '-self' {iuuenis} i̯uu̯ɛnis 'young' {laudare} lau̯dārɛ 'to praise'

E6 Intervocalic {i} such as in {cuius} was geminate /i̯i̯/.

{cuius} *ku̯i̯i̯us* 'whose?' {peior} pɛi̯i̯or 'worse' {maior} mai̯i̯or 'bigger'

{aio} ai̯i̯o 'I say'

3 The Place of Articulation

● **Where in the mouth are language sounds formed?**

This book describes the sound changes within the Latin language, and therefore we must familiarize ourselves with some methods of describing sounds. The sounds of human languages are classified according to two fundamental variables: their place of articulation and their manner of articulation. The location at which a sound is produced inside the mouth is known as the **place of articulation**, and the way the sound is produced is known as the **manner of articulation**. Say aloud the words *cool* and *kinship* and pay attention to the position of the tongue while articulating the two initial k-sounds. Do the same for the word-pair *interest* and *think*, and pay attention to the position of the tongue while articulating the two nasal sounds written {n}. Do not go on reading before doing this exercise.

The {c} in *cool* is a velar /k/ and is articulated further back in the mouth than the palatal /k̂/ in *kinship*. That is because the k-sound adapts to the place of articulation of the vowel that follows. The /u/ written {oo} in *cool* is a back or velar vowel, and the /i/ in *kinship* is a front or palatal vowel. Also, the {n} in *think* is articulated further back than the first {n} in *interesting* because the nasal adapts to the place of articulation of the consonant following. The {k} in *think* is a velar /k/, whereas the first {t} in *interest* is an alveolar /t/, and that is why the n-sound in *think* is a velar n-sound and the n-sound in *interest* is an alveolar n-sound. These two n-sounds are written with the same grapheme {n} in English and Latin, but linguists use the symbol [ŋ] to refer to the velar nasal in order to avoid confusion. This is also the reason for the transcription *i̯uŋgō* for {iungo} 'I join' introduced in unit 2.

● **The following illustration shows the places of articulation which are important for this book.**

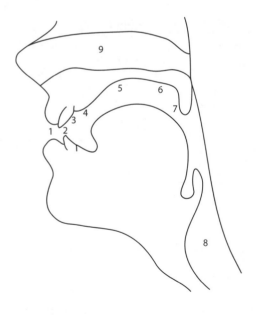

	Place	Description
1	labial	The lips
1/2	labiodental	Lower lip and incisors
2	interdental	Between the teeth
3	dental	The teeth
4	alveolar	The teeth-ridge
5	palatal	The hard palate
6	velar	The soft palate
7	uvular	The uvula
8	glottal	The vocal folds
9	nasal	The nasal cavity

The Manner of Articulation

● **Different sounds are produced at the same place of articulation**

Touch your larynx with your fingers. Now pronounce the s-sound in *silver* and draw out the sound. Repeat this exercise with the word *reason*, also with a long {s}. What do you notice? What is the difference between the s-sound in *silver* and the s-sound in *reason*? Do not go on reading before thinking about this for a moment.

You can noticeably feel your throat vibrating while articulating the s-sound in *reason*, whereas no vibration accompanies the articulation of the s-sound in *silver*. That is why the s-sound in *reason* is classified as voiced and noted [z] to distinguish it from the voiceless /s/ in *silver*. Both sounds are written with the same grapheme {s} in English. /s/ and [z] are articulated at the same place of articulation but differ in their manner of articulation. Therefore, sounds are not only classified according to their place but also according to their manner of articulation. The following table lists the manners of articulation which are relevant for this book.

Manner of articulation	Description
Consonant and vowel	Consonants are articulated with a complete or partial closure of the vocal tract, in contrast to vowels which are articulated with an open vocal tract.
Stop / Plosive	A complete closure of the vocal tract causes the airflow to stop. When this closure is opened, air escapes rapidly and the sounds /k/, /t/, /p/ or /g/, /d/, /b/ are produced depending on the position of the tongue. Stop consonants are also called plosive consonants.
Nasal	Air is exhaled partially or completely through the nose. According to the position of the tongue, a velar nasal [ŋ] like in *iuŋgō* 'I join', a dental nasal /n/ like in *teneō* 'I hold', or a labial nasal /m/ like in *moneō* 'I admonish' is formed.
Continuant	The continuants /r/, /l/, /m/, /n/, /f/, /s/, /u̯/, /i̯/ may be articulated for a longer period of time.
Fricative	A partial closure of the vocal tract causes the articulation of fricative consonants like /s/ or /f/. Fricatives are also called spirants or stridents.
Lateral	Alveolar /l/ and its velar variant [ɫ] are lateral sounds. The airstream escapes along the sides of the tongue while the tongue blocks the airstream in the middle.
Voiced	While articulating a vowel, a nasal, or /b/, /d/, /g/, /u̯/, /i̯/, /r/, /l/, [ɫ], [z], the vocal cords vibrate and cause a sonorous sound. All other sounds are voiceless.
Trill	A characteristic feature of Latin and Spanish is the alveolar trill consonant /r/, which is articulated while the tongue vibrates against the teeth-ridge.
Approximant	The approximant consonants /u̯/ and /i̯/ are also called semivowels because they have an intermediate position between vowels and fricative consonants.
Velarization	'Dark' [ɫ] and /u̯/ were articulated with an additional raising of the tongue against the soft palate. This coarticulation is called velarization.

4   Phonemes, Phones and Allophones

The human speech organs enable us to produce a broad variety of sounds of which every language uses only a small part to distinguish words. This choice of possible sounds is called the **phoneme inventory** of a language. The sounds which are used to differentiate words are called **phonemes**. Many languages possess a phoneme inventory of about 30 to 40 phonemes; there are, however, languages with extremely few or many phonemes. The language of the Pirahã-tribe in the Amazone region of Brasil counts only 10 to 13 phonemes, according to the classification scheme used. The Khoisan language !Xoõ, which is spoken in Botswana and Namibia, has more than 150 phonemes. Depending on the classification scheme used, Latin has between 25 and 28 phonemes, of which 10 are vowels.

● **Minimal pairs and oppositions**

In this book, a practical and simple **definition of the term phoneme** is used: if it is possible to change the meaning of a word by exchanging one sound with another, such as in *sīdus* 'star' and *nīdus* 'nest', then both the exchanged and the newly inserted sound are called phonemes of that language. Both phonemes are said to form an opposition in the phonological system of the language. If two words differ in meaning only by the contrast of one phoneme, they constitute a minimal pair.

● **Phones are the actual realizations of abstract phonemes**

In English, there exist regional variations of the pronunciation of the phoneme /r/. Depending on the dialect, /r/ can be articulated as an alveolar approximant [ɹ], as a postalveolar or retroflex approximant [ɻ], as a labiodental approximant [ʋ], as an alveolar flap [ɾ], or as an alveolar trill [r] (notation according to IPA). Each of these realizations of r-sounds is called a phone of the phoneme /r/. A phone is the concrete pronunciation of an abstract phoneme that can change the meaning of a word and constitutes a unit within the phoneme system of the language. Phones are not phonemes because by changing one of the r-sounds in a word, e.g. the English *for* pronounced as [fɔr] or [fɔɹ] or [fɔɻ], one does not change the meaning. Phonemes are written in /slashes/, while their corresponding phones are written in [square] brackets.

[r]   [ɹ]

/r/

[ʋ]   [ɾ]

The English phoneme /r/
and some of its allophones.

● **Allophones are variant phones of a phoneme**

Phones that are assigned to the same phoneme are called **allophones**. All of the above mentioned phones of the phoneme /r/ are allophones. The Latin phoneme /l/ had the two complementarily distributed allophones [l] ~ [ł] (cf. unit 5). In this book, the correlation /l/ :: [l] ~ [ł], which means that the phoneme /l/ had the two realizations [l] and [ł], is simplified by saying that the phoneme /l/ had a velar allophone [ł]. Instead of the correlation /s/ :: [s] ~ [z], it is said that the phoneme /s/ had an allophone [z].

Defining Latin Consonant Phonemes

Search for minimal pairs in the following jumbled list and insert them at the correct position in the table. Then cross out the words in the list. Some words in the list appear twice.

---

serō 'I join', *rapiō* 'I snatch', *tōtus* 'whole', *rēks* {rex} 'king', *nīdus* 'nest', *mōns* 'mountain', *lōtus* 'washed', *seku̯ī* {sequi} 'to follow', *lūmen* 'light', *lēks* {lex} 'law', *terō* 'I rub', *sum* 'I am', *kapiō* {capio} 'I grasp', *mōs* 'habit', *tam* 'there', *kūr* {cur} 'why?', *terō* 'I rub', *niger* 'black', *sub* 'under', *nūmen* 'nod', dat./abl. sg. *hortō* 'garden', 1. ps. perf. *sekuī* {secui} 'I cut', *sīdus* 'star', *fūr* 'thief', *hortus* 'garden', *pōns* 'bridge', *tam* 'there', *a̯nnus* {agnus} 'lamb', *ortus* 'originated', *nam* 'for', *piger* 'lazy', *dōs* 'gift', *portō* 'I carry', *u̯īu̯us* {uiuus} 'alive', *u̯īsus* {uisus} 'seen', *i̯am* {iam} 'already', *annus* 'year', *ferō* 'I carry'

Opposition	Minimal Pair
s :: t	*serō* :: *terō*
s :: n	
u̯ :: u	*seku̯ī* {sequi} :: *sekuī* {secui}
l :: t	
n :: l	
n :: t	
l :: r	
p :: h	
n :: p	
h :: Ø	*hortus* ::
d :: m	
r :: k {c}	
f :: t	
p :: m	
k :: f	
n :: ŋ	*annus* :: *aŋnus* {agnus}
b :: m	
u̯ :: s	
i̯ :: t	

⇦ The Latin continuation of the PIE labiovelars */kʷ/ and */gʷ/ are the phoneme combinations /ku̯/ and /gu̯/ because there are not enough minimal pairs to corroborate the status of /kʷ/ and /gʷ/ as individual phonemes. Furthermore, the minimal pairs can be interpreted as showing the opposition /u̯/ :: /u/ (cf. unit 33).

⇨ Only the educated language of the upper class contrasted initial /h/ with words that began with a vowel. The common speech had already lost initial /h/ by the 4ᵗʰ century BC.

⇦ {g} was pronounced [ŋ] before {n} (cf. unit 23). The phonemic status of [ŋ] is disputed because of the absence of convincing examples of oppositions.

5   Feature Structures of Latin Consonants

By using the classification of place and manner of articulation, all the sounds of a language can be unambiguously described. The Latin phoneme /b/ is a voiced labial stop which can be noted in abstract linguistic notation as: b [+stop, +labial, +voiced]. The enumeration of phonological features that describe a sound is called the feature structure of the sound. The following table lists all the features of Latin consonant phonemes with their main allophones.

	Labial				Labio-dental	Dental					Alve-olar		Pala-tal	Velar				Glot-tal
	p	b	m	u̯	f	s	[z]	t	d	n	l	r	i̯	k	g	[ŋ]	[ɫ]	h
Stop	+	+	-	-		-	-	+	+	-	-	-	-	+	+	-	-	-
Nasal	-	-	+	-		-	-	-	-	+	-	-		-	-	+	-	-
Continuant	-	-	+	+	+	+	+	-	-	+	+	+	+	-	-	+	+	-
Fricative	-	-	-	-	+	+	+	-	-	-	-	-		-	-	-	-	+
Lateral	-	-	-	-		-	-	-	-	-	+	-		-	-	-	+	-
Voiced	-	+	+	+	-		-	+	-	+	+	+	+	+	-	+	+	+	-
Approxim.	-	-	-	+		-	-	-	-	-	-	-	+	-	-	-	-	-
Trill	-	-	-	-		-	-	-	-	-	-	+		-	-	-	-	-
Velarized	-	-	-	+		-	-	-	-	-	-	-		-	-	+	+	-

● **Additional remarks for individual sounds**

- The nasal /n/ had an allophone [ŋ] before velar /g/ and /k/. [ŋ] can also be the result of the assimilation of /g/ before a nasal consonant (SCN 17.5). /m/ is an individual phoneme but it can also be an allophone of /n/ before /b/ or /p/. Nasals always assimilate to the place of articulation of the consonant following.
- The lateral sound /l/ had a velar allophone [ɫ] before /a/, /o/, /u/, in the final position and before a consonant if the consonant was not /l/ (SCN 28).
- The labial approximant /u̯/ had a velar coarticulation [u̯ᵞ] and could equally be classified as a labialized velar approximant.
- The voiceless fricative /s/ was voiceless in all positions. In voiced surroundings, it had the voiced allophone [z] (SCN 15), which was lost with compensatory lengthening of the preceding vowel (SCN 2.2), or by rhotazism, which is the development of [z] to /r/ (SCN 26).
- The Latin continuation of the PIE labiovelars */kʷ/ and */gʷ/ are considered to be sequences of the two phonemes /ku̯/ and /gu̯/, which is described by SCN x4. For more information see unit 33.
- The classification of /s/, [z], /t/, /d/, /n/ as dental sounds follows the analysis of Latin grammarians found in Sturtevant 1940. These sounds could also have been alveolar sounds.
- The Romance languages do not show any traces of the phoneme /h/ because it was lost early in all positions. Only upper-class society continued to use this sound, albeit artificially (cf. SCN x6.9c and SCN x8.12c).

Exercises

E1 Add the features of the consonants. Start with the place of articulation.

b [+   labial,   +   stop   , +   voiced   ]   **p** [+_____ , +_____]

d [+_____ , +_____ , +_____]   **t** [+_____ , +_____]

r [+_____ , +_____ , +_____ , +_____]

n [+_____ , +_____ , +_____ , +_____]

E2 Which consonants are represented by the feature structures?

___ [+palatal, +continuant, +voiced, +approximant]

___ [+labial, + continuant, +voiced, +approximant, +velarized]

___ [+glottal, +fricative]   ___ [+labiodental, +continuant, +fricative]

E3 Which feature separates the allophonic pairs?

1. **n** [+dental, +nasal, + continuant, +voiced]   ::   **ŋ** [+velar, +nasal, +continuant, +voiced]

2. **l** [+alveolar, + continuant, +lateral, +voiced] :: **ł** [+velar, +continuant, +lateral, +voiced]

Answer: _____

COVER-SYMBOLS

Upper case cover symbols help to group together sounds that exhibit similar features. This can be quite useful when sound change rules do not apply only to single sounds but to all sounds that exhibit similar features. A cover symbol stands for whatever element of the group described by the cover symbol. In this book, the following cover symbols are used:

C = (p, t, k, b, d, g, m, n, ŋ, r, l, ł, f, s, z, h, i̯, u̯) is used for a random consonant.

G = (b, d, g, m, n, ŋ, r, l, ł, z, i̯, u̯) is used for a random voiced consonant.

D = (b, d, g) is used for a random voiced stop.

T = (p, t, k) is used for a random voiceless stop.

P = (p, b, m, u̯, f) is used for a random labial or labiodental consonant.

N = (n, ŋ, m) is used for a random nasal.

R = (r, l) is used for a sonant.

The term sonant groups together the lateral sound /l/ as well as the rhotic sound /r/.

V = (a, e, i, o, u, ā, ē, ī, ō, ū) is used for a random vowel.

V̄ = (ā, ē, ī, ō, ū) is used for a random long vowel.

V̆ = (a, e, i, o, u) is used for a random short vowel.

6 Latin Vowels and Diphthongs

● **Long and short vowels differed in their vowel height**

Like consonants, vowels too can be described in terms of place and manner of articulation. The position of a vowel in the mouth is described starting from the central position of the tongue while articulating the vowel /a/. By pushing the tongue forwards, the palatal, or front vowels, /e/ and /i/ are formed. By retracting the tongue backwards, the velar, or back vowels, /o/ and /u/ are formed, which are additionally characterized by the feature of roundedness. The central vowel /a/ can have a slightly more palatal or velar articulation and is usually said to have been a velar vowel in Latin. Latin long and short vowels did not differ only in quantity but also in quality, which is a common feature accompanying vowel length also found in other languages like German. The long vowels were slightly higher than their corresponding short vowels except for /a/ and /ā/, which did not differ in their quality. This means that a vowel pair like /u/ :: /ū/ as in the minimal pair *domus* [dɔmʊs] 'house' :: gen. sg. *domūs* [dɔmuːs] 'of the house', which is given on the next page, was not only differentiated by the feature of length but also by the fact that short /u/ was phonetically the vowel [ʊ], whereas long /ū/ was [uː], which is a similar but identical vowel. This difference of vowel height can be deduced from statements made by Latin grammarians and the subsequent development of the Latin vowel system in the Romance languages. The following diagram displays the tongue position on the horizontal axis and the vowel height on the vertical axis. IPA notation is given in square brackets.

● **Feature structures of Latin vowels**

		tongue position = place of articulation				
		front		**central**	**back**	
		long	short		long	short
vowel height	high	ī [iː]	i [ɪ]		ū [uː]	u [ʊ]
	high-mid	ē [eː]			ō [oː]	
	low-mid	(VL ẹ̄ [ɛː])	e [ɛ]		(VL ǭ [ɔː])	o [ɔ]
	low			a [a] / ā [aː]		

● **Additional remarks for individual sounds**

- Next to labials, /i/ was allophonically rounded to a sound like [y] or [ɨ], as in German *küssen* [kʰysn] 'to kiss' or the Rumanian *cârnat* [kɨrnat] 'sausage' (cf. SCN 8.5, SCN 8.6, SCN 9.12a, SCN 9.23). In this book, [y] is used. This rounded pronunciation can be reconstructed on the basis of statements made by Roman grammarians as well as variant spellings such as {optimus/optumus} and {artifex/artufex}, in which {u} and {i} are interchanged before labial sounds.

- The VL vowels /ẹ̄/ and /ǭ/ were the result of the monophthongization of /ae̯/ (SCN 10.7) and /au̯/ (SCN 10.1), and were distributed diatopically, diastratically and diaphasically. The non-urban population, speakers of lower social status, and speakers in informal speech situations appear to have preferred the monophthongized forms already in classical times. The use of the etymologically older diphthongs was restricted to the cultivated language of the upper class, to educated speakers, and to formal speech situations.

- ● Monophthong / Diphthong / Monophthongization

A single vowel is sometimes called a **monophthong** in order to differentiate it more clearly from two vowels within one syllable, known as a **diphthong**. Since a syllable can have only one vowel as its nucleus (cf. unit 7), the other vowel is weakened to one of the Latin semivowels /i̯/, /u̯/ and /e̯/, and transcribed with a semi-circle beneath. Already in CL times, there existed the monophthongized counterparts /ę̄/, /ǭ/, /ę̄/ of the CL diphthongs /ae̯/, /au̯/, /oe̯/. The development from a diphthong to a monophthong is known as **monophthongization**. This is one of the characteristics which separates Classical Latin from Old Latin on the one hand, and Classical Latin from Vulgar Latin on the other. These processes will be dealt with in detail in chapters 19 and 20. The sound change of monophthongization proceeds via a gradual assimilation of vowel and semivowel and ends with the subsequent contraction of the two elements forming a long vowel (cf. SCN 11).

- ● Compensatory lengthening

After a consonant has been lost, a **compensatory lengthening** of the preceding vowel might occur. This process can be illustrated with the word *īdem* {idem} 'the same', which is derived from *is* 'he' and can be traced back to *isdem*, which is also used by some authors. In this case, the /i/ was lengthened in order to compensate for the loss of /s/.

Defining Latin Vowel Phonemes

E1 Vowel length was a phonologically distinctive feature of Classical Latin. Search the following list for minimal pairs which differ only in vowel length, and transfer them into the table below. Cross out used words.

> ~~*mālus* 'apple tree'~~, *plaga* 'net', ~~*malus* 'bad'~~, ~~*latus* 'side'~~, *sōlum* 'alone', *plāga* 'hit', *regeris* 'you are governed', *turrīs* 'the towers', *ēs* 'you eat', *ōs* 'mouth', *lēu̯is* 'smooth', *es* 'you are', *regēris* 'you will be governed', *datis* 'you give', *turris* 'tower', *populus* 'people', *leu̯is* 'light', *lātus* 'carried', *līber* 'free', *domūs* 'of the house', *lūstrum* 'lustration', *datīs* dat. abl. pl. of *datus* 'given', *pōpulus* 'poplar', *os* 'bone', *solum* 'ground', *fugit* 'he flees', *liber* 'book', *domus* 'house', *lustrum* 'puddle', *fūgit* 'he has flown'

Opposition	Example 1	Example 2	Example 3
a :: ā	*malus :: mālus*	*latus ::*	
e :: ē			
i :: ī			
o :: ō			
u :: ū			

7   Syllabification of Latin Words

● **Syllable structure**

The phonemes of a language are organized into larger rhythmic patterns known as syllables. A syllable usually consists of a vocalic nucleus which accounts for the acoustic phase of the highest sonority within the syllable. Due to the loss of vowels, it is possible that nasals or liquids glide into the nucleus position (see unit 34). Syllable nuclei rarely consist of other consonants as for example the /s/ in German *Pssst* 'Be quiet!'. The syllable nucleus can be surrounded to the left by a consonantal syllable onset and to the right by a consonantal syllable offset, known as a coda. The first syllable of a word is called initial syllable, the last one final syllable, and the syllables in between are known as medial syllables. The following chart shows the words *pulmentum* 'relish of meat' and *urbs* 'city' according to their syllabic structure.

Initial syllable			Medial syllable			Final syllable		
Onset	Nucleus	Offset	Onset	Nucleus	Offset	Onset	Nucleus	Offset
p	*u*	*l*	*m*	*e*	*n*	*t*	*u*	*m*
	u	*rbs*						

● **Phonotactic structure of Latin words**

The structure of Latin syllables allows up to three consonants in the offset, such as in *striŋ.gō* {stringo} 'I press together', of which the first must be the fricative /s/ and the third a liquid. The syllable offset may also consist of three consonants, of which the first must be a liquid or a nasal, the medial a stop, and the last an /s/, such as in *urbs*. In the initial position, /s/ was avoided before /m/, /n/, /r/, /l/ so that in prehistoric times /s/ disappeared in this position (SCN 30.12). The medial /s/ disappeared in historic times with compensatory lengthening of the preceding vowel (SCN 2.2). Exceptions are loan words such as *smaragdus*.

● **Syllabification rules**

Rule 1: There can be only one nucleus per syllable. The nucleus is most often a vowel. An adjacent vowel either transforms into a consonantal semivowel or becomes the nucleus of the next syllable.

Rule 2: A single consonant following a vowel always belongs to the next syllable.

Rule 3: The last of two or more medial consonants belongs to the next syllable. Exceptions to this rule are the so called 'muta cum liquida' groups /br/, /pr/, /dr/, /tr/, /gr/, /kr/, as well as /ku̯/, which fully belong to the next syllable

Rule 4: Compound words are separated according to their word formation, thus *adesse* 'to help' is syllabified as *ad.es.se* instead of *a.des.se*.

● **Syllable types**

A syllable without a consonantal offset ends with a vowel and is known as an **open** syllable. If it is a short vowel, the syllable is additionally known as a **short** or **light** syllable. A syllable ending with a consonant is known as a closed syllable, which necessarily is a **long** or **heavy** syllable. Syllables that end with a long vowel or a diphthong are **long** or **heavy** syllables, too.

Exercises

ATTENTION In this book, syllables are separated with the syllable separator sign {.} in order to avoid confusion with the morpheme separator sign {-}.

E1 Transcribe the graphemes and separate the syllables afterwards.

1. {factus}   :: *faktus* :: *fak.tus*   2. {aedes}   :: *aędēs* :: *aę.dēs*

3. {confectus} ::_____ ::_____   4. {laudare} ::_____ ::_____

5. {gaudia}   ::_____ ::_____   6. {uirtutem}::_____ ::_____

7. {mulierem}   ::_____ ::_____   8. {filiolus} ::_____ ::_____

9. {ornamentum} ::_____ ::_____   10. {attingo} ::_____ ::_____

E2 Insert the syllable-separated words of exercise 1 into the tables below.

Monosyllabic words

Initial syllable			Final syllable		
Onset	Nucleus	Offset	Onset	Nucleus	Offset
	a	ę	d	ē	s

Trisyllabic words

Initial syllable			Medial syllable			Final syllable		
Onset	Nucleus	Offset	Onset	Nucleus	Offset	Onset	Nucleus	Offset
k	ō	n	f	e	k	t	u	s

Words having four syllables

Initial syllable			Medial syllable			Medial syllable			Final syllable		
On-set	Nu-cleus	Off-set	On-set	Nu-cleus	Off-set	On-set	Nu-cleus	Off-set	On-set	Nu-cleus	Off-set
m	u		l	i			e		r	e	m

8   Accentuation of Latin Words

● **From the preclassic initial accent to the classical penultimate accentuation**

A stress accent is defined as the increase of air pressure while articulating the accented vowel within a syllable. Until about the 5ᵗʰ century BC, Early Latin had a stress accent on the first syllable, similar to the accent found in English and German. This can be deduced from the phenomena of syncope (the expulsion of an unstressed vowel, cf. unit 13) and vowel weakening (the raising of an unstressed vowel, cf. units 14/15). By the time of Classical Latin, the accentuation had changed to a system known as the rule of the penult. This rule states that the penultimate syllable was always stressed if it was long. If the penultimate syllable was short, the antepenult was stressed. The change from the initial stress accent to the rule of the penult accentuation system is indicated by rule Ac1.

● **Accent rules for Classical Latin**

1. Monosyllabic words can only be stressed on their one syllable:
   mél {mel} 'honey'   *ṓs* {os} 'bone'   *nóks* {nox} 'night'

2. Disyllabic words are stressed on their first syllable:
   kántō {canto} 'I sing'   *hómō* {homo} 'man'   *kánis* {canis} 'dog'

3. Words of three or more syllables are stressed on the penultimate syllable if this syllable is long:
   orā́tor {orator} 'speaker' *laudā́re* {laudare} 'to praise' *laudābā́mus* {laudabamus} 'we praised'

4. Words of three or more syllables are stressed on the antepenultimate syllable if the penultimate syllable syllable is short: *agríkola* {agricola} 'farmer' *ánima* {anima} 'soul'
   kálidus {calidus} 'hot'

● **The addition of enclitic words influenced the accent position**

Enclitic words such as *ku̯e* {que} 'and' are unaccented. If such an enclitic word was added to an accentuated word, the accent position shifted to the syllable preceding the enclitic word even if the vowel of this syllable was short. That way, the juxtaposition of *ómnēs* + *que* becomes *omnḗsque* and *ómnia* + *que* became *omniáque*. In contrast, words like *úndiku̯e* {undique} 'allover', *ítaku̯e* {itaque} 'and so' or *úbinam* 'where in the world' were regularly accentuated because their medial syllables were light.

● **Exceptions to the accentuation rules**

Sometimes, former trisyllabic words that had been stressed on the penult lost their last syllable due to the production of a disyllabic word through syncope or apocope. In these cases, the original place of accentuation was preserved, although its position was on the last syllable. Examples: **1.** {illace} *illā́ke* > (4.3) *illā́k* {illac} 'there' or {adhuce} *adhū́ke* > (4.3) *adhū́k* {adhuc} 'until now', which are formed with the particle {c}, shortened from {ce}. **2.** Words like {uidesne} *u̯idḗsne* > (15.2) **u̯idḗzne* > (2.1) **u̯idḗne* > (4.3) *u̯idḗn* {uiden} 'do you see?', which are formed with the particle {n}, shortened from {ne}. **3.** Words like {arpinatis} *Arpinā́tis* > (4.2) **Arpinā́ts* > (16.4) **Arpinā́ss* > (39.7) *Arpinā́s* {arpinas} 'from Arpinum'. **4.** Shortened perfect forms such as {audiuit} *au̯dī́u̯it* > (40.2) **au̯dī́it* > (1.1) **au̯díit* > (3.1) *au̯dī́t* {audit} 'he heard', which can be found in poetic language as well as in Vulgar Latin.

Exercises

E1 Transcribe and accentuate the following exceptions to the rule of the penult.

A {nostras} _____ 'from our area'

B {samnis} _____ 'from Samnium'

C *illī̆ke* > _____ {illic} 'there'

D *posthā̆ke* > _____ {posthac} 'from now on'

E 3. ps. sg. perf. *fūmā̌u̯it* > _____ {fumat} 'he smoked'

E2 Rule Ac1 describes the accent shift from initial to penultimate accent.

A {arceo} *árkeō* 'I repel' :: *éks-arkeō* > (8.1) *ékserkeō* > (Ac1) _____ {exerceo} 'I exercise'

B {carpo} *kárpō* 'I pluck' :: *dís-karpō* > (8.1) *dískerpō* > (Ac1) _____ {discerpo} 'I tear into pieces'

C {tracto} *tráktō* 'I drag' :: *dḗ-traktō* > (8.1) *dḗtrektō* > (Ac1) _____ {detrecto} 'I refuse'

E3 The muta cum liquida groups (/br/, /pr/, /dr/, /tr/, /gr/, /kr/) did not cause positional length of the preceding vowel in CL. In VL, however, these consonants caused positional length of the preceding vowel, causing a change of the accent position, which is indicated by rule Ac2.

A CL {colubra} *kó.lu.bra* > (Ac2) VL _____ 'female snake' > sp. *culebra* 'snake'

B CL {integrum} *ín.te.grum* > (Ac2) VL _____ 'untouched' > sp. *entero* 'whole'

C CL {tenebras} _____ > (Ac2) VL *te.néb.ras* 'darkness' > sp. *tinieblas*

Labeling the accent position with accent signs

The accent position of Latin words is automatically arrived at according to the rules given on the opposite page except for exceptions noted. Thus only the preclassic forms still bearing the initial accent as well as the form following rule Ac1 is furnished with an accent sign. Likewise, the PIE accent position is only marked if it is different from the preclassic initial accent position.

This book uses the following accent rules

Ac0: The morphologically caused free PIE accent transforms into the initial accent:
PIE *patḗr* > (Ac0) PIT *pátēr* > CL *pater* 'father'

Ac1: The initial accent transforms into the rule of the penult accentuation:
EL *éks-erkeō* > (Ac1) CL *eks-érkeō* {exerceo} 'I exercise'

Ac2: A muta cum liquida group closes a preceding syllable in VL:
CL *ín.te.grum* > (Ac2) VL *in.tég.rum* 'undamaged'

9   Modeling Sound Changes

● **Formulas for describing systematic sound changes**

The sounds of a language are not static but rather are subject to changes that can be illustrated by the development from OL *gnōskō* {gnosco} 'I learn' to CL *nōskō* {nosco}, in which the initial /g/ was lost before /n/. This sound change can be represented by the following formula:

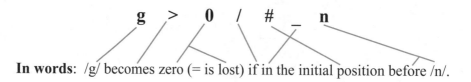

$$\mathbf{g} \quad > \quad \mathbf{0} \quad / \quad \mathbf{\#} \quad \_ \quad \mathbf{n}$$

In words: /g/ becomes zero (= is lost) if in the initial position before /n/.

● **Notation of sound changes**

The derivational operator > indicates the direction of the sound change, and zero represents the loss of the concerned sound. This loss is limited to a certain environment which is noted after the slash. The underscore is a placeholder for the sound to the left side of the derivational operator, and the hash represents a word boundary. The combinations consisting of hash and underscore represent the left word boundary #_, which corresponds to the initial sound of a word, and the right word boundary _#, which corresponds to the final sound of a word.

● **A derivation chain**

The formula g > 0 / #_n can be used to describe the development from *gnōskō* to *nōskō*. Therefore, it is placed in round brackets between the derivational operator and the word derived by the formula. This expression is complemented by the spelling of the words in curly brackets:

OUTPUT

$$\{\text{gnosco}\} \quad \text{OL} \; (\textit{gnōskō}) \; > \; (\text{g} > 0 \, / \, \#\_\text{n}) \quad \text{CL} \; (\textit{nōskō}) \; \{\text{nosco}\}$$

INPUT

The expression is read in the following way: "the {gnosco} written Old Latin form *gnōsko* was transformed by sound change g > 0 / #_n to the Classical Latin form *nōskō*, which was written {nosco}".

Instead of writing the derivation formula, the equivalent SCN-number from the index can be used and written into the round brackets. The SCN-index lists all the sound changes which are of concern for Latin historical phonology. By doing so, the following expression is obtained: {gnosco} *gnōskō* > (30.2) *nōskō* {nosco}. As can be seen from the index and the derivation chain below, SCN 30.2 is a complex sound change and can be divided into two phases. Often the output of a derivation chain is at the same time the input for another transformation. The asterisk of *ŋnōskō* implies that this form is not attested like *gnōskō* and *nōskō* but can be reconstructed as an intermediate step.

$$> (\ldots) \; \textit{gnōskō} \; > \; (\text{30.2a}) \; *\textit{ŋnōskō} \; > \; (\text{30.2b}) \; \textit{nōskō} \; > \; (\ldots)$$

Definitions of Fundamental Sound Changes

Assimilation: An assimilation is the harmonization of one or more phonological features of two sounds. These sounds can be two vowels (SCN 6), two consonants (SCN 12–22), or vowel and consonant (e.g. SCN 9.9, 9.23, 28.3). One speaks of regressive assimilation if the first sound is harmonized to the second sound, and of progressive assimilation if the second sound is harmonized to the first sound. Regressive assimilations such as in *ad-ferre* > *af-fere* 'to bring' are very common in Latin. Units 22 to 24 illustrate these sound changes in detail.

Dissimilation: One s peaks of dissimilation if in a sequence of similar sounds or sounds that share similar features the sounds lose similarity. The word *merīdiēs* goes back to *medī-diēs* 'middle of the day' and shows that the sequence of two non-adjacent d-sounds was dissimilated by changing the first one to /r/. Just as for assimilations, one can differentiate progressive (SCN 23.10/11) and regressive dissimilations (SCN 23.1–23.8). Unit 25 takes a closer look at these dissimilation processes.

Deletion / Loss: The sound changes SCN 30 to SCN 40 describe the deletion or loss of sounds, which can be seen in the development of OL *gnōskō* 'I know' to CL *nōskō* (SCN 30.2) or OL *forktis* {forctis} 'strong' to CL *fortis* (SCN 34.1). It is possible to model the deletion of sounds by assuming a deep-structural assimilation followed by a simplification of the newly formed double consonant. For more information see chapters 28–30.

Exercises

E1 Add either the SCN-rule or the description.

SCN	Rule	Description
16.1	p > f / _f	/p/ becomes /f/ before /f/.
16.2	p > s / _s	
30.6	d > 0 / #_i̯	
27.2	u̯ > u / C_C	
28.2		/l/ becomes velar [ł] in the final position after a vowel.
29.2	0 > p / m_l	
35.1		/b/ is lost between /r/ and /m/.
30.9		/p/ is lost in the initial position before /s/.
40.5	u̯ > 0 / _(o, ō, u, ū)	
9.15	o > e / #u̯_(s, t, rC)	
8.15	i > [y] {u/i} / _(f, m, b)	/i/ becomes [y] before /f/, /m/ or /b/. This sound was written {u} or {i}.
34.1	k {c} > 0 / r_t	
x9.2	m > b / #_r	
x8.12c	h > 0 / V_V	

10   Vowel Shortening

- ## SCN 1.1
  Ṽ > V / _V   A vowel before a vowel is shortened: *vocalis ante vocalem corripitur*

In Old Latin, one regularly finds long vowels that are shortened in Classical Latin, e.g. OL *fūit* {fuit} 'was' with a long /ū/ found in Plautus in comparison to CL *fuit* {fuit} with a short /u/. This sound change, known as *vocalis ante vocalem corripitur* "a vowel before a vowel is shortened", was used in Latin poetry as well as in common speech. It is namely this occurrence that can explain some of the paradigm irregularities in which long vowels alternate with short vowels. One can thus compare the infinitive *au̯dī-re* {audire} 'to hear' with a long /ī/ to the 1. ps. sg. *au̯diō* {audio} 'I hear' with a short /i/ and find that the preform of *audiō* was **audī-ō* with a long /ī/. Furthermore, nominal forms such as *grūs*, *gruis* 'crane', which show vowel length alternations between the nom. and the gen., can be traced back to a more regular paradigm *grū-s*, **grū-is* lacking variation in quantity.

- ## SCN 1.3
  V̆CV̄ > V̆CV̆   The correptio iambica

In Plautus, the imperatives OL *ama* {ama} 'love!' and OL *i̯ube* {iube} 'command!' with a short vowel in the second syllable are found, although *amā* and *i̯ubē* with a long vowel would have been expected. The reason for this is that the second syllable of a iambic sequence could be shortened in certain positions in Old Latin poetry. This rule was probably an adaption of common speech (cf. Sommer 1977:104) and affected highly frequently occurring words such as {ego} *egō* > *ego* {ego} 'I', {uolo} *u̯olō* > *u̯olo* {uolo} 'I want' or {fero} *ferō* > *fero* {fero} 'I carry'. These examples bear witness to the fact that the Latin writing system did not display this sound change so that these conclusions can only be drawn via a metrical analysis of the words.

- ## SCN 1.4
  Ṽ > V / _C#   Shortening of long vowels in final syllables except before /s/

Old Latin regularly has long vowels in final syllables that are shortened in Classical Latin. In Plautus, the forms OL *arāt* {arat} for CL *arat* {arat} 'he plows' as well as OL *solēt* {solet} for CL *solet* {solet} 'he is accustomed to do' are attested. If one takes *arāre* {arare} and its paradigmatic forms 1. sg. *arō* {aro}, 2. sg. *arās* {aras}, 3. sg. *arat* {arat} as an example and traces back the 3. sg. to its preform *arāt* {arat} with a long /ā/, the paradigm becomes more regular, because there is no variation of vowel quantity between the 2. sg. and 3. sg. The 1. sg. *arō* can be traced back to the preform **árā-ō* containing a long vowel, which developed via a shortening of the vowel **árā-ō* > (1.1) **áraō* and the contraction **áraō* > (3.4) *árō* {aro} to the classical form. The starting point **árā-ō* still bears the preclassic initial stress accent position (cf. unit 13/14). By looking at the 2. sg. *arās* {aras} 'you plow', one sees that this vowel shortening did not take place before /s/. In Plautus, one can also find long vowels in the final syllables of nouns such as *uksōr* {uxor} 'wife' and *au̯ktōr* {auctor} 'producer', which are shortened in CL *uksor* {uxor} and *au̯ktor* {auctor}. The classic paradigm *au̯ktor, au̯ktōris* can thus be traced back to an older paradigm *au̯ktōr, au̯ktōris* {auctor, auctoris} showing no variation in vowel quantity.

> **TIP**   It is useful to study units 22 to 24 at an early stage. The sound changes described there are very frequent and fundamental for an understanding of Latin historical phonology.

Exercises

E1 Do you know the exceptions to SCN 1.1 *vocalis ante vocalem corripitur*?

_____

E2 Add the SCN-number of the vowel shortening as well as the spelling.

SCN	OL	CL	Spelling	
1.1	*fūimus*	*fuimus*	{	}
	ūtār	*ūtar*	{	}
	īerō	*ierō*	{	}
	tenēt	*tenet*	{	}
	u̯elīt	*u̯elit*	{	}
	fūisset	*fuisset*	{	}
	adnūit	*adnuit*	{	}
	fidēī	*fideī*	{	}
	seru̯āt	*seru̯at*	{	}
	memorāt	*memorat*	{	}
	fūerim	*fuerim*	{	}
	tinnīt	*tinnit*	{	}

E3 Add the missing forms by using SCN 1.3.

A {domi} *domī* > (1.3) _____ 'at home'

B *_____ > (1.3) *bene* {bene} 'well'

C *modōd* > (38.3) *modō* > (1.3) _____ {modo} 'only'

D OL {sibei} *sibei̯* > (10.8/9) *sibī* > (1.3) _____ {sibi} 'oneself'

E {_____} _____ > (1.3) *mihi* {mihi} 'me'

F {_____} _____ > (1.3) *tibi* {tibi} 'you'

G {ibi} *ibī* > (1.3) _____ {_____} 'there'

H {puta} *putā* 'think!' > (1.3) _____ {_____} 'for example'

SCN 1.2 V̄ > V /_RC Osthoff's law

A long vowel was shortened in a sequence consisting of a long vowel plus a resonant plus a consonant. This sound change affected the 3. ps. pl. *laу̯dānt > laу̯dant*, the vowel shortening of which cannot be explained by SCN 1.4 because SCN 1.4 affected only syllables which were closed by one consonant. This produced the alternating pattern 1. ps. pl. *laу̯dāmus* :: 3 ps. pl. *laу̯dant*, which is essential for the verbal inflection. The comparison of Lat. *perna* 'ham' to Skr. *pā́rṣṇi* 'heel' enables to reconstruct the preform *pērna* with a long /ē/. Likewise, *u̯entus* {uentus} 'wind' goes back to *u̯ēntus* with a long /ē/; this form had once been an nt-participle with the meaning 'blowing'.

11   Vowel Lengthening

- **SCN 2.1 V > V̄ / _n(f,s)**
  The COSOL-Rule: loss of /n/ before /s/ and /f/ with compensatory lengthening

The nasal /n/ was only weakly articulated before /s/ and probably caused a nasalization of the preceding vowel. This nasalization, however, was also weakly articulated so that both it and the /n/ could be completely lost, causing a compensatory lengthening of the preceding vowel. OL *konsoł* {consol} 'consul' first became *koⁿsoł* by the weakening of the articulation of /n/, then *kõsoł* by the nasalization of the preceding vowel, and finally *kōsoł* by the loss of the nasalization and compensatory lengthening o > ō. This form is attested in inscriptions such as {cosol} and in the CL abbreviation {cos} for 'consul'. In Latin spelling, however, the {n} still existed, and probably it had also not been completely lost in all strata of the language so that CL *kōnsuł* {consul} exhibits the vowel lengthening as well as the nasal /n/, which had been lost in common speech. This means that CL *kōnsuł* has a long vowel, which is the effect of the loss of the nasal, as well as the nasal that had caused the vowel lengthening because it had been reintroduced into the word. Even in the oldest inscriptions, one can find examples of the omission of /n/ before /s/, which means that this sound change happened at a very early period of the language. Furthermore, Cicero is said to have spoken *forēsia* and *hortēsia* for written {forensia} and {hortensia}, according to the Roman grammarian Velius Longus. The Romance languages also do not show any trace of /n/ before /s/. The same sound change happened before /f/, which can be exemplified by *inferus > īnferus* {inferus} 'the lower'.

- **SCN 2.2 z > 0 / _G + compensatory lengthening**
  Loss of [z] before voiced consonants with compensatory lengthening

The fricative /s/ was allophonically pronounced [z] in voiced surroundings before being lost, whereby causing a compensatory lengthening of the preceding vowel. The preclassic forms OL *kozmis* {cosmis} 'courteous' and OL *ozmen* {osmen} 'omen', in which {s} probably stood for [z], were pronounced *kōmis* {comis} and *ōmen* {omen} in CL. One can assume the following development: {cosmis} *kosmis* > (15.1) *kozmis* {cosmis} > (2.2) *kōmis* {comis} as well as {osmen} *osmen* > (15.1) *ozmen* {osmen} > {2.2} *ōmen* {omen}. In comparison to SCN 2.1, which describes the loss of /n/ before /s/, one finds the inverted context of /s/ being lost before /n/. Before other voiced consonants, /s/ was also pronounced [z] and vanished, whereby causing a compensatory lengthening of the preceding vowel, which can be seen by comparing the different variants of the prefix *dis-* in *dispōnō* {dispono} 'I arrange' and *distulī* {distuli} 'I delayed' in contrast to *dīgerō* {digero} 'I carry away' and *dīmittō* {dimitto} 'I let go'.

- **SCN 2.3 *agō* :: *agtus > āktus***
  Lachmann's law

The participles *āktus* {actus} 'done' and *lēktus* {lectus} 'read' have long vowels, whereas their derivational bases *agō* {ago} and *legō* {lego} do not show any long vowels in the corresponding positions. Analogous to the proportion of the 1. ps. sg. prs. and its corresponding PPP, exemplified by *fakiō* {facio} 'I do' :: *faktus* {factus} 'done', the expected outcome of the above forms would be *aktus** and *lektus** with short vowels.

If the verbal stem ended with a voiced stop -*g* or -*d*, the preceding vowel of the verb was lengthened in its PPP. The exact process of this sound change, known as Lachmann's law, has been strongly debated among linguists (cf. footnote SCN 2.3) because there are also counterexamples that do not show the respective lengthening. In cases like {iungo} *i̯uŋgō* 'I join' :: *i̯ūŋktus* {iunctus} 'joined', this lengthening process coincides with the vowel lengthening according to SCN 2.4 because one regularly finds long vowels before the consonant cluster /ŋkt/. In the case of *i̯ūŋktus*, one therefore finds a double condition of the vowel length, which is absent in *i̯uŋgō*.

Exercises

E1 **Derive the forms.**

A {consol} *konsoł* > (2.1) _____ > (9.18) _____ {_____} 'consul'

B {contuli} *kon-tulī* 'I collected' :: **konferre* > (2.1) _____ {_____} 'to collect'

C **insīdiae̯* > (2.1) _____ {_____} 'snare, trap'

D {maneo} *maneō* 'I stay' :: *mansī* > (2.1) _____ {_____} 'I stayed'

E2 **Model the loss of /s/ via intermediate voiced [z].**

A {aes} *aes* 'ore' :: **aesnos* > (15.2) **aeznos* > (2.2) **_____ > (9.18) _____ {_____} 'of copper, of bronze' **B** {cascus} *kaskus* 'very old' :: **kasnos* > (15.2) **kaznos* > (2.2) **_____ > (9.18) _____{_____} 'grey' **C** {fas} *fās* 'divine law' :: **fasnom* > (15.2) **faznom* > (2.2) **_____ > (9.18) _____ {_____} 'sanctuary' **D** **nisdos* > (15.5) **nizdos* > (2.2) **_____ > (9.18) _____ {_____} 'nest' **E** {sedo} *sedō* 'I sit' :: **si-sd-ō* > (15.5) **si-zd-ō* > (2.2) _____ {sido} 'I settle' **F** *is* 'this' :: {isdem} *isdem* > (15.5) **izdem* > (2.2) _____ {idem} 'the same' **G** **i̯ūsdeks* > (15.5) **i̯ūzdeks* > (2.2) _____ {_____} 'judge'

E3 **Apply Lachmann's law before the assimilation of voice (cf. footnote SCN 2.3).**

A {lego} *legō* 'I read' :: PPP **legtus* > (2.3) **_____ > (12.7) _____ {_____} 'read' **B** {iungo} *i̯uŋgō* 'I join' :: PPP **i̯uŋgtus* > (2.3/2.4) **_____ > (12.7) _____ {_____} 'joined' **C** {fungo} *fuŋgō* 'I perform' :: PPP **fuŋgtus* > (2.3/2.4) **_____ > (12.7) _____ {_____} 'performed' **D** {frango} *fraŋgō* 'I break' :: PPP **fragtus* > (2.3) **_____ > (12.7) _____ {_____} 'broken' **E** {sancio} *saŋki̯ō* 'I sanctify' :: PPP **saŋktus* > (2.4) _____ {_____} 'sanctified' **F** {uincio} *u̯iŋki̯ō* 'I chain' :: PPP **u̯iŋktus* > (2.4) _____ {_____} 'chained'

The frequent rule SCN 9.18 o > u / _C(C)#

A chain of derivations often ends with SCN 9.18, which describes the raising of /o/ to /u/ in final syllables and thus affected all words belonging to the frequent o-stems. For example, the form *kaskus* {cascus} stems from former **kaskos*, which will be presented in the exercises as follows: **kaskos* > (9.18) *kaskus* {cascus} 'old'.

12

<h2 style="text-align:center">Vowel Contraction</h2>

● **Vowels came into contact because of the loss of intervocalic consonants**

A vowel contraction is the fusion of two individual vowels, resulting in one long vowel. The quality of the resulting vowel depends on the length (quantity) and color (quality) of the contracted vowels. Often vowels came into contact as a result of the loss of intervocalic /i̯/ (SCN 40.1), /u̯/ (SCN 40.2) and /h/ (SCN x.8.12c). The resulting hiatus was thus resolved by the contraction of the vowels.

● **SCN 3.1 V+V > V̄   Contractions of vowels having the same quality**

The contraction of two vowels of the same quality but of a different quantity resulted in a long vowel of the same quality. If the first of the vowels was long, it was shortened according to SCN 1.1 before the contraction. Examples for this process are the short perfect forms such as {audiuit} *audíu̯it* > (40.2) **audíit* > (1.1) *audíit* > (3.1) *audít* {audit} 'he heard' or formations with prefixes such as {prehendo} *prehendō* > (x8.12c) **preendō* > (3.1) *prēndō* {prendo} 'I seize'.

● **SCN 3.2 a+e > ā. SCN 3.3 a+ē > ē   Contractions with /a/ as the first vowel**

The result of a vowel contraction, in which the first vowel was /a/, depended on the quantity of the second vowel. In the case of a short vowel following, the /a/ prevailed, in the case of a long vowel following, it was the quality of the long vowel following that prevailed. This explains the forms of the indicative and subjunctive of the a-conjugation: 2. ps. sg. ind. **lau̯dā̯i̯es* > (40.1) **lau̯dāes* > (1.1) **lau̯daes* > (3.2) *lau̯dās* {laudas} 'you praise' vs. 2. ps. sg. sub. **lau̯dā̯i̯ēs* > (40.1) **lau̯dāēs* > (1.1) **lau̯daēs* > (3.3) *lau̯dēs* {laudes} 'you shall praise'.

● **SCN 3.5 o+a > ō. SCN 3.6 o+e > ō Contractions of vowels having different qualities**

Normally, the quality of the first vowel prevailed. Compound verbs of *emō* {emo} 'I take' such as **prō-emō* > (1.1) **proemō* > (3.6) *prōmō* {promo} 'I take out' or **kō-emō* > (1.1) **koemō* > (3.6) *kōmō* {como} 'I arrange' serve as examples for contractions with /o/ as the first vowel. An example for /e/ as the first vowel is furnished by the compound verb **dē-habeo* > (x8.12c) *dēabeo* > (1.1) **deabeo* > (3.7) *dēbeo* 'I owe' derived from *habeō* {habeo} 'I have'. The diphthong /ae̯/ {ae} prevailed when a vowel followed as well. In this manner, *prae̯tor* {praetor} 'leader' can be explained as a compound of *iter* {iter} 'way' going back to **prae̯-itor* > (3.8) *prae̯tor* {praetor}.

● **No contraction took place if the second vowel was /i/ or /u/**

Vowels were not always contracted when they occured in the hiatus position. If the second vowel was /i/ or /u/, the hiatus remained, such as in *ne.u.ter* {neuter} 'neither', or a diphthong was formed such as in *dei̯n.de* {deinde} 'thereafter'. If the contracted forms were no longer comprehensible, or the phonological relation to their derivational base was disturbed, the contractions could be undone. This ambition for clarification produced forms such as *de-esse* {deesse} and *ko-operīre* {cooperire} besides their regularly contracted forms *dēsse* {desse} and *kōperīre* {coperire}. Furthermore, the non-contracted forms of the gen. sg. of the o-declination such as *kōnsiliī* {consilii} and *imperiī* {imperii} are younger than their contracted counterparts *kōnsilī* {consili} and *imperī* {imperi} and had been formed afterwards.

Exercises

E1 Before contracting the vowels, you might have to shorten the first vowel

A {ire} *īre* 'to go' :: inf. perf. *i-isse* > (3.1) _____ {_____} 'having gone'

B {alo} *alō* 'I nourish' :: *prō-olēs* > (1.1) *_____ > (3.1) _____ {_____}

'descendants' **C** {lauo} *lau̯ō* 'I wash' :: Perf. *lau̯ā-u̯ī* > (40.2) *laāu̯ī* > (3.1) _____

{_____} 'I washed' **D** {hortor} *hortor* 'I urge' :: *ko-hors* > (x8.12c) *ko-ors* > (3.1)

_____ {_____} 'cohort' **E** {os} *ōs, ōris* 'face' :: *ko-ōram* > (3.1) _____

{_____} 'publicly' **F** {diues} *dīu̯es* 'rich' :: gen. sg. *dīu̯itis* > (40.2) *dīitis* > (1.1)

*_____ > (3.1) _____ {_____} **G** {obliuiscor} *oblīu̯īskor* 'I forget' :: PPP

oblīu̯itus > (40.2) *_____ > (1.1) *_____ > (3.1) _____ {_____}

'forgotten'

E2 Add the missing forms.

A *hiems* 'winter' :: *bi-himos* > (x8.12c) *biimos* > (3.1) *_____ > (9.18) _____

{_____} 'of two winters' **B** {si uis} *sī u̯īs* > *sīu̯īs* > (40.2) *_____ > (1.1)

*_____ > (3.1) _____ 'if you like' **C** {uiuus} *u̯īu̯us* 'alive' :: *u̯īu̯ita* > (40.2)

*_____ > (1.1) *_____ > (3.1) _____ {_____} 'life' **D** *trei̯es*

> (40.1) *trees* > (3.1) _____ {_____} 'three' **E** {homo} *homō* 'human being'

:: *ne-hemō* > (x8.12c) *_____ > (3.1) *_____ {_____} 'nobody'

F {deleo} *dēleō* 'I destroy' :: *dēlēu̯eram* > (40.2) *_____ > (1.1) *_____ > (3.1)

_____ {_____} 'I had destroyed'

These sound changes appear in the exercises		
SCN 1.1	V̄ > V / _V	A vowel before a vowel is shortened.
SCN 9.18	o > u / _C(C)#	Raising of /o/ to /u/ in closed final syllables.
SCN 40.1	i̯ > 0 / V_V	Loss of intervocalic /i̯/.
SCN 40.2	u̯ > 0 / V₁_V₁	Loss of /u̯/ between vowels of similar quality.
SCN x8.12c	h > 0 / V_V	Loss of intervocalic /h/.

13   Syncope and Apocope / Deletion of Vowels

- **SCN 4.1 V̆ > 0 / C_C   A short unaccented vowel is lost between two consonants**

Syncope is the ejection of a short vowel between two consonants. The Greek word *synkopḗ* means "clashing" and describes the coming together of consonants that had previously been separated by a vowel. An example of a syncopated form is *kaldus* {caldus} 'warm', which originated from the non-syncopated form *kalidus* {calidus}. Syncopated and non-syncopated forms could exist side by side; the non-syncopated form was often a sign of a higher style of language. These variants were diastratically and diaphasically distributed in the language system. The coexistence of syncopated and non-syncopated forms was also used for grammatical or semantic differentiations. The syncopated *suprā* {supra} 'above' was used as an adverb and a preposition, while the non-syncopated *superus* {superus} 'the upper' was used as an adjective. A similar relation is seen in *aliter* {aliter} 'different' and *alter* {alter} 'the other'; the first was used as an adverb and the second one as an adjective.

- **Accentuation as the engine of the syncope**

The explanation for the phenomenon of syncope is the assumption that in prehistoric times Latin was accentuated differently than in classical times, when the place of accentuation was governed by rule of the penult (cf. unit 8). There must have been a phase in which the first syllable was accentuated in the place of the penult. Due to the intensity of this prehistoric stress accent on the first syllable, the following syllables of the word were stressed less and tended to vanish. The second syllable was most often syncopated because it directly followed the stressed first syllable. An unstressed vowel was completely deleted by the syncope, whereas the process of vowel weakening caused the vowel raising which will be dealt with in the next two chapters. A vowel could only vanish completely if the remaining phonological information of the word was sufficient to transfer its meaning correctly. Therefore, syncope and vowel weakening are directly related processes in Latin language history.

> **INFO**   The syncope can be dated to the 5th century BC. But also numerous syncopes must have occurred in later times, judging from the further evolution of Latin in the Romance languages.

- **SCN 4.3 V̆ > 0 / C_#   Apocope: Ejection of a short final vowel**

Short vowels in the final position could be eliminated, too. Examples are the short forms *dīk* {dic} 'say!', *dūk* {duc} 'lead!', *fak* {fac} 'do!' and *fer* {fer} 'carry!', which are sporadically attested as OL {dice, duce, face, fere}. The co-existence of the synonymous forms *neku̯e* {neque} and *nek* {nec} 'and not yet' can be explained by apocope as well. First, *neku̯e* was apocopated to **neku̯* if the following word started with a consonant. Afterwards, the final /u̯/ of **neku̯* was lost regularly before a consonant by SCN 40.3. The development was: *neku̯e* + C > (4.3) **neku̯* > (40.3) *nek* {nec}. An analogous development with an additional assimilation according to SCN 18.4 is seen in *atku̯e* {atque} and its variant *ak* {ac}, which can be derived as follows: *atku̯e* + C > (18.4) *akku̯e* > (4.3) *akku̯* > (40.3) *akk* > (39.6) *ak* {ac} 'and'.

Exercises

E1 Separate the words using the syllable separation operator {.} before syncopating the second syllable.

A {positus} *positus* > *po.si.tus* > (4.1) *postus* {postus} 'placed' **B** {aliter} *aliter* > _____

> (4.1) _____ {_____} 'one of two' **C** {calidus} *kalidus* > _____ > (4.1)

_____ {_____} 'hot' **D** {ualide} *u̯alidē* > _____ > (4.1) _____

{_____} 'much' **E** {auis} *au̯is* 'bird' :: *au̯ispeks* > (4.1) _____ {_____}

'augur'

E2 After the syncope, long vowels are shortened according to Osthoff's law (SCN 1.2 V̄ > V / _RC).

A {nauis} *nāu̯is* 'ship' :: {nauita} *nāu̯ita* > (4.1) * _____ > (1.2) _____

{_____} 'sailor' **B** {gauisus} *gāu̯isus* 'happy' :: *gāu̯ideō* > (4.1) * _____ > (1.2)

_____ {_____} 'I am happy' **C** {rauis} *rāu̯is* 'hoarseness' :: *rāu̯ikos* > (4.1)

rāu̯kos > (1.2) *rau̯kos* > (9.18) *rau̯kus* {raucus} 'hoarse' **D** {rego} *regō* 'I erect' :: abl. sg. *ēregō*

> (4.1) * _____ > (1.2) _____ {_____} 'in consequence of'

E3 For experts: consonant clusters resulting from syncope are assimilated or simplified.

A {date} *date* 'give!' :: *ke-date* > (4.1) * _____ > (12.5) _____ {_____}

'look!' **B** {sitis} *sitis* 'thirst' :: *sitikos* > (4.1) * _____ > (18.4) * _____ > (9.18)

_____ {_____} 'dry' **C** {dico} *dikō* 'I speak' :: *prá̯edikō* > (4.1) * _____

> (12.6) * _____ > (18.4) * _____ > (39.1) _____ {_____}

'herald' **D** {rego} *regō* 'I erect' :: *perregō* > (4.1) * _____ > (39.2) _____

{_____} 'I go on' **E** {positus} *positus* 'placed' :: *po-sinō* > (4.1) * _____ > (15.2)

* _____ > (2.2) _____ {_____} 'I place'

New SCN-rules in exercise 3		
SCN 12.5	**d > t / _t**	Voiced /d/ becomes voiceless /t/ before voiceless /t/.
SCN 12.6	**d > t / _k**	Voiced /d/ becomes voiceless /t/ before voiceless /k/.
SCN 15.2	**s > z / _n**	Voiceless /s/ becomes voiced [z] before voiced /n/.
SCN 18.4	**t > k / _k**	/t/ becomes /k/ before /k/.
SCN 39.1	**C₁ > 0 / V̄_C₁**	A double consonant is simplified after a long vowel or a diphthong.
SCN 39.2	**C₁ > 0 / _C₁C₂**	A double consonant is simplified before a consonant.

Vowel Weakening I

● **Initial stress accent > vowel weakening > accent change**

If the vowel was not syncopated, the strong initial stress accent of the 5th century BC caused raising and fronting of the vowels following the stressed first syllable. This process is referred to as vowel weakening, and the result in CL was in open syllables mostly /i/, which can be seen in word pairs such as {capere} *kapere* :: *akkipere* {accipere} or {regere} *regere* :: *korrigere* {corrigere}. This sound change was often accompanied by assimilations as in *akkipere*, which is derived from **adkipere*. For methodological reasons, these assimilations are always put before the vowel weakening in this book, even if the two processes occurred simultaneously or one after the other because the exact chronology cannot be determined. After the weakening of the vowel, the accent position shifted from the initial position **ákkipere* and **kórrigere* to the penult or antepenult (rule Ac1) of the classical forms *akkípere* {accipere} 'I accept' and *korrígere* {corrigere} 'I set right'.

● **Raising and fronting of unstressed vowels**

The initial stress accent caused /a/ to become /e/ in all unstressed syllables except in the final position (SCN 8.1. lines 1–5 and 9). Moreover, /o/ was fronted to /e/ in all unstressed syllables except before [ɫ], which also affected the diphthong /oi̯/ (SCN 8.2. lines 6–8). /e/ was preserved in closed syllables (lines 3–5), after /i/ (line 7) as well as before /r/ (line 9). In open medial syllables, first original /e/, and then /e/ that had been weakened out of /a/ or /o/ became /i/ (SCN 8.3. lines 1/2/6). Furthermore, /u/ was fronted to /i/ (SCN 8.4. line 10). Before labial sounds other than /u̯/, the sounds /i/ and /u/ could develop a rounded allophone [y] (SCN 8.5/6. line 2), which can be reconstructed out of spelling variants like {artifex, artufex}. More detailed descriptions can be found in Sihler 1995:60 and Weiss 2009:120.

● **Developments ca. 500–400 BC**

	Preform	Assimilation	SCN 8.1 a > e	SCN 8.2 o > e	SCN 8.3 e > i	SCN 8.4 u > i	SCN 8.5/6 i/u > y
1	**ád-kapiō*	**ákkapiō*	**ákkepiō*		**ákkipiō*		
2	**ád-rapiō*	**árrapiō*	**árrepiō*		**árripiō*		**árrypiō*
3	**ád-lai̯dō*	**állai̯dō*	**állei̯dō*				
4	**ád-taŋgō*	**áttaŋgō*	**átteŋgō*				
5	**éks-kau̯ssō*		**éks-keu̯ssō*				
6	**nóu̯otāts*			**nóu̯etāts*	**nóu̯itāts*		
7	**sókiotāts*			**sókietāts*			
8	**u̯íroi̯*			**u̯írei̯*			
9	**péparai̯*			**péperei̯*			
10	**káputes*					**kápites*	

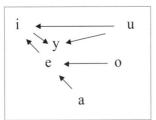

This chart illustrates the vowel changes. /u/ and /i/ cannot be raised further, but only rounded to [y]. No other vowel moved into the position of /a/ because /a/ is the lowest of the given vowels.

Exercises

INFO   SCN Ac1 describes the shift of the Early Latin initial stress accent to the classical rule of the penult.

E1 In closed medial syllables, /a/ is raised to /e/.

A {annus} *annus* 'year' :: *bí-annium* > (8.1) * _____ > (Ac1) _____

{_____} 'time of two years' **B** {arma} *arma* 'weapons' :: *ín-armis* > (8.1) * _____

> (Ac1) _____ {_____} 'unarmed' **C** {carpo} *karpō* 'I plug' :: *éks-karpō* > (8.1)

* _____ > (Ac1) _____ {_____} 'I discard'

E2 In open medial syllables, /e/ is raised to /i/ and /u/ is fronted to /i/.

A {placet} *plaket* 'it is pleasing' :: *dísplaket* > (8.1) * _____ > (8.3) _____

{_____} 'it is not pleasing' **B** {medius} *medius* 'medial' :: *dímedios* > (8.3)

* _____ > (Ac1) * _____ > (9.18) _____ {_____} 'by half'

C {rego} *regō* 'I govern' :: *díregō* > (8.3) _____ {_____} 'I straighten' **D** {peto}

petō 'I strive for' :: *kompetum* > (8.3) _____ {_____} 'crossroads' **E** {lego} *legō*

'I read' :: *élegō* > (8.3) _____ {_____} 'I choose' **F** {statuo} *statuō* 'I put up' ::

réstatuō > (8.1) * _____ > (8.3) * _____ > (Ac1) _____ {_____}

'I restore' **G** {cornu} *kornu* 'horn' :: *kornu-ger* > (8.4) _____ {_____} 'having

horns' **H** {manus} *manus* 'hand' :: *manuka* > (8.4) _____ {_____} 'sleeve'

E3 Before labial sounds except /u̯/, the vowels /i/ and /u/ are rounded to [y] and spelled {i} or {u}.

A {manus} *manus* 'hand' :: *mánu-pulus* > (8.6) *mánypulus* > (Ac1) *manýpulus* {manipulus}

'handful' **B** *opos* 'work' + *fakiō* :: *opo-fak-s* > (8.1) * _____ > (8.2) * _____ >

(8.3) * _____ > (8.5) _____ {_____} 'craftsman' **C** {ars} *ars* + *fakiō* ::

arti-faks > (8.1) * _____ > (8.5) _____ {_____} 'artist' **D** *optemos* >

(8.3) * _____ > (8.5) * _____ > (9.18) _____ {_____} 'the best'

15

● **Developments before and until the accent shift**

The vowel /e/ was raised to /i/ before [ŋ] (SCN 8.7), which inevitably occurred only in closed syllables because [ŋ] was the allophone of /n/ before /g/ and /k/ as well as the result of the assimilation of /g/ before /n/. The vowel /e/ was backed to /o/ before /u̯/ (SCN 8.9) and further raised to /u/ in open syllables (SCN 8.11). SCN 8.9 had been active in stressed syllables already by Proto-Italic times (SCN 9.10). This sound change is the reoccurring tendency to assimilate the place of articulation of /e/ to /u̯/. Analogous to the development of /e/ before velarized /u̯/, the vowel /e/ was also backed to /o/ before velar [ł] (SCN 8.8) before it was further raised to /u/ (SCN 8.10). Later on, /o/ was raised to /u/ even in unstressed closed syllables that did not end in /u̯/ or [ł], as can be seen from the development of OL *indostruus* to CL *industrius* 'industrious'. SCN 8.7, 8.8, 8.9 and 8.10 reoccurred in initial syllables in later times, too. In this book, the accent shift from the initial position to the penult is applied after the application of rule SCN 8.

● **Developments ca. 400–300 BC**

		SCN 8.7	SCN 8.9	SCN 8.8	SCN 8.10	SCN 8.11	Ac1
	Preform	e > i / _ŋ	e > o / _u̯	e > o / _ł	o > u / _ł	o > u / _u̯	**Accent**
1	*átteŋgō	áttiŋgō					attíŋgō
2	*ábleu̯ō		*áblou̯ō			*ábluu̯ō	
3	*éks-keu̯ssō		*ékskou̯ssō				*eks-kóu̯ssō
4	*dḗsełtōr			*dḗsołtōr	*dḗsułtōr		*dēsúłtōr
5	*ókkełō			*ókkołō	*ókkułō		

● **The 4ᵗʰ century BC accent shift**

The reasons for the accent shift from the initial to the penult position are still uninvestigated. One possible reason could have been the attempt to level accentual differences between simple and compound verbs. The effects of vowel weakening are seen mainly in compound verbs which had been stressed on the prefix in Early Latin times. This tendency to level out accentual variation in verbal paradigms became even more popular in late VL, when, in addition to the phenomenon of recomposition, which is the substitution of the vowel of a weakened form by the vowel of a corresponding non-weakenend form, also the regular CL accent position of compound forms was replaced by the accent position of the corresponding simple verbs. During the time of the accent shift, it is likely that many words existed with variant accentuation such as in *dḗsołtōr /*dēsółtōr, so that the context of vowel weakening in unstressed syllables could be transferred to stressed syllables as well. Nearly all of the above described sound changes, which originated in unstressed syllables, can be found also in stressed initial syllables in later times.

Sound change	e > i / _ŋ	e > o / _u̯	e > o / _ł	o > u / _ł
In medial syllables	8.7	8.9	8.8	8.10
In initial syllables	9.6	9.10/10.2	9.9	9.21

Exercises

E1 /e/ is raised to /i/ before [ŋ].

A {frango} *fraŋgō* 'I break' ::*kónfraŋgō > (8.1) * _____ > (8.7) * _____ >

(Ac1) _____ {_____} 'I break into pieces' **B** {pango} *paŋgō* 'I fix' :: *súbpaŋgō

> (12.1) * _____ > (8.1) _____ > (8.7) _____ > (Ac1) _____

{_____} 'I fix below'

E2 /e/, which originated from /a/, is backed to /o/ before /u̯/ or [ɫ], and then raised to /u/.

A {lauo} *lau̯ō* 'I wash' :: *ablau̯ō > (8.1) * _____ > (8.9) * _____ > (8.11)

_____ {_____} 'I wash' **B** {pauio} *pau̯iō* 'I hit' :: *dépau̯iō > (8.1) *_____

> (8.9) * _____ > (8.11) * _____ > (Ac1) _____ {_____} 'I

cudgel' **C** *nou̯os > (9.18) *nou̯us* {nouus} 'new' :: *dē-nou̯ōd > (8.11) * _____ > (38.3)

_____ {_____} 'anew' **D** *sēd-doɫōd > (39.1) * _____ > (8.10)

* _____ > (38.3)* _____ {_____} 'zealous' **E** {sicilia} *Sikilia* 'Sicily' ::

*Sikeɫos > (8.8) *_____ > (8.10) *_____ > (9.18) _____ {_____}

'Sicilian'

E3 /a/ is raised to /e/ in closed final syllables.

A {remus} *rēmus* 'oar of a ship' + *agō* :: *rēm-ag-s > (13.6) * _____ > (8.1) _____

{_____} 'rower' **B** {primus} *prīmus* 'first' + *kaput* 'head' :: *prīmo-kaps > (4.1) *

_____ > (19.11) *_____ > (8.1) _____ {_____} 'leading person'

These SCN rules appear in the exercises		
SCN 9.18	o > u / _C(C)#	Raising of /o/ to /u/ in closed final syllables.
SCN 12.1	b > p / _p	Voiced /b/ becomes voiceless /p/ before voiceless /p/.
SCN 13.6	g > k / _s	Voiced /g/ becomes voiceless /k/ before voiceless /s/.
SCN 19.11	m > ŋ / _k	The labial nasal /m/ becomes velar [ŋ] before velar /k/.
SCN 38.3	d > 0 / V̄_#	/d/ is lost in the final position after a long vowel.
SCN 39.1	C₁ > 0 / V̄_C₁	A double consonant is simplified after a long vowel.

● **SCN 9.5 e > i / _ ŋ. SCN 9.6 e > i / _mb**
Raising of /e/ to /i/ before nasal consonants

The sound change e > i occurs regularly before the velar nasal [ŋ], which was the allophonic variant of /n/ before the velar stops /g/ and /k/ (SCN 19.4/19.5), as well as the result of the assimilation of /g/ before /n/ (SCN 17.5). After /e/ had become /i/ before [ŋ] in unstressed positions such as in *kónteŋgō > (8.7) *kóntiŋgō > (Ac1) kontíŋgō {contingo} 'I reach', the vowel /e/ in initial syllables aligned with this development later on. The word sīŋnum {signum} 'sign' originally meant 'something carved or cut' and can be linked to the verbal form sekō {seco} 'I cut'. The preforms of {signum} are as follows: *seknom > (14.5) *segnom > (17.5) *seŋnom > (9.6) *siŋnom > (2.5) *sīŋnom > (9.18) sīŋnum {signum}. After /k/ had become /g/ before voiced /n/ by SCN 14.5, and after /g/ had been further assimilated to [ŋ] by SCN 17.5, the condition for the sound change e > i / _ŋ had been produced. After /e/ had become /i/, this /i/ was lengthened by SCN 2.5.
The regular transition of /e/ to /i/ can also be found before /mb/, which is revealed by words such as *ember > (9.5) imber 'rain' and *lembos > (9.5) *limbos > (9.18) limbus 'fringe', the preforms of which can be derived by external reconstruction.

● **SCN 9.8 e > i / _C#   Vowel weakening in final syllables**

Just as in medial syllables, vowels in final syllables were also subject to vowel weakening. This development, however, cannot be explained by the effect of a strong initial accent because the initial accent had already shifted to the CL accentuation pattern at the time the weakening of final syllables occurred. Words consisting of two syllables might nevertheless have been directly affected by the initial accent because the unaccented final syllable directly followed the stressed initial syllable. The important function of carrying morphological information preserved unstressed vowels in final syllables intact longer than in medial syllables. Therefore, one finds many inscriptional forms of the gen. sg. of the consonant stems such as OL Kēreres {cereres} or OL Ịūnōnes {iunones} in contrast to the corresponding CL forms Kēreris and Ịūnōnis, in which the vowel of the final syllable was raised to /i/. Analogous to the change of /e/ to /i/, which can be dated to the end of the 4th century BC, the change of /o/ to /u/ such as in *opos > (9.18) opus 'work' occurred a little later around the middle of the 3rd century BC.

● **SCN 9.14a i > e / _#   Final /i/ was lowered to /e/**

The development was precisely the opposite in the case of a final /i/, which was lowered to /e/. The comparison of mare 'ocean' with its plural maria 'oceans' leads to the preform *mari for mare, which shows that a final -e of the neuter i-stems originated out of -i. Furthermore, the imperative of the third conjugation i-stems such as *kapi > (9.14) kape {cape} 'take!' exhibits this sound change, although in this case one could also think of a formation in analogy to other third conjugation forms such as rege 'govern!'.

The sound changes

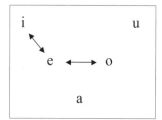

e > i and i > e concern the place and the manner of articulation. The sound changes e > o and o > e concern only the place of articulation, whereas the manner of articulation remains unchanged.

Exercises

E1 The raising of /e/ to /i/ was caused by velar [ŋ], which originated from assimilation.

A {decus} *dekus* 'honor' :: *deknos* > (14.5) * _____ > (17.5) * _____ > (9.6)

* _____ > (2.5) * _____ > (9.18) _____ {_____} 'worthy'

B {lego} *legō* 'I collect' :: *legnom* > (17.5) * _____ > (9.6) * _____ >

* _____ > (9.18) _____ {_____} 'firewood' **C** {tego} *tegō* 'I cover'

:: *tegnom* > (17.5) * _____ > (9.6) * _____ > (2.5) * _____ > (9.18)

_____ {_____} 'piece of lumber'

E2 Reconstruct the preforms of the CL forms that have a final /e/.

A * _____ > (9.14a) *sedīle* {_____} 'chair' **B** * _____ > (9.14a) *breųe*

{_____} 'short' **C** * _____ > (9.14a) *forte* 'brave' **D** * _____ > (9.14a)

ante {_____} 'before' **E** {_____} _____ > (1.3) * _____ >

(9.14a) *here* {_____} 'yesterday'

E3 Some dialectal variants have /i/ instead of CL /e/.

A {commercium} *kommerkium* > (9.4) _____ {_____} 'commerce' **B**

{stercus} *sterkus* > (9.4) _____ {_____} 'manure' **C** {Mercurius} *Merkurius*

> (9.4) _____ {_____} 'God of commerce' **D** *penna* > (9.3) _____

'feather' **E** {uellus} *ųellus* > (9.3) _____ {_____} 'fur' **F** {uetulus} *ųetulus* >

(9.3) _____ {_____} 'elderly' **G** {uespillo} *ųespillō* > (9.3) _____

{_____} 'undertaker'

Vowel weakening in the hiatus position

VL exhibits the 'consonantification' of /i/, /e/ and /u/ to the semivowels /i̯/, /e̯/ and /u̯/ in the hiatus position. This development can be regarded as a continuation of the general tendency of vowel weakening. In CL *gau̯dia* 'joys', it was the vowel /i/, and in *u̯īnea* 'vineyard', it was the vowel /e/ that became /i̯/ and produced the disyllabic forms *gau̯di̯a* and *u̯īni̯a* (via *u̯īnea* > *u̯īnia* > *u̯īni̯a*). This tendency can be detected quite early in the Annals of Ennius, where the usually trisyllabic gen. pl. {auium} *au̯ium* 'of the birds' counts as disyllabic in *au̯i̯um* (Ann. 89), and the trisyllabic {quattuor} *ku̯attuor* 'four' counts as disyllabic in *ku̯attu̯or* (Ann. 88). Furthermore, CL poets took advantage of this linguistic possibility, which can be seen in the disyllabic abl. *abi̯ete* for usually trisyllabic *abiete*, which is derived from *abiēs* {abies} 'fir tree' and can be found in Vergil. An example of /e/ being weakend to /e̯/ can be seen in the examples *e̯ōrundem* for *eōrundem* 'their' in Ennius (Ann. 200) and *au̯re̯a* for *au̯rea* 'golden' in Vergil (Aen. VII 190).

The Sound Change e > o

- **SCN 9.9 e > o / _ ł   /e/ is backed to /o/ and further raised to /u/ in closed syllables next to velar [ł]**

Before the vowels /o/, /u/, /a/, before a consonant (but not before another /l/), and in the final position, palatal /l/ had a velar allophone [ł]. This velar [ł] was articulated further back in the throat than palatal /l/ and thus caused an adjacent palatal /e/ to become velar /o/, which can be regarded as an assimilation of the place of articulation. At first, this sound change only affected unstressed /e/ such as in *ób-kelō > (12.3+18.2) *ókkelō > (8.8) *ókkołō, which later on became ókkułō {occulo} 'I hide' by SCN 8.10. Furthermore, a secondary unstressed /e/, which had originated out of /a/ by vowel weakening, was affected: *désaltōr > (8.1) *déseltōr > (8.8) *désoltōr > (8.10) *désultōr > (Ac1) dēsúltor {desultor} 'circus-rider' (cf. unit 14/15). But due to the accent change of the 4th century BC, also stressed initial syllables started to share the same development. Thus CL u̯olō {uolo} 'I want' can be traced back to the preform *u̯elō, by comparison with the infinitive u̯elle {uelle}. In closed syllables, this newly formed /o/ was further raised to /u/, as it had previously been raised in unstressed positions: *u̯elt > (9.9) *u̯olt > (9.21) u̯ult {uult} 'he wants'. In open syllables before [ł], /o/ remained unchanged, which can be seen from u̯olō {uolo}, which did not become ˣu̯ułō.

- **SCN 9.10 e > o / _u̯   /e/ is backed to /o/ before velar /u̯/**

From very early on, /e/ was backed to /o/ next to velar /u̯/. The PIE diphthong */eu̯/ had already become */ou̯/ in Proto-Italic times, because all Italic languages share this sound change. All the examples of the rarely occuring Latin group /eu̯/ have a secondary origin and stem either from */ēu̯/ or arose by SCN 36.1 and SCN x8.10. This sound change e > o / _u̯ can therefore be proven only by external reconstruction, as all Latin words already exhibit the result of the change *eu̯ > ou̯. By the comparison with Greek néos < *néu̯os, CL nou̯us {nouus} 'new' can be traced back to *neu̯os. The development was: *neu̯os > *nou̯os > *nou̯us.

This sound change e > o / _u̯ cannot be dated to a specific time but seems rather to have had a general effect in Latin language history, because one also finds the development of secondary /e/ to /o/ next to /u̯/: *áblau̯ō > (8.1) *ábleu̯ō > (9.9) *áblou̯ō, which became ablu̯ō {abluo/abluuo} 'I wash off' later on. Weakened diphthongs (au̯ > eu̯) shared the same development as in *éks-kau̯ssō > (8.1) *éks-keu̯ssō > (8.9) *éks-kou̯ssō > (Ac1) *ekskóu̯ssō > (10.3) *ekskǭssō > (10.4) ekskūsō {excuso} 'I excuse'. Even stressed /e/ such as in *bréu̯ma, which had originated out of *bréu̯ima {breuima} by syncope, was backed to /o/, which resulted in *bróu̯ma before /ou̯/ became /ū/, resulting in brūma {bruma} 'summer solstice'.

- **SCN 9.11 e > o / u̯_C(C)a,o,u   /e/ was backed to /o/ after /u̯/ due to vowel assimilation**

The so called o-umlaut affected /e/ when it occured after /u̯/ and one of the velar vowels /a/, /o/, /u/ followed in the next syllable. EL {duenos} du̯enos changed via *du̯onos to CL bonus {bonus} 'good', whereas the related form bene {bene} 'well' was not affected because it goes back to *du̯enēd, in which the required phonological context is not given. Most examples showing this sound change can only be reconstructed by external reconstruction, which proves this sound change to be very old.

Exercises

E1 Velar [ɫ] caused the velarization of /e/ to /o/ which remained in open syllables.

A {uelle} u̯elle 'to want' :: *u̯eltis > (28.1) * _____ > (9.9) _____ > (9.19)

_____ {_____} 'you want' **B** *ku̯elō > (28.3) * _____ > (9.9)

* _____ > (40.5) _____ {_____} **C** *helos > (28.3) * _____ >

(9.9) _____ > (9.18) _____ {_____} 'green vegetables'

E2 For experts only: further changes take place after the o-umlaut.

A *su̯epnos > (9.11) * _____ > (40.5) * _____ > (14.2) * _____ >

(17.2) * _____ > (9.18) _____ {_____} 'sleep' **B** *ku̯eku̯ō > (9.11)

* _____ > (40.5) _____ {_____} 'I cook' **C** *su̯esōr > (9.11)

* _____ > (40.5) * _____ > (15.6) * _____ > (26.1) * _____

> (1.4) _____ {_____} 'sister' **D** *su̯ekrūs > (9.11) * _____ > (40.5)

* _____ > (A: ū > u) _____ {_____} 'mother-in-law' **E** *su̯ekords > (9.11)

* _____ > (40.5) * _____ > (13.4) * _____ > (16.4) * _____

> (39.7) _____ {_____} 'sorrowless' **F** *u̯emō > (9.11) _____

{_____} 'I vomit'

These SCN rules appear in the excercises		
SCN 1.4	V̄ > V / _C#	Shortening of long vowels in final syllables.
SCN 13.4	d > t / _s	Voiced /d/ becomes voiceless /t/ before voiceless /s/.
SCN 14.2	p > b / _n	Voiceless /p/ becomes voiced /b/ before voiced /n/.
SCN 15.6	s > z / V_V	Intervocalic voiceless /s/ becomes voiced [z].
SCN 16.4	t > s / _s	Voiceless /t/ becomes /s/ before /s/.
SCN 17.2	b > m / _n	Labial /b/ becomes /m/ before /n/.
SCN 26.1	z > r / V_V	Rhotazism followed SCN 15.6.
SCN 28.1	l > ɫ / _C	/l/ has a velar allophone [ɫ] before a consonant.
SCN 28.3	l > ɫ / _(a, o, u)	/l/ has a velar allophone [ɫ] before the velar vowels /a/, /o/ and /u/.
SCN 39.7	s > 0 / s_#	A double consonant was simplified in the final position.
SCN 40.5	u̯ > 0 / _(o, ō, u, ū)	/u̯/ was lost before phonetically similar velar vowels.
SCN A	**Analogical change**	The sound change happened in analogy to other forms (cf. unit 32).

- **SCN 9.15 o > e / u̯_(rC, s, t)**   Dissimilation of /o/ to /e/ next to /u̯/

Many Old Latin forms such as *u̯oster* {uoster} and *u̯otō* {uoto} have o-vocalism while their corresponding CL forms *u̯ester* {uester} 'your' and CL *u̯etō* {ueto} 'I veto' have e-vocalism. The sound change u̯o > u̯e probably started at the beginning or in the middle of the 2nd century BC and had the opposite effect of the so called o-umlaut, which happened some centuries earlier and transformed EL {duenos} *du̯enos* via SCN 9.11 to *du̯onos*, before it developed further to CL *bonus* 'good' (cf. the preceding chapter). While the o-umlaut can be regarded as an assimilation of the place of articulation of /e/ to /u̯/, the transformation of /o/ to /e/ next to /u̯/ such as in *u̯oster > u̯ester* seems to be a dissimilatory tendency caused by the initial /u̯/.

- **SCN 9.16/17/18/19 o > u / _N**   Raising of /o/ to /u/ in different positions

CL *uŋkus* {uncus} 'hook' and *umbilīkus* {umbilicus} 'navel' can be traced back to *oŋkos and *ombilīkus by external reconstruction and exhibit the sound change o > u next to the nasals [ŋ] and /m/. The development before [ŋ] was more consistent than before /m/, but for both contexts one can find counterexamples such as *domus* 'house', *loŋgus* {longus} 'long' and *toŋgeō* {tongeo} 'I know' without the respective sound changes. This vowel raising took place around the end of the 3rd century BC and also affected final syllables, which can be seen in the examples acc. sg. {honc} *hoŋk > huŋk* {hunc} 'this' and {consentiont} *kōnsentiont > kōnsentiunt* {consentiunt} 'they agreed'. A preceding /u̯/ delayed the sound change o > u by dissimilation until about 50 BC (SCN 9.19), which means that the change of *kōnsentiont > kōnsentiunt* happened earlier than the change of *seku̯ontur > (9.19) seku̯untur* {sequuntur} 'they follow'.

- **SCN 9.21 o > u / _ɫC**   /o/ is raised to /u/ in closed syllables before [ɫ]

By comparing the Old Latin forms *koɫpa* {colpa} 'guilt' and *moɫta* {molta} 'punishment' to their CL cognates *kuɫpa* {culpa} and *muɫta* {multa}, one finds that the /o/ was raised to /u/ before velar [ɫ]. This sound change also affected the /o/ that had originated from /e/ and can thus be regarded as the final step of the tendency to raise vowels before [ɫ]. An example for this development is furnished by: *u̯elt > (28.1) *u̯eɫt > (9.9) *u̯oɫt > (9.14) u̯uɫt* {uult} 'he wants'. The same result had already been reached in unstressed syllables earlier, as can be seen from examples such as *tetoɫai̯ > (8.1) *tetoɫei̯ > (8.10) *tetuɫei̯ > (10.8/9) tetulī* {tetuli} 'I brought' and *okkoɫō > (8.10) okkuɫō* {occulo} 'I hide'.

- **Symmetries of vowel developments**

The phonemes of a language constitute a system in which all elements have a mutual relation and influence each other. Modifications that affected one element within the phoneme system could therefore be transferred to elements with similar features. The raising of the vowels e > i and o > u before the velar nasal [ŋ], as well as in the final position before a consonant, are examples that show how elements can develop symmetrically within a phoneme system.

Symmetrical developments of /o/ and /e/			
SCN 9.16	o > u / _ŋ	SCN 9.6	e > i / _ŋ
SCN 9.18	o > u / _C(C)#	SCN 9.8	e > i / _C#

Exercises

E1 Reconstruct the OL preforms.

A OL {_____} _____ > (9.15) *dīu̯ertium* {diuertium} 'divorce' **B** OL

{_____} _____ > (9.15) *u̯erteks* {uertex} 'whirl' **C** OL {_____}

_____ > (9.15) *u̯errō* {uerro} 'I sweep' **D** OL {_____} _____ (The prefix

{ar-} is an OL dialect variant of {ad-} before labial sounds.) > (9.15) *ad-u̯ersum* {aduersum} 'against'

E OL {_____} _____ > (9.15) *u̯ertō* {uerto} 'I turn' **F** OL {_____}

_____ > (9.15) *reu̯ertus* {reuertus} 'come back'

E2 Before [ɫ], /e/ was backed to /o/ and then raised to /u/.

A {uelle} *u̯elle* 'want' :: *u̯eltis* > (28.1) * _____ > (9.9) _____ > (9.21)

_____ {_____} 'you want' **B** *polenta* 'peeled barley' :: *pols* > (28.1)

* _____ > (9.21) _____ {_____} 'pap' **C** *pollen* 'fine flour' :: *polu̯is* >

(28.1) * _____ > (9.21) _____ {_____} 'dust' **D** {consol} *kōnsol* > (28.2)

_____ > (9.18) _____ {_____} 'consul'

E3 Reconstruct the preforms.

A {_____} _____ > (9.19) *seku̯untur* {sequuntur} 'they follow' **B** {_____}

_____ > (9.18) *probāu̯ērunt* {probauerunt} 'they approved' **C** _____ > (9.18)

suum 'his own' **D** {_____} _____ > (9.16) *huŋk* {hunc} 'this' **E** {_____}

_____ > (9.18) *dōnum* {donum} 'gift' **F** {_____} _____ > (9.16/9.19)

au̯uŋkulus {auunculus} 'oncle' **G** {_____} _____ > (28.1) _____ >

(9.21/9.19) *u̯uɫnus* {uulnus} 'wound' **H** {_____} * _____ > (28.1) _____

> (9.21/9.19) *u̯uɫgus* {uulgus} 'ordinary people' **I** {uolua} * _____ > (28.1) _____

> (9.21/9.19) *u̯uɫu̯a* {uulua} 'womb'

The lateral sound /l/ and its allophone [ɫ]		
SCN 28.1	l > ɫ / _C	/l/ has a velar allophone [ɫ] before a consonant.
SCN 28.2	l > ɫ / _#	/l/ has a velar allophone [ɫ] in the final position.
SCN 28.3	l > ɫ / _(a,o,u)	/l/ has a velar allophone [ɫ] before the velar vowels /a/, /o/ and /u/.

19 Monophthongizations in Medial and Final Syllables

- **Development of the i-diphthongs /ei̯/, /ai̯/ and /oi̯/ in medial and final syllables**

The Early Latin Forum-inscription attests the dat. sg. *rēgei̯* {recei}, which corresponds to the dat. sg. CL *rēgī* {regi} from *rēks* {rex} 'king'. The development of the ending shows that CL /ī/ can be traced back to an earlier /ei̯/. One can furthermore postulate the intermediate step /ē/ within the evolution ei̯ > ī, which is evidenced by the final {e} of the inscriptional form OL *ploi̯rymē* {ploirume}, which corresponds to CL *plūrimī* 'most' and goes back via *ploi̯rymoi̯* (SCN 8.2) to *ploi̯rymei̯*. Cf. line 1 of the table below.

The formation of the 1. ps. sg. perfect ending can also be explained by the development ei̯ > ē > ī shown in line 2 of the table below. The vowel weakening in the 5 century BC caused an unstressed /a/ to become /e/ (column B), but did not affect a stressed /a/. By this process, also the diphthong /ai̯/ became /ei̯/ and shared the further evolution of /ei̯/. This affected e.g. the dat. and abl. pl. of the a-stems (line 3) or compound verbs (line 4). Unstressed /oi̯/ merged with /ei̯/ as well and shared the same further evolution (line 5), because /o/ had also been affected by vowel weakening, as can be seen in the earlier example *ploi̯rymoi̯* > (8.2) *ploi̯rymei̯*. Column D of the table describes the accent shift from the initial position to the penult position. From then on, the further development of stressed and unstressed /ei̯/ was the same.

- **The development of the u-diphthongs /eu̯/, /au̯/ and /ou̯/ in medial and final syllables**

In the case of original /eu̯/ (line 6) and /eu̯/, which originated from /au̯/ due to vowel weakening (line 7, column B), the /e/ was backed to /o/ producing /ou̯/ (column C). This rule must already have been active in Proto-Italic and taken effect again and again in the course of Latin language history. A newly formed /ou̯/, as well as original /ou̯/, monophthongized (column E) to long /ō/ and were raised to /ū/ in a second step (column F). For both the i-diphthongs and the u-diphthongs, the development from diphthong to monophthong proceeded via the intermediate steps /ē/ and /ō/, which were subsequently raised to /ī/ and /ū/ (cf. SCN 11).

- **Developments ca. 500–400 BC (columns B, C), 400–300 (column D), 300–200 (column E), 200–100 (column F)**

	A	B SCN 8.1/8.2	C SCN 8.9	D Ac1	E SCN 10.8/10.3	F SCN 10.9/10.4
	Preform	a/o > e	e > o / _u̯	Accent	ei̯ > ē / ou̯ > ō	ē > ī / ō > ū
1	EL *rēgei̯*				*rēgē*	*rēgī*
2	*memenei̯*				*meminē*	*meminī*
3	*terrai̯s*	*terrei̯s*			*terrēs*	*terrīs*
4	*állai̯dō*	*állei̯dō*		*alléi̯dō*	*allēdō*	*allīdō*
5	*u̯iroi̯*	*u̯irei̯*			*u̯irē*	*u̯irī*
6	*korneu̯s*		*kornou̯s*		*kornōs*	*kornūs*
7	*éks-kau̯ssō*	*éks-keu̯ssō*	*éks-kou̯ssō*	*eks-kóu̯ssō*	*ekskōssō*	*ekskūssō*
8	*ábdou̯kō*			OL *abdóu̯kō* *	*abdōkō*	*abdūkō*

Exercises

E1 Trace the development of /ai̯/ in medial syllables. The development of /ai̯/ in initial syllables, which will be discussed in the next unit, is shown to the left of the comparation operator {::}.

A *ai̯stimō* > (10.6) > *aẹstimō* {aestimo} 'I estimate' :: *éks-ai̯stimō* > (8.1) * _____ >

(Ac1) * _____ > (10.8) _____ > (10.9) _____ {_____} 'I

estimate' **B** *lai̯dō* > (10.6) *laẹdō* {laedo} 'I injure' :: *ád-lai̯dō* > (20.4) * _____ > (8.1)

* _____ > (Ac1) * _____ > (10.8) * _____ > (10.9) _____

{_____} 'I bump at' **C** *ólai̯u̯a* > (8.1) * _____ > (Ac1) * _____ > (10.8)

* _____ > (10.9) _____ {_____} 'olive tree' **D** {aequus} *aẹku̯us* 'even'

:: *ín-ai̯ku̯os* > (8.1) * _____ > (Ac1) * _____ > (10.8) * _____ > (10.9)

* _____ > (9.18) _____ {_____} 'uneven' **E** {taedet} *taẹdet* 'he is tired

of' :: *dís-tai̯d-to-m* > (12.5) * _____ > (x3) * _____ > (8.1) * _____ >

(Ac1) * _____ > (10.8) _____ > (10.9) * _____ > (39.1) * _____

> (9.18) _____ {_____} 'he is strongly tired of' **F** *kai̯dō* > (10.6) *kaẹdō* {caedo}

'I cut' :: *ké-kai̯dai̯* > (8.1) * _____ > (Ac1) * _____ > (10.8) * _____ >

(10.9) _____ {_____} 'I chopped'

E2 Trace the development of /au̯/ in medial syllables.

A {causa} *kau̯sa* 'cause' :: *éks-kau̯ssō* > (8.1) * _____ > (8.9) * _____ > (Ac1)

* _____ > (10.3) * _____ > (10.4) * _____ > (39.1) _____

{_____} 'I apologize' **B** {fraudo} *frau̯dō* 'I betray' :: *dé̄-frau̯dō* > (8.1) * _____ >

(8.9) * _____ > (Ac1) * _____ > (10.3) * _____ > (10.4) _____

{_____} 'I betray' **C** {claudo} *klau̯dō* 'I close' :: * ín-klau̯dō > (8.1) * _____ >

(8.9) * _____ > (Ac1) * _____ > (10.3) * _____ > (10.4) _____

{_____} 'I close sth. within'

SCN 20.4	**d > l / _l**		/d/ becomes /l/ before /l/.
SCN 39.1	$C_1 > 0 / \bar{V}\_C_1$		A double consonant is simplified after a long vowel or diphthong.
SCN x3	***tt > ss**		This sound change is arrived at by means of external reconstruction.

- **SCN 10.3/10.4 oṷ > ǭ > ū**
The diphthong /oṷ/ was monophthongized to /ǭ/ and raised to /ū/

The diphthong /oṷ/ originated from */oṷ/ and */eṷ/, which had become /oṷ/ by SCN 9.10/10.2. Both shared the same further development. Old inscriptions and texts still attest unaltered /oṷ/, which can be seen e.g. in OL *loṷkos* {loucos} 'clearing' and OL *noṷtrīks* {noutrix} 'wet nurse'. Analogous to the intermediate step /ē̦/ of the development of OL /ei̯/ to CL /ī/, one can posit the intermediate step /ǭ/ of the development of OL /oṷ/ to CL /ū/, which is attested in the inscriptional form {locina} for OL {loucina}, which became CL *lūkīna* {lucina} 'goddess of childbirth' (cf. Weiss 2009:103). Examples: *loṷkos* > (10.3) **lǭkos* > (10.4) **lūkos* > (9.18) *lūkus* {lucus}, and *noṷtrīks* > (10.3) **nǭtrīks* > (10.4) *nūtrīks* {nutrix}.

- **SCN 10.1/10.6/10.7 ai̯ > ae̦ > ē̦**
The diphthongs /aṷ/ and /ai̯/

In initial syllables, the diphthong /ai̯/ was monophthongized via /ae̦/ to VL /ē̦/, whereas in CL this development halted at the stage /ae̦/ with a lowered second element of the diphthong. Also the development of /aṷ/ halted at /ao̦/ {au} in CL (cf. footnote SCN 10.1), whereas the VL monophthongization aṷ > ǭ was very common already in classical times. This is seen in numerous complementary variants such as {codex} *kǭdeks* :: *kaṷdeks* {caudex} 'book' or {colis} *kǭlis* :: *kaṷlis* {caulis} 'stalk'. The language of the elite used /ao̦/ {au} and /ae̦/ {ae}, whereas in popular speech /ǭ/ and /ē̦/ were preferred, leading to a diastratic distribution of the variant forms.

- **SCN 10.8/10.9 ei̯ > ē̦ > ī**
Diphthongal /ei̯/ was monophthongized to /ē̦/ and subsequently raised to /ī/

The diphthong /ei̯/ was monophthongized to /ē̦/ and subsequently further raised to /ī/ in both initial and medial syllables. The intermediate step /ē̦/ can be found in the word *deus* {deus} 'God', which stems from **dei̯u̯os*, of which the EL Duenos inscription attests an acc. pl. *dei̯u̯ōs* {deiuos}. After having reached the intermediate step **dei̯u̯os* > (10.8) **dē̦u̯os* by monophthongization, /u̯/ was lost by SCN 40.5 **dē̦u̯os* > **dē̦os*, which developed to **deos* by SCN 1.1 and further to *deus* by SCN 9.18. The development ei̯ > ē̦ > ī can be seen in the adjective *dīu̯us* {diuus}, which stems from **dei̯u̯os,* too. In this case, /u̯/ was analogically restored in the nominative in analogy to other paradigmatic forms such as the gen. *dīu̯ī*.

- **SCN 10.10/11 oi̯ > oe̦ > ǭ > ū**
Diphthongal /oi̯/ was monophthongized to /ǭ/ and subsequently raised to /ū/

In initial syllables, /oi̯/ was monophthongized via /oe̦/ to /ǭ/, and then joined the further development of /ū/ as can be seen in the change of OL *oi̯nos* to CL *ūnus* {unus} and OL *oi̯tile* to CL *ūtile* {utile}. After initial /f/ or /p/, it remained as {oe} if /i/ or /ī/ did not follow in the next syllable. In this case, it normally developed via /ǭ/ to /ū/. Examples for the retention of /oe̦/ are: **foi̯dos* > (10.10) **foe̦dos* > (9.18) *foe̦dus* {foedus} 'alliance' and **Poi̯nos* > (10.10) **Poe̦nos* > (9.18) *Poe̦nus* {poenus} 'Punic'. Examples for the change of /oi̯/ to /ū/ caused by /i/ in the next syllable are: **Poi̯nikos* > (10.10) **Poe̦nikos* > (10.11) **Pǭnikos* > (10.4) **Pūnikos* > (9.18) *Pūnikus* {punicus} 'Punic' and **poi̯niō* > (10.10) **poe̦niō* > (10.11) **pǭniō* > (10.4) *pūniō* {punio} 'I punish'.

> **INFO** In the initial sequence #u̯oi̯- attested in **u̯oi̯kos* > (10.12) **u̯ei̯kos* > (10.8) **u̯ē̦kos* > (10.9) **u̯īkos* > (9.18) *u̯īkus* {uicus} 'settlement', the /o/ of the diphthong /oi̯/ changed to /e/ by SCN 9.15, creating the diphthong /ei̯/, which joined the normal development of ei̯ > (10.8) ē̦ > (10.9) ī.

Exercises

E1 Add either the CL or the VL form.

A CL _____ > (10.1) VL *lōrẹola* 'a little triumph' **B** CL *aụrikula* > (10.1) VL _____

'earlobe' **C** CL _____ > (10.1) VL *Ōlus* 'a name' **D** CL _____ > (10.1) VL *plōdere*

'to applaud' **E** CL *plaụstrum* > (10.1) VL _____ 'wagon'

E2 Trace the development of OL /eị/ to CL /ī/.

A {_____} *deus* 'god' :: *deịụos* > (10.8) *_____ > (10.9) *_____ >

(9.18) _____ {_____} 'divine' **B** *deịkō* > (10.8) *_____ > (10.9)

_____ {_____} 'I say' **C** {feido} *feịdō* > (10.8) *_____ > (10.9)

_____ {_____} 'I believe' **D** OL {_____} *seị* > (10.8) *_____ > (10.9)

_____ {_____} 'if' **F** OL {sibei} *sibeị* > (10.8) *_____ > (10.9) _____ >

(1.3) _____ {_____} 'oneself' **G** {abeis} *ab-eịs* > (10.8) *_____ > (10.9)

_____ {_____} 'you go away' **H** {_____} *keịụis* > (10.8) *_____

> (10.9) _____ {_____} 'citizen' **I** {uirtutei} *ụirtūteị* > (10.8) _____ >

(10.9) _____ {_____} dat. sg. 'virtue'

E3 Trace the context-sensitive development of OL /oị/ to either CL /oẹ/ or CL /ū/.

A OL {loidos} *loịdos* > (10.10) *_____ > (10.11) *_____ > (10.4)

*_____ > (9.18) _____ {_____} 'game' **B** {coiraueront} *koịrāụẹront* >

(10.10) *_____ > (10.11) *_____ > (10.4) *_____ > (9.18) _____

{_____} 'they cared for' **C** OL {moerum} *moẹrom* > (10.11) *_____ >

(10.4) *_____ > (9.18) _____ {_____} 'wall' **D** OL {moinicipiom}

moịnikipiom > (10.10) *_____ > (10.11) *_____ > (10.4) *_____ > (9.18)

_____ {_____} 'town' **E** OL {oetantur} *oẹtantur* > (10.11) *_____ >

(10.4) _____ {_____} 'they use' **F** *foịdos* > (10.10) *_____ > (9.18)

_____ {_____} 'contract'

Anaptyxis and Vowel Assimilation

- **SCN 5 0 > V / C_C (V=u, i)**   Anaptyxis as the counterpart to syncope

Many languages break up consonant clusters in order to facilitate their pronunciation by inserting vowels between the consonants. This phenomenon is called anaptyxis and functions as a counterpart to syncope, which elides vowels between consonants. The inserted vowels are known as anaptyctic vowels. In Latin, the consonant clusters /kl/, /gl/, /pl/ and /bl/ were subject to anaptyxis, a phenomenon seen in the development of the word *perīklum* {periclum} to *perīkulum* {periculum} 'danger'. Both forms were used as poetic variants to fit the syllable count of a line. If the {l} following the consonant was a palatal /l/, the anaptyctic vowel was /i/, as seen in *faklis* > (5.1) *fakilis* {facilis} 'easy'. If it was a velar [ł], the anaptyctic vowel was /u/, as seen in *perīklum* > (5.2) *perīkułum*. In VL, the suffixes *-kułum* {-culum} and *-bułum* {bulum} such as in *stabułum* {stabulum} were again regularly syncopated, which can be seen by their further development in the Romance languages. The use of these suffix variants was distributed diastratically and diatopically throughout the language system.

- **SCN 7 V$_1$...V$_2$ > V$_1$...V$_1$**   Progressive vowel assimilation

In VL, one finds the two forms *karkar* {carcar} and *ānsar* {ansar} for CL *karker* {carcer} 'prison' and CL *ānser* {anser} 'goose'. Both cases exhibit the assimilation of the /e/ in the second syllable to the /a/ of the first syllable. If a sound in a word takes on features from another sound, one speaks of assimilation. The linguistic phenomenon exemplified in this case is known as a distant progressive assimilation, because the first vowel progressively transfers its quality onto a non-adjacent vowel. Another example is *kalamitās* {calamitas} 'misfortune', which must have evolved from *kalimitās**, in which the vowel /i/ is expected as a result of vowel weakening. The same applies to *alaker, alakris* {alacer, alacris} 'happy', which should have been *aliker**, *alekris**, according to regular sound changes. The regular form **alékris* (cf. accent rule Ac2 in unit 8), however, must have also existed, because it is presupposed by the further development to Italian *allegro* and Old Provencial *alegre*.

> **INFO**   Vowel assimilations occur rarely, compared to the consonant assimilations, which are described in the next chapters.

- **INFO: SCN 9.22 o > a / _u̯**   The rule of Thurneysen and Havet

External reconstruction reveals a Latin sound change o > a / _u̯. The Greek forms *lóō* < **lou̯ō* 'I bathe' and *koéō* < **kou̯eō* 'I hear' enables to reconstruct the preforms **lou̯ō* and **kou̯eō* for CL *lau̯ō* {lauo} 'I wash' and *kau̯eō* {caueo} 'I beware'. In Greek, intervocalic /u̯/ was lost (cf. unit 37, line 24). A phonetic similar case is seen in the development of long ō > ā / _u̯ (cf. SCN 30). The preform of *flāu̯us* {flauus} 'golden yellow' can be reconstructed as **flōu̯os* by comparison with *flōrus*. Another example is *oktāu̯us* {octauus} 'the eigth', which goes back to **oktōu̯os*. The initial /o/, however, might also have changed the following /ō/ to /ā/ by dissimilation.

Exercises

E1 The sound of the anaptyctic vowel is defined by the sound following.

A *popłus* > (5.2) _____ {_____} 'people' **B** *pōtłom* > (28.4) *_____ >

(5.2) *_____ > (9.18) _____ {_____} 'drinking cup' **C** {piaclum} *piākłum*

> (5.2) _____ {_____} 'sin offering' **D** {uinclum} *u̯iŋkłum* > (5.2) _____

{_____} 'binding rope' **E** *stabłum* > (5.2) _____ {_____} 'stable' **F**

stablis > (5.1) _____ {_____} 'solid' **G** {iuglans} *i̯ūgłāns* > (5.2) _____

{_____} 'walnut' **H** *faklis* > (5.1) _____ {_____} 'easy' **I** {extemplo}

ekstempłō > (5.2) _____ {_____} 'instantly'

E2 Reconstruct the preforms by using the rule of Thurneysen and Havet.

A *_____ > (9.22) *_____ > (9.18) _____ {cauus} 'hollow'

B *_____ > (9.22) _____ {faueo} 'I favor'

E3 Examples for regressive vowel assimilation.

A {semper} *sem-per* 'always' :: *semlis* > (5.1) *_____ > (7.1) _____

{_____} 'similar' **B** *nesī* > (7.1) _____ {_____} 'if not' **C** {hilum}

hīlum 'shred' :: *ne-hīl* > (7.1) *_____ > (x8.12c) *_____ > (3.1) _____

{_____} 'nothing' **D** *ne-mios* > (7.1) *_____ > (9.18) _____ 'too much'

E *meliom* > (7.1) *_____ > (9.18) _____ 'millet'

E4 Examples for progressive vowel assimilation.

A {passer} _____ > (7.3) VL _____ {_____} 'sparrow'

B {farferus} _____ > (7.3) VL _____ {_____} 'horsefoot'

SCN 5.1	**0 > i / C_l**	An anaptyctic /i/ is inserted before a palatal /l/.
SCN 5.2	**0 > u / C_ł**	An anaptyctic /u/ is inserted before a velar [ł].
SCN 7.1	**e...i > i...i**	/e/ assimilates to a non-adjacent following /i/.
SCN 7.3	**a...e > a...a**	/e/ assimilates to a non-adjacent preceding /a/.

Assimilation of Consonants I

● **SCN 19.3 n > m / _m   One sound assimilates to another sound**

This paragraph deals with the development of {inmolo} *inmolō* 'I make a sacrifice' to its variant form *immolō* {immolo} by SCN 19.3. The sound change n > m / _m is known as an assimilation because /n/ assimilates to /m/ and becomes /m/ itself. In the world's languages, assimilations are a universal phenomenon which brings about an ease of articulation. It is easier to pronounce *immolō* than *inmolō* because our articulatory organs do not need to put up articulatory energy to differentiate two different nasals from one another. Which feature changes during the assimilation n > m / _m can be seen easily from the feature structures of the involved sounds:

SCN 19.3   n [+nasal, +<u>dental</u>, +voiced] > m [+nasal, +<u>labial</u>, +voiced]

The place of articulation of the nasal shifts from dental to labial, all the other features remain unchanged. The two sounds /n/ and /m/ are very similar anyway because they differ only in one feature. The next example is the assimilation of {adtuli} *adtulī* > (11.5) *attulī* {attuli} 'I brought', and again the analysis starts by looking at the feature structures of the involved sounds:

SCN 12.5   d [+plos, +dental, +<u>voiced</u>] > t [+ plos, +dental, -<u>voiced</u>]

The only difference between the two sounds /d/ and /t/ is the feature of voice. During this assimilation, it is not the place of articulation that changes, such as in SCN 19.3, but it is the manner of articulation, because voiced /d/ becomes voiceless /t/ in contact with voiceless /t/. This sound change can be traced to a more general rule which states that a voiced consonant becomes voiceless in contact with a voiceless consonant following:

SCN 12   C [+voiced] > [-voiced] / _ [-voiced]

● **SCN 22.1–22.3 z > R / R_   Regressive and progressive assimilations**

By stating which sound in a sequence of sounds assimilates to another sound within the sequence, assimilatory processes can be classified more clearly. If the first sound assimilates to the second sound, such as in the examples above, one speaks of regressive assimilation. If, in the above examples, the second sound had assimilated to the first sound, the forms *innolō** and *addulī** would have been produced. This was prevented because their phonetic relation to the simple verbs *molō* {molo} and *tulī* {tuli} would have been lost. Progressive assimilations are rarely found in Latin. Examples for progressive assimilations are the sequences /ls/ and /rs/, which can be reconstructed for the preforms **u̯el-se* and *fer-se, which later on became *u̯elle* 'want' and *ferre* 'carry'. The morpheme *-se* is the old ending of the infinitive, still preserved in *es-se* 'to be', but changed to *-re* in *laudā-re*, *monē-re*, *au̯dī-re* by rhotazism. At first, voiceless /s/ developed to its voiceless allophone [z] in contact with /r/ or /l/. The sound [z] was extremely unstable and assimilated rapidly to the preceding liquid. The development can be described as **u̯else* > (15.7) **u̯elze* > (22.1) *u̯elle* {uelle} and *ferse > (15.8) *ferze > (22.2) *ferre* {ferre}.

Exercises

E1 Examples for regressive assimilations.

A {_____} *loku̯or* 'I speak' :: *adloku̯or* > (20.4) _____ {_____} 'I speak

to' **B** {lustro} *lūstrō* 'I illuminate' :: *inlūstris* > (21.2) _____ {_____} 'illuminated'

C {moueo} _____ 'I move' :: *admou̯eō* > (17.3) *_____ > (19.3) _____

{_____} 'I move to' **D** {rado} *rādō* 'I scrape' :: *rādlom* > (20.4) *_____ > (9.18)

_____ {_____} 'scraping knife'

E2 Examples for progressive assimilations via intermediate voiced [z].

A {facilis} *fakilis* 'easy' :: **fakil-simus* > (15.7) *_____ > (22.1) _____

{_____} 'very easy' **B** {acer} *aker* 'sharp' :: **aker-simus* > (15.8) *_____ > (22.2)

_____ {_____} 'very sharp' **C** {uelim} *u̯elim* 1. sg. pres. subj. :: pres. inf. **u̯el-se*

(-*se* is the ending of the inf. such as in *es-se*) > (15.7) *_____ > (22.1) _____

{_____} 'want'

E3 Lachmann's law is applied before the assimilation of voice (cf. footnote SCN 2.3).

A {scribo} *skrībō* 'I write' :: **skrib-tus* > (2.3) *_____ > (12.2) _____

{_____} 'written' **B** {rego} *regō* 'I govern' :: **reg-tus* > (2.3) *_____ > (12.7)

_____ {_____} 'governed' **C** {ago} *agō* 'I drive' :: **agtus* > (2.3) *_____

> (12.7) _____ {_____} 'driven'

These rules appear in the exercises		
SCN 2.3	**V > V̄ / _(d, g)tus**	Lachmann's law states a lengthening process in some PPPs.
SCN 12.2	**b > p / _t**	Voiced /b/ becomes voiceless /p/ before voiceless /t/.
SCN 12.7	**g > k / _t**	Voiced /g/ becomes voiceless /k/ before voiceless /t/.
SCN 15.7	**s > z / l_**	Voiceless /s/ is voiced to [z] after /l/.
SCN 17.3	**d > n / _m**	Voiced /d/ becomes /n/ before /m/.
SCN 19.3	**n > m / _m**	Dental /n/ becomes labial /m/ before labial /m/.
SCN 20.4	**d > l / _l**	/d/ becomes /l/ before /l/.
SCN 21.2	**n > l / _l**	/n/ becomes /l/ before /l/.
SCN 22.1	**z > l / l_**	[z] becomes /l/ after /l/.
SCN 22.2	**z > r / r_**	[z] becomes /r/ after /r/.

23

- **SCN 19   N > N [+place] / _C [+place]   Nasal before stop consonant**

The /n/ of the negation prefix *in-* always assimilated to the place of articulation of the consonant following. Before the dental stops /d/ and /t/, it remained such as in *indīkō* {indico} 'I indicate' and *inter* {inter} 'between', before the labial stops /b/ and /p/, it became /m/ such as in *imbuō* {imbuo} 'I moisten' and *improbus* {improbus} 'wicked', and before velar /g/ and /k/, it became the velar nasal [ŋ] such as in *iŋgrātus* {ingratus} 'unpleasant' and *iŋkīdō* {incido} 'I cut into'. The Latin writing system did not reflect velar [ŋ] but used the grapheme {n}, which was normally used for writing the dental nasal /n/. A stop consonant does only allow the articulation of a homorganic nasal before it because the phonological opposition of nasals is nullified before stop consonants.

- **SCN 14   C [-voiced] > C [+voiced] / _ N   Stop consonant before nasal**

A stop was also assimilated to a nasal if placed directly before it. Examples for this process are {submoueo} *submoueō* > (17.1) *summoueō* {summoueo} 'I separate' and {adnuo} *adnuō* > (17.4) *annuō* {annuo} 'I nod', which show that /b/ became /m/ by assimilating to a following /m/, and /d/ became /n/ by assimilating to a following /n/. Also /g/ transformed into homorganic [ŋ] before nasals. This change g > ŋ / _n was, however, not spelled, but it can be inferred from non-standard orthography inscriptions.

The next lines deal with the relation of *legō* {lego} 'I collect' and *līŋnum* {lignum} 'piece of lumber', which goes back to a preform **legnom*. The development can be modeled as **legnom* > (17.5) **leŋnom* > (9.6) **liŋnom* > (2.5) **līŋnom* > (9.18) *līŋnum* {lignum}. At first, /g/ became [ŋ] before /n/ (SCN 17.5), and subsequently /e/ became /i/ before [ŋ] (SCN 9.6) and was additionally lengthened (SCN 2.5). A second example for these sound changes is furnished by the etymological word pair *dekus* {decus} 'grace, beauty' and *dīŋnus* {dignus} 'worthy', which goes back to a preform **deknos*. The analogous development was: **deknos* > (14.5) **degnos* > (17.5) **deŋnos* > (9.6) **diŋnos* > (2.5) **dīŋnos* > (9.18) *dīŋnus* {dignus}. In this case, /k/ became /g/ before /n/ (SCN 14.5) before the further development was identical to that of *līŋnum*. CL /i/ was pronounced [ī] before [ŋ] by SCN 2.5, whereas VL /i/ was not lengthenend in this position, because the Romance languages do not confirm this development (cf. Meiser 1998:79; Sihler 1995:76).

> **VL-INFO**   The consonant cluster /ŋn/ was extremely instable because of the distance between the places of articulation of [ŋ] and /n/. That is why both sounds were subject to a mutual assimilation yielding geminate palatal /ɲɲ/, which is seen from Romance words such as Italian *leɲɲio* {legno} 'wood' and *deɲɲio* {degno} 'worthy'.

- **Syncope and assimilation**

Sometimes, the consonants, which were subject to assimilation, came into contact after a short vowel had been emitted between them by the process of syncope. One such example is the derivation **sitikos*, which is based on *sitis* {sitis} 'thirst' and developed via > (4.1) **sitkos* > (18.4) **sikkos* > (9.18) to *sikkus* {siccus} 'dry'.

Exercises

E1 Assimilate the place of articulation of the nasal to the consonant following.

A {eum} *eum* 'him' :: *eum-dem* > (19.8) _____ {_____} 'the same' **B** {tam}

tam 'there' :: *tam-dem* > (19.8) _____ {_____} 'finally' **C** {quam} *ku̯am*

'how?' :: *ku̯am-dō* > (19.8) _____ {_____} 'when?' **D** {clam} *klam* 'secretly' ::

klam-kułum > (19.11) _____ {_____} 'secretly'

E2 Assimilate the stop to the nasal following.

A {daps} *daps* 'meal' :: *dapnom* > (14.2) *_____ > (17.2) *_____ > (9.18)

_____ {_____} 'loss' **B** {scabillum} *skabillum* 'small chair' :: *skabnom* >

(17.2) *_____ > (9.18) _____ {_____} 'stool' **C** {sopor} *sopor* 'deep

sleep' :: *su̯epnos* > (9.11) *_____ > (40.5) *_____ > (14.2) *_____

> (17.2) *_____ > (9.18) _____ {_____} 'sleep' **D** *seknom* > (14.5)

*_____ > (17.5) *_____ > (9.6) *_____ > (2.5) *_____ > (9.18)

_____ {_____} 'sign'

E3 Syncope of the final syllable brings about the consonant cluster which is subsequently assimilated.

A gen. sg. {artis} *artis* 'of the art' :: nom. sg. *artis* > (4.2) *arts* > (16.4) *arss* > (39.7) *ars*

{ars} 'art' **B** gen. sg. {montis} *montis* 'of the mountain' :: nom. sg. *montis* > (4.2) *_____

> (16.4) *_____ > (39.7) *_____ > (2.1) _____ {_____}

'mountain' **C** {do} *dō* 'I give' :: nom. sg. *dōtis* > (4.2) *_____ > (16.4) *_____ >

(39.7) _____ {_____} 'gift' **D** {damno} *damnō* 'I condemn' :: *damnãtos* > (4.2)

*_____ > (16.4) _____ > (39.7) _____ {_____} 'condemned'

SCN 2.1	$V > \bar{V} /$ _n(f,s)	Vowel lengthening before /nf/ and /ns/ in CL.
SCN 2.5	$i > \bar{i} /$ _ŋn	Vowel lengthening before /ŋn/ in CL but not in VL.
SCN 4	$V > 0 /$ C_C	Syncope in medial (4.1) and final syllables (4.2) deletes a short vowel.
SCN 9.6	$e > i /$ _ŋ	/e/ is raised to /i/ before velar [ŋ].
SCN 9.11	$e > o /$ u̯_C(C)V	This vowel assimilation is caused by velar vowels.
SCN 39.7	$s > 0 /$ s_#	Double consonants are simplified in the final position.
SCN 40.5	$u̯ > 0 /$ _(ŏ,ŭ)	/u̯/ is lost before the velar vowels /o/, /ō/, /u/, /ū/.

● **Etymological spelling versus phonetic spelling**

The 1. sg. perf. *nūbsī* > (13.2) *nūpsī* {nupsi} 'I married', which is derived from *nūbō* {nubo} 'I marry', as well as the 1. sg. perf. *skrībsī* > (13.2) *skrīpsī* {scripsi} 'I wrote', which is derived from *skrībō* {scribo} 'I write', both exhibit the assimilation of voiced /b/ to voiceless /p/ because of the following /s/. The result of the assimilation was actually spelled in the words. In forms like {plebs}, however, which was pronounced *pleps*, it was avoided to spell the stem formant of the nominative differently from the other cases, and thus the spelling {pleps} was avoided because of its contrast to the gen. {plebis}. Spellings like these are known as etymological spellings. Inscriptions like {pleps}, {optinuit} or {optulit} confirm the reconstructed pronunciation, even if forms like *obtinuit* 'he obtained' or *obtulit* 'he offered' were mandatory in official orthography (cf. Niedermann 1953:139).

● **Unattested intermediate steps of sound changes**

The description of sound changes oftes involves intermediate steps which are not attested but can be assumed because of lingustic reasons. In these cases, the sound changes are said to have a subtle or deep structure. In all the assimilation processes, in which /d/ assimilates to an /s/ following, one can suppose that at first the feature of [+voice] assimilated, by which /d/ became */t/. Secondly, the feature [+fricative] assimilated, by which */t/ became the fricative /s/ before /s/. Examples of this process are furnished by s-perfect forms of verbs that end in a stop consonant: {claudo} *klaud̯ō* 'I close' :: *klaud̯-s-ī* > (13.4) *klaud̯tsī* > (16.4) *klaud̯ssī* > (39.1) *klaud̯sī* {clausi} 'I closed'. Another example is {suadeo} *su̯ādeō* 'I recommend' :: *su̯ādsī* > (13.4) *su̯ātsī* > (16.4) *su̯āssī* > (39.1) *su̯āsī* {suasi} 'I recommended'. The simplification of double consonants after long vowels or diphthongs (SCN 39.1) is described in unit 26.

It is also possible to assume an intermediate step in the case of a voiceless sound assimilating to a voiced sound. By comparing *u̯annus* {uannus} 'winnow' to the related *u̯atillum* {uatillum} 'small shovel', the preform *u̯atnos* for *u̯annus* can be reconstructed, whereby the /t/ of the preform *u̯atnos* is reconstructed on the basis of the /t/ in *u̯atillum*. The development that led to the classical form was *u̯atnos* > (14.4) *u̯adnos* > (17.4) *u̯annos* > (9.18) *u̯annus* {uannus}. At first, /t/ became /d/ in contact with voiced /n/, secondly, /d/ assimilated completely to the /n/ following.

● **SCN 39 $C_1C_1 > C_1 / \bar{V}\_$ Simplification of double consonants**

The above presented assimilation processes often produced so called geminate or double consonants, which were simplified again after long vowels or diphthongs. An example is furnished by the form *prōsum* {prosum} 'I help', which is based on *sum* {sum} 'I am' and goes back to a preform *prōdsum*, as can be seen from the infinitive *prōdesse*. The inserted /d/ is merely a transition consonant which eliminates the hiatus of the two vowels surrounding it. The details of the development from the preform *prōdsum* to CL *prōsum* are *prōdsum* > (13.4) *prōtsum* > (16.4) *prōssum* > (39.1) *prōsum* 'I help'. After /d/ had become /t/ because of the following voiceless /s/, the /t/ assimilated completely to the /s/ following, thus producing a double consonant /ss/. This double consonant was again simplified to /s/ after the preceding long vowel.

Exercises

E1 Fill the gaps with the intermediate steps of the assimilations.

A {sum} *sum* 'I am' :: *adsum* > (13.4) *atsum > (16.4) *assum* {assum} 'I am there' **B** gen. sg.
{pedis} *pēdis* 'of the foot' :: nom. sg. *pēds > (13.4) *_____ > (16.4) *_____
> (39.7) _____ {_____} 'foot' **C** *hod-ke > (12.6) *_____ > (18.4)
*_____ > (4.3) * _____ > (39.6) _____ {_____} 'this' **D** {quid}
ku̯id 'what?' :: **ku̯id-ku̯am* > (12.6) *_____ > (18.4) _____ {_____}
'anything' **E** {_____} *ku̯id* 'what?' :: **ku̯id-pe* > (12.4) *_____ > (18.3)
_____ {_____} 'of course' **F** {idcirco} *idkirkō* > (12.6) *_____ > (18.4)
_____ {_____} 'that is why' **G** {_____} *seku̯or* 'I follow' :: {adsequor}
_____ > (13.4) *_____ > (16.4) _____ {_____} 'I reach'

E2 Fill the gaps with the intermediate steps of the assimilations.

A {_____} *ferō* 'I carry' :: *ad-ferō > (13.3) *_____ > (16.3) _____
{_____} 'I bring' **B** gen. sg. {uirtutis} *u̯irtūtis* 'of the virtue' :: **u̯irtūt-s* > (16.4)
*_____ > (39.7) _____ 'virtue' **C** gen. sg. {_____} *noktis* 'of the night' ::
*nokts > (16.4) *_____ > (39.7) _____ {_____} 'night' **D** {laudo} *lau̯dō*
'I praise' :: **lau̯d-s* > (13.4) *_____ > (16.4) *_____ > (39.7) _____
{_____} 'praise' **E** {_____} *sedeō* 'I sit' :: *dēseds > (13.4) *dēsets > (16.4)
*_____ > (39.7) _____ {_____} 'sitting aside' **F** {supra} *suprā*
'above' :: *supmos > (14.1) *_____ > (17.1) *_____ > (9.18) _____
{_____} 'the highest' **G** {glubo} *glūbō* 'I peel' :: *glūbma > (17.1) *_____ >
(39.1) _____ {_____} 'hull'

SCN 4.3	e > 0 / C_#	A final short vowel is lost.
SCN 12.4	d > t / _p	Voiced /d/ becomes voiceless /t/ before voiceless /p/.
SCN 12.6	d > t / _k	Voiced /d/ becomes voiceless /t/ before voiceless /k/.
SCN 17.1	b > m / _m	Labial /b/ becomes /m/ before /m/.
SCN 18.3	t > p / _p	/t/ becomes /p/ before /p/.
SCN 18.4	t > k / _k	/t/ becomes /k/ before /k/.
SCN 39.1	C₁ > 0 / V̄_C₁	Double consonants are simplified after a long vowel.
SCN 39.7	s > 0 / s_#	Double consonants are simplified in the final position.

CONSONANTS

51

25 Dissimilation / Dissimilatory Deletion of Sounds / Haplology

- **SCN 23   X...X > Y...X   Dissimilation as the counterpart to assimilation**

The prefix *re-* 'again' is not used with Latin verbs which start with /r/ because the language avoided the sequence of two r-sounds, which was difficult to pronounce. If a speaker had built a form *rerēgnāre** from *rēgnāre* {regnare} 'to govern', it would probably have been transformed into *lerēgnāre** or *relēgnāre**, through the exchange of one /r/ by the similar sound /l/. The deletion of one sound in a sequence of two similar sounds, or the deletion of similar features in a sequence of two similar sounds, is called dissimilation. It is the exact counterpart to an assimilation, in which a sequence of two sounds becomes more similar by harmonizing some or all of the phonological features of the involved sounds.

- **SCN 23.9   l...l > l...r   Complimentary distribution of the suffix variants *-ālis* and *-āris***

The two synonymous suffix variants *-ālis* and *-āris*, which derive adjectives from nouns, are complimentarily distributed in Latin. The suffix *-āris* is used if there is already an /l/ in the word, and the suffix *-ālis* is used if there is already an /r/ in the word. Examples are *auksilium* {auxilium} 'help' and the change of *auksiliālis** to *auksiliāris* {auxiliaris} 'helpful', and *kōnsul* {consul} 'consul' and the change of *kōnsulālis** to *kōnsulāris* {consularis} 'consular' both via SCN 23.9.

> **INFO**   The medial /r/ in *merīdiēs* {meridies} 'noon' originated by dissimilation from *medī-diēs*. This form originally designated 'the middle of the day'. Independently from dissimilations, an analogous sound change d > l occurs in other words such as *olēre* 'to smell', which can be traced back to the preform *odēre*, by comparing it to the related *odor* 'smell' (cf. SCN 23.2).

- **SCN 24   X...X > Ø...X   Dissimilatory deletion of sounds**

If a sequence of two similar sounds is not changed by dissimilation but by the complete loss of one of the two sounds, one speaks of dissimilatory deletion. CL *taberna* {taberna} 'hut' can be traced back to *traberna* and subsequently connected to *traps* {trabs} 'beam' (SCN 24.1). In this case, the sequence of the two non-adjacent r-sounds caused the first r-sound to disappear. In *praęstīgiaę* {praestigiae} 'delusion', however, it was not the first but the second r-sound that disappeared. This word is derived from *praęstriŋgō* {praestringo} 'to blind' and can be traced back to *praęstrīgiaę* via SCN 24.2. A complete loss of a consonant can also be found in the sequence *st...st*, as can be seen in the example *opstetrīks* {obstetrix} > (24.6) VL *opsetrīks* {obsetrix} 'midwife'.

- **Haplology is the loss of identical or similar syllables**

Another strategy to avoid similar sequences of sounds was the deletion of a whole syllable in a sequence of identical or similar syllables. Examples for this process are furnished by the reduplicated perfect of compound verbs such as *respopondī* > *respondī* {respondi} 'I answered', which shows the loss of the reduplication syllable when compared to the simple verb perf. *spopondī* {spopondi} 'I promised'. In some texts, the regular forms are occasionally found. Another example is the noun *honestās* {honestas} 'honor', which is derived from *honestus* 'honorable' and goes back to a preform *honestitās*. The sequence *titā* was simplified to *tā*. In a similar process *konsuetūdō* {consuetudo} 'custom', which is derived from *konsuētus* {consuetus}, had been simplified from *konsuēto-tūdō*. Likewise, *stipendium* 'contribution' goes back to *stipi-pendium*.

Exercises

E1 Dissimilate the forms.

A {caelum} *kaelum* 'sky' :: **kaeluleus* > (23.1) _____ {_____} 'blue' **B** {pales}

Palēs 'goddess of shepherds' :: *Palīlia* > (23.1) _____ {_____} 'celebration

for the goddess Palēs' **C** {flagellum} *flagellum* > (23.1) VL _____ {_____}

'whip' **D** {lunalis} **lūnālis* > (23.9) _____ {_____} 'moonly' **E** **mīlitālis*

> (23.9) _____ {_____} 'of a soldier' **F** **singulālis* > (23.9) _____

{_____} 'singular' **G** {monimentum} *monimentum* > (23.6) VL _____

{_____} 'monument'

E2 Reconstruct the preforms.

A {_____} *flagellum* 'whip' :: **_____* > (23.9) **_____* > (9.18)

flagrum {_____} 'whip' **B** {_____} *skalpō* 'I scrape' :: **_____* > (23.9)

*_____ > (9.18) *skalprum* {_____} 'chisel' **C** {_____} *premō* 'I press'

:: **_____* > (23.10) **preslom* > (15.3) **_____* > (2.2) **_____* > (9.18)

prēlum {_____} 'press, winepress' **D** {_____} *rādō* 'I scrape' :: **_____*

> (23.10) **_____* > (20.4) **_____* > (9.18) *rāllum* {_____} 'scraping

knife'

E3 Add the phonological formula into the brackets.

A {culter} *kulter* 'knife' :: VL **kultellus* > (_____) *kuntellus* {cuntellus} 'small knife' **B**

{peregrinus} *peregrīnus* > (_____) VL *pelegrīnus* {pelegrinus} 'foreign' **C** {meretrix}

meretrīks > (_____) *menétrīks* {menetrix} (VL-accentuation) 'prostitute' **D** {fragrare}

fragrāre > (_____) VL *flagrāre* {flagrare} 'to smell' **E** {genui} *genuī* 'I brought forth' ::

*genmen > (_____) *germen* {germen} 'sprout'

E4 Add the formula of the dissimilatory deletion.

A {caluor} *kaluor* 'I play a trick' :: **kaluilla* > (_____) *kauilla* {cauilla} 'trick'

B {trabs} *traps* 'beam' :: **traberna* > (_____) *taberna* {taberna} 'hut'

26   Double Consonants

- **SCN 1.5 $\bar{V}C_1 > VC_1C_1$ Formation of double consonants according to the littera-rule**

Double consonants were often formed according to the littera-rule which describes the change from OL *lītera* {leitera} to CL *littera*. In this case, the spelling {ei} of the Old Latin form is to be interpreted as a long /ī/. The name of the God of the sky {iupiter} *Iūpiter* > (1.5) *Iuppiter* {iuppiter} is another example for this development, in which a long vowel is shortened and its length transferred onto the following consonant. By doing so, the syllabic structure of the word remains intact, because a long vowel, as well as a short vowel plus a double consonant, counts as a heavy syllable.

- **SCN 39.1 $C_1C_1 > C_1 \, / \, \bar{V}\_$ Simplification of double consonants after a long vowel or a diphthong**

Double consonants were often shortened after a long vowel or a diphthong, because it takes some articulatory effort to pronounce a double consonant, which is phonetically a long consonant, after a long vowel. Examples for this simplification are furnished by verbs such as *sēkēdō* {secedo} 'I go away' which are formed with the prefix *sēd-* 'aside, apart, away, without'. The development was: **sēd-kēdō* > (12.6) **sētkēdō* > (18.4) **sēkkēdō* > (39.1) *sēkēdō* {secedo}. The assimilation of the /d/ to the /k/ following produced the double consonant /kk/, which was simplified to a single /k/ after the long /ē/. Another example is the development of *sēdulō* {sedulo} 'busy', which is derived from *dolor* 'ache, pain', and originally meant something like 'without pain': **sēd-dolōd* > (39.1) **sēdolōd* > (8.10) **sēdulōd* > (38.3) *sēdulō*. An exeption to this rule is geminate /ll/, which remains after a long vowel in words such as *u̯īlla* {uilla} 'country house' or *nūllus* {nullus} 'not any'.

- **SCN 39.2 $C_1C_1 > C_1 \, / \, \_C_2$ Simplification of double consonants before a consonant**

Double consonants were also simplified before another consonant. This can be seen from *diskindō* {discindo} 'I tear apart', which goes back to **dis-skindō* via SCN 39.2. Spellings like {occresco} and {opprimo}, which were probably pronounced *okrēskō* and *oprimō*, are known as etymological spellings. This rule is particularly important for the explanation of deep-structural assimilations in elision processes (SCN 31–33. Unit 30).

- **SCN 39.3/4 $C_1C_1 > C_1 \, / \, R\_$ Simplification of double consonants after continuant**

Double consonants were also simplified after a continuant sound. An example is the compound form *koŋkidī* {concidi} 'I fell', which is derived from *kekidī* {cecidi} 'I fell'. The development was: **koŋ-ke-kid-ī* > (4.1) **koŋkkidī* > (39.4) *koŋkidī* {concidi}.

- **SCN 39.5 $C_1C_1 > C_1 \, / \, \_\acute{V}$ Simplification of double consonants according to the mamilla-rule**

The mamilla-rule states that double continuants (R, /s/, /f/) were simplified before a stressed syllable. An example is *mamílla* 'teat', which goes back to **mammílla*, which is derived from *mamma* 'breast'. Another example is **opmíttō* > (14.1) **obmíttō* > (17.1) **ommíttō* > (39.5) *omíttō* {omitto} 'I omit'. Analogy, however, leveled out forms quite often such as in *gallı̆na* 'hen', which is derived from *gallus* 'cock'. But even in these cases, a simplified pronunciation is very probable despite the spelling of the double consonant. VL even shows the simplification of stop consonants e.g. in VL *sakellus* {sacellus} 'small sack', which is derived from *sakkus* {saccus} 'sack' and goes back to **sakkellus*.

> The simplification of double consonants in the final position is described in unit 29.

Exercises

E1 Add the missing forms according to the littera-rule.

A *bāka* {baca} :: _____ {_____} 'berry' **B** _____ {_____} ::

mukkus {muccus} 'snot' **C** *sūkus* {sucus} :: _____ {_____} 'juice' **D** *kīpus* {cipus}

:: _____ {_____} 'pale, stake, post' **E** *kūpa* {cupa} 'barrel' :: *kuppa* {cuppa}

'cup' **F** _____ {_____} :: *stlatta* {stlatta} 'merchant vessel' **G** _____

{_____} :: *littus* {littus} 'beach'

E2 Double consonants were simplified after a long vowel or a diphthong.

A {paro} *parō* 'I provide' :: **sēdparō* > (12.4) **_____* > (18.3) **_____* >

(39.1) _____ {_____} 'I separate' **B** {pono} *pōnō* 'I put' :: **sēdpōnō* > (12.4)

*_____ > (18.3) **_____* > (39.1) _____ {_____} 'I set aside'

C {praedico} *praędikō* 'I declare' :: **praędikō* > (4.1) **_____* > (12.6) **_____*

> (18.4) **_____* > (39.1) _____ {_____} 'herold' **D** {accusso} *akkūssō*

> (39.1) _____ {_____} 'I accuse' **E** {_____} _____ > (39.1)

kuaęsō {quaeso} 'I ask for' **F** {claudo} *klaųdō* 'I close' :: **klaųd-to-s* > (12.5) **klaųttos* > (x3)

*klaųssos > (39.1) **_____* > (9.18) _____ {_____} 'closed' **G** {haussi}

haųssī > (39.1) _____ {_____} 'I drew up'

E3 A double consonant was simplified before a consonant.

A **ad-spīrō* > (13.4) **_____* > (16.4) **_____* > (39.2) _____

{_____} 'I breathe' **B** **adstō* > (13.4) **_____* > (16.4) **_____* > (39.2)

_____ {_____} 'I stand at' **C** **disstō* > (39.2) _____ {_____} 'I

am distant'

E4 Simplify the double consonant according to the mamilla-rule.

A {canna} *kanna* 'reed' :: **kannālis* > (39.5) _____ {_____} 'channel' **B** {currus}

kurrus 'chariot' :: **kurrūlis* > (39.5) _____ {_____} 'of a chariot' **C** {far} *far*

'spelt' :: **farrīna* > (39.5) _____ {_____} 'flour'

27 The Fricative /s/ and Its Allophone [z]

● **SCN 2.2 z > 0 / _D**   The fricative [z] was lost before voiced sounds with compensatory lengthening

In voiced surroundings, the voiceless fricative /s/ had a voiced allophone [z] (SCN 15), which is pronounced like the {s} in English *reason*. This sound [z], however, was extremely instable and disappeared with compensatory lengthening of the preceding vowel if [z] was placed between a vowel and a consonant. The development can be seen in the pronominal form *īdem* {idem} 'the same' which is derived from *is* {is} 'this one': *isdem* > (15.5) **izdem* > (2.2) *īdem* {idem}. In preclassical Latin, {s} was actually written before {n} in forms such as EL {cosmis} 'friendly' and OL {osmen} 'omen'. The development s > z, however, had probably already started in Proto-Italic so that these two forms have to be phonologically interpreted as *kozmis* and *ozmen*, before they developed to CL *kōmis* {comis} and CL *ōmen* {omen} by the loss of [z] and compensatory lengthening. If placed between two vowels, [z] became /r/, which is described in the next paragraph.

● **SCN 26.1 z > r / V_V**   Rhotazism is the development of [z] to /r/

According to Cicero, a person called L. Papīsius Crassus was the first in his family to call himself Papīrius instead of Papīsius, in the year 312 BC. Equally, Appius Claudius Caecus, who was consul from 307 to 296 BC, replaced the spelling Valesii by Valerii and Fusii by Furii (cf. Niedermann 1953:103). Family names and personal names are usually very resistant against changes, which means that the sound change SCN 26.1 z > r / V_V must have been carried through completely at that time. As said before, the change from /s/ to [z] in voiced surroundings had probably already started in Proto-Italic so that the development z > r can be regarded as the final result of a more ancient sound change. The words OL *āza* {asa} 'altar' and OL *fēziae* {fesiae} 'holidays', which correspond to CL *āra* {ara} and CL *fēriae* {feriae}, still show the archaic state in which [z] was spelled {s} between vowels. The sound change of intervocalic [z] to /r/ is called rhotazism, and is responsible for paradigm irregularities such as in *flōs, flōris* 'flower', in which the nominative has an /s/ while the oblique cases have an /r/ as the stem formant. The /r/ of the genitive was originally an /s/, and the preform of *flōris* was **flōsis*.

● **Exceptions to Rhotazism**

The compound verb *dēsinō* {desino} 'I cease' is derived from *sinō* {sino} 'I let' and does not show rhotazism although the /s/ is placed between vowels because the regularly expected form *dērinō** would have lost its phonological relation to its derivational base *sinō*. For the same reason, *dēsunt* {desunt} 'they are not there' did not change to *dērunt**. In these cases, analogy prevented the forms to divert too much from their base forms. In some words such as *miser* 'miserable' or *Kaęsar* {caesar}, rhotazism was prevented due to the final /r/, which had a dissimilatory effect. A counterexample, however, is *soror* {soror} 'sister', which goes back to **sozōr*. In this case, the final /r/ did not prevent rhotazism. Loanwords such as *asinus* 'donkey' or *kisium* {cisium} 'light two-wheeled vehicle' found their way into Latin after rhotazism had ceased to be active, so that their intervocalic /s/ was not changed, but stayed intact. Words such as *dēsuper* {desuper} 'from above', which were formed after the time of rhotazism, were also not subject to this sound change.

Exercises

E1 Explain the development of the prefix *trāns-* to its positional variant *trā-* before voiced sounds. Tip: The lost nasal (SCN 2.1) was not analogically restituted.

_____

_____

E2 The verb *gerō* {gero} 'I carry' has a perfect form *gessī* {gessi} 'I carried'. What is the reason of the two different stems *ger-* and *ges-* if one assumes that the present form was enlarged with the ending *-ō* and the perfect form with the tempus morpheme *-s-* and the ending *-ī*?

_____

_____

E3 How can *herī* {heri} 'yesterday' and *hes-ternus* {hesternus} 'of yesterday' be etymologically connected?

_____

_____

E4 The fricative /s/ was lost via intermediate [z] with compensatory lengthening.

A {dumetum} *dūmētum* 'undergrowth' :: **dusmos* > (15.1) *_____ > (2.2) *_____

> (9.18) _____ {_____} 'undergrowth' **B** {positus} *positus* 'placed' :: **posinō* >

(4.1) *_____ > (15.2) *_____ > (2.2) _____ {_____} 'I put' **C**

{gusto} *gustō* 'I taste' :: **dēgusnō* > (15.2) *_____ > (2.2) _____ {_____}

'I taste' **D** {egestas} *egestās* 'indigence' :: **egesnos* > (15.2) *_____ > (2.2) *_____

> (9.18) _____ {_____} 'indigent' **E** {premo} *premō* 'I press' :: **preslom* >

(15.3) *_____ > (2.2) *_____ > (9.18) _____ {_____} 'press,

wine press' **F** {quasillum} *kṷasillum* 'small basket' :: **kṷaslom* > (15.3) *_____ > (2.2)

*_____ > (9.18) _____ {_____} 'basket'

> **INFO** The /s/ in *kaṷsa* {causa} 'cause', *kāsus* {casus} 'accident' and *dīṷīsiō* {diuisio} 'distribution' originated by the simplification of the geminate /ss/. According to the Roman grammarian Quintilian, Cicero wrote these words as {caussa, cassus, diuissio}.

28

Loss of Initial Consonants

● **SCN 30.2 g > 0 / #_n**   Loss of initial /g/ before /n/

The OL form *gnōskō* {gnosco} 'I know' with initial /g/ before /n/ became CL *nōskō* {nosco} through the loss of the initial /g/. The related CL form *īŋnōtus* {ignotus} 'unknown' still has the {g}, which was pronounced [ŋ] before /n/ (see unit 23). Initial /gn/ remained only in the personal name CL *Gnaẹus*, of which the archaic abl. sg. OL *Gnaiụōd* {gnaiuod} is attested in an inscription. Personal names, as well as place names, are usually very conservative and resist language change. The development from the OL to the CL form was *Gnaiụōd* > (10.6) **Gnaẹụōd* > (40.5) **Gnaẹōd* > (38.3) CL *Gnaẹō* {gnaeo}. In the word *kognōmen* {cognomen} 'epithet', a non-etymological /g/ was inserted either in analogy to the pattern *nātus* :: *kognātus* ~ *nōmen* :: *kognōmen*, or due to folk etymology with *gnōscō* {gnosco}.

● **SCN 30.6 d > 0 / #_i̯**   The God of the sky lost its initial /d/

The form OL *Di̯oụem* {diouem} is inscriptionally attested in the 4th century BC. In CL *I̯oụem* {iouem}, the initial consonant cluster was simplified through the loss of the initial /d/. This rule was also active in the medial position where one finds a similar development due to the assimilation dị > ii̯ (SCN x11.2): **pedi̯ōs* > (x11.2) **pei̯i̯ōs* > (A: gen. *pei̯i̯ōr-is*) **pei̯i̯ōr* > (1.4) *pei̯i̯or* {peior} 'worse'.

● **SCN x6.9c h > 0 / #_V**   Initial /h/ was lost as early as the 4th century BC

The loss of an initial aspirate -known as *psilosis*, which comes from Greek *psīlós* 'bald'- is attested in the course from OL to CL. Due to this change, OL *harēna* {harena} became CL *arēna* {arena} 'sand' and OL *hānser* {hanser} became CL *ānser* {anser} 'goose'. After the /h/ had been lost, the educated speech tried to reintroduce it into the language system, which eventually led to misspellings like {humor} for *ūmor*, because the speakers did not know anymore in which words the initial /h/ had been lost. The Romance languages do not show any trace of the phoneme /h/ which was lost even before the time of rhotazism in the 4th century BC (cf. Meiser 1998:105). It vanished also in medial positions such as in {prehendo} *prehendō* > (x8.12c) **preendō* > (3.1) *prēndō* {prendo} 'I take hold of'.

● **SCN 37.2 t > 0 / #s_l**   Simplification of the OL initial consonant cluster /stl/

CL *lokum* {locum} 'place' and acc. sg. *lītem* {litem} 'quarrel' go back to the attested OL forms *stlokum* {stlocum} and *stlītem* {stlitem}. In these cases, the medial /t/ between /s/ and /l/ was probably ejected and the newly formed cluster /sl/ developed to /l/, according to SCN 30.12. The development was: *stlokum* > (37.2) **slokum* > (30.12) *lokum*, and can be found also in the medial position with a phonologically similar context: **post-ne* > (37.3) **posne* > (15.2) **pozne* > (2.2) *pōne* {pone} 'behind'. Another example is: **póstmoi̯riom* > (37.3) **pósmoi̯riom* > (15.1+2.2) **pǒ́moi̯riom* > (8.1) **pǒ́mei̯riom* > (Ac1) **pōméi̯riom* > (10.8) **pōmēriom* > (9.18) *pōmērium* {pomerium} 'open space around a city'.

● **SCN 40.11 du̯ > b / #_**   CL *bonus* goes via **duonos* back to *du̯enos*

The initial group /du̯/ was simplified to /b/. The forms OL *du̯onōro(m)* {duonoro} and EL *du̯enos* {duenos} were pronounced *bonōrum* and *bonos* in CL. In the medial position, the cluster was retained in words such as *perduellio* 'high-treason' and *perduellis* 'enemy'. Horaz and Ovid even used the archaic form *duellum* for *bellum* 'war'.

Exercises

E1 The initial OL groups /gn/ and /stl/ were simplified.

A OL {gnatus} *gnātus* > (30.2a) **ŋnātus* > (30.2b) *nātus* {_____} 'born' **B** OL {gnotus}

gnōtus > (30.2a) **_____* > (30.2b) _____ {_____} 'known' **C** OL {gnauus}

gnāu̯us > (30.2a) **_____* > (30.2b) _____ {_____} 'busy' **D** **stlātos*

> (37.2) **_____* > (30.12) **_____* > (9.18) _____ {_____}

'broad' **E** {tollo} *tollō* 'I bear' :: **stlātos* > (37.2) **_____* > (30.12) **_____* >

(9.18) _____ {_____} 'carried'

E2 The initial EL and OL group /du̯/ became CL /b/.

A EL {duenos} *du̯enos* > (9.11) **_____* > (40.11) **_____* > (9.18) _____

{_____} 'good' **B** OL {duonorom} **du̯onōrom* > (40.11) _____ {_____}

C **du̯enēd* > (40.11) **_____* > (38.3) **_____* > (1.3) _____ 'well' **D**

{duellom} *du̯ellom* > (40.11) **_____* > (9.18) _____ {_____} 'war' **E**

{duo} *duō* 'two' :: *du̯is* > (40.11) _____ {_____} 'twice' **F** {duidens} *du̯idēns* >

(40.11) _____ {_____} 'having two teeth'

E3 The following examples are based on external reconstruction.

A **snō* > (30.12) _____ {_____} 'I swim' **B** **u̯lōrum* > (40.7) _____

{_____} 'reigns' **C** **u̯rādiks* > (40.7) _____ {_____} 'root' **D** **ksentos*

> (30.8) **_____* > (9.18) _____ {_____} 'tangled' **E** **ksnéu̯ātlā* > (30.8)

*_____ > (30.12) **_____* > (1.6) **_____* > (9.10) **_____* >

(28.3) **_____* > (28.4) **_____* > (Ac1) **_____* > (5.2) _____

{_____} 'clipping blade' **F** **psternu̯ō* > (30.7) _____ {_____} 'I

sneeze' **G** **psablom* > (30.7) **_____* > (28.3) **_____* > (5.2) **_____* >

(9.18) _____ 'sand' **H** **dlongos* > (30.5) **_____* > (9.18) _____ 'long'

I **knīdōs* > (30.1) **_____* > (30.2a) **_____* > (30.2b) **_____* > (A: gen.

nidōris) **_____* > (1.4) _____ {_____} 'steam' **J** **slūbrikus* > (30.12)

_____ {_____} 'lubricious'

29

Loss of Final Consonants

- **SCN 38.1/38.2 m/s > 0 / V_#   Weak pronunciation of /m/ and /s/ in the final position**

Many inscriptions of the 3rd century BC display forms like OL *oino* {oino} and OL *optimo* {optimo}, which reveal a loss of a final /m/ in opposition to the respective forms CL *ūnum* 'one' and CL *optimum* 'the best', in which final /m/ is written. Latin grammarians describe the reduced pronunciation of /m/ in the final position, too. In inscriptions of the 3rd century BC, one can also find the frequent omission of a final /s/ in forms such as OL *Kornēlio* {cornelio} for CL *Kornēlius* {cornelius} and OL *Fou̯rio* {fourio} for CL *Fūrius* {furius}. A reduced pronunciation of /s/ in the final position is also inferred from the fact that in the Old Latin poetry of Plautus and Ennius a final /s/ often did not cause positional length of the preceding vowel. The official CL orthography, however, reintroduced the spelling of final /m/ and /s/, because of their highly important morphological function of denoting the ending of the accusative and nominative (cf. Sommer 1977:220–223).

- **SCN 38.3 d > 0 / V̄_#   Loss of final /d/ after a long vowel**

Some OL forms, which end in a long vowel followed by /d/, lost the final -*d* in CL. Examples are abl. sg. forms such as OL *magistrātūd* or OL *sententiād*, the 2nd imperative of the 3rd person such as OL *datōd* {datod} 'he shall give' or OL *suntōd* {suntod} 'they shall be', as well as the acc. sg. of certain pronouns such as OL *mēd* or OL *tēd*, which became *mē* and *tē* in CL.

- **SCN 39 C₁C₁ > C₁ / _#   Simplification of final consonant clusters**

Final double consonants were always simplified in CL. This can be seen in the developments of *far* 'spelt' and *fel* 'bile', which can be traced back to **farr* and **fell* via SCN 39.8, by comparing them to the gen. *farris* and *fellis*. In some cases, metrical analysis even provides a proof for former OL final double consonants. In Plautus and Terence, the final syllable of *es* {es} 'you are' and *mīles* {miles} 'soldier' always counts as heavy, and it is not until Ennius that it counts as light. The comparison of *mīles* to the oblique cases *mīlit-is, mīlit-ī* enables us to reconstruct the preform **mīlet-s* for the nominative, which developed via SCN 16.4 to **mīless* and further on to CL *mīles* via SCN 39.7. The final /s/ must thus have been heard and counted as a double consonant in Old Latin times. Double /ss/, which was spelled as a simple {s}, was also never subject to the weakening process SCN 38.2, which is described in the first paragraph of this page. Another example for the simplification of final double consonants is *hok* {hoc} 'this', which must have been pronounced **hokk* because its syllable still counts as long in Vergil. The etymology of the words confirms this analysis, because *hok* comes from **hodke* via the stages: **hodke* > (12.6) **hotke* > (18.4) **hokke* > (4.4) *hokk* {hoc} > (39.6) *hok* {hoc} (cf. Meiser 1998:113/114).

> **INFO** If /i/ became final by the loss of final /s/, it was lowered to /e/ by SCN 9.14.
> **A** *magis* > (38.2) **magi* > (9.14) *mage* 'more'
> **B** *potis* > (38.2) **poti* > (9.14) *pote* 'possible'.

Exercises

E1 Add the missing forms of the ablative and imperative.

A OL {_____} _____ > (38.3) *magistrātū* {magistratu} **B** OL {_____}

_____ > (38.3) *datō* {_____} **C** OL {_____} _____ > (38.3)

suntō {_____} **D** OL {_____} _____ > (38.3) *sententiā* {_____}

E OL {_____} _____ > (38.3) *u̯iolātō* {_____} **F** OL {_____}

_____ > (38.3) *likētō* {_____} 'will be allowed'

E2 Double consonants are simplified in the final position.

A *mīlets* > (16.4) *_____ > (39.7) _____ {_____} 'soldier' **B** *kustōds*

> (13.4) *_____ > (16.4) *_____ > (39.7) _____ {_____}

'guardien' **C** EL *sakros* > (4.2) *_____ > (6.1) *_____ > (6.2) *_____

> (15.9) *_____ > (22.3) *_____ > (39.8) _____ {_____}

'holy' **D** *ākris* > (4.2) *_____ > (6.1) *_____ > (6.2) *_____ > (15.9)

*_____ > (22.3) *_____ > (39.8) _____ {_____} 'sharp'

E *hodke* > (12.6) *_____ > (18.4) *_____ > (4.3) *_____ > (39.6)

_____ {_____} 'this'

E3 Compare the nominative and the genitive and reconstruct the preforms.

A gen. sg. {ossis} *ossis* 'of the bone' :: nom. sg. *_____ > (39.7) *os* {os} 'bone'

B gen. sg. {cordis} *kordis* 'of the heart' :: nom. sg. *_____ > (38.5) *kor* {cor} 'heart'

C gen. sg. {lactis} *laktis* 'of the milk' :: nom.sg. *_____ > (38.4) *lak* {lac} 'milk'

SCN 4.2	**V > 0 / C_s#**	Syncope in final syllables.
SCN 4.3	**V > 0 / C_#**	Apocope is the loss of a final vowel.
SCN 6.1	**r > r̥ / C_C**	/r/ becomes syllabic [r̥] by syncope.
SCN 6.2	**r̥ > er**	Emergence of an anaptyctic vowel besides syllabic [r̥].
SCN 12.6	**d > t / _k**	Voiced /d/ becomes voiceless /t/ before voiceless /k/.
SCN 13.4	**d > t / _s**	Voiced /d/ becomes voiceless /t/ before voiceless /s/.
SCN 15.9	**s > z / r_#**	/s/ is voiced to [z] after /r/ in the final position.
SCN 16.4	**t > s / _s**	/t/ becomes /s/ before /s/.
SCN 18.4	**t > k / _k**	/t/ becomes /k/ before /k/.
SCN 22.3	**z > r / r_#**	Final [z] assimilates to preceding /r/.

30   Simplification of Medial Consonant Clusters

- **SCN 31 T > 0 / _sC (T=p,t,k)   The Espresso-Rule**

In consonant clusters like /kst/, /pst/, /tst/, /ksk/, which consist of a stop plus /s/ plus a stop, the medial /s/ was ejected. Due to this sound change, words such as **apsportō* > (31.1) *asportō* {asporto} 'I take away' and **opstendō* > (31.1) *ostendō* {ostendo} 'I show' were formed. There are, however, also words such as *ekstrā* {extra} 'on the outside' and *tekstus* {textus} 'texture', which have the respective clusters, but in these cases the clusters with medial /s/ were remodeled in analogy to *eks* {ex} 'out of' and *teksō* {texo} 'I weave'. Furthermore, these backformations existed only in the educated speech and in written Latin. The Romance languages clearly attest **sestus* and **estra* as the VL forms.

This rule was also applied to consonant clusters like /ksl/ or /ksn/, which have a liquid or a nasal after the /s/. The comparison of *aksilla* {axilla} 'armpit' to *āla* {ala} 'armpit' shows that the second form can be traced back to a preform **aksla*. After the loss of the cluster initial stop consonant, the /s/ was voiced to [z] and subsequently lost with compensatory lengthening of the preceding vowel. The development was: **aksla* > (32.3) **asla* > (15.3) **azla* > (2.2) *āla* {ala}.

The word *lūna* {luna} 'moon' is an example of the same development before /n/ and can be traced back to the preform **louksnā*, which corresponds exactly to Avestan *raoxšna-* 'shining' and Old Prussian *lauxnos* 'stars'. The intermediate steps were **louksnā* > (1.6) **louksna* > (32.1) **lousna* > (15.2) **louzna* > (10.3) **lōzna* > (10.4) **lūzna* > (2.2) *lūna*, whereby the exact relative chronology of the monophthongization (SCN 10.3 and 10.4) and the loss of [z] (SCN 2.2) cannot be determined.

- **SCN 34 k > 0 / R_(t,s)   /k/ is lost between a liquid and a consonant**

The OL form {forctis} *forktis* 'strong' lost the medial /k/ on its way to CL *fortis*. In this case, it is possible to model the loss *forktis* > (34.1) *fortis* as the effect of a deep structural assimilation with the subsequent simplification of the newly formed double consonant: *forktis* > (18.6) **forttis* > (39.3) *fortis*. The perfect forms *fulsī* and *mersī* of *fulgeō* {fulgeo} 'I flash' and *mergō* {mergo} 'I immerse' go back to **fulgsī* and **mergsī*. The development was **fulgsī* > (13.6) **fulksī* > (34.3) *fulsī* as well as **mergsī* > (13.6) **merksī* > (34.3) *mersī*. After /g/ had lost the feature [+voice] before voiceless /s/, the newly formed /k/ was lost between the liquid and the /s/. The development modeled as an assimilation reads like **fulgsī* > (13.6) **fulksī* > (16.6) **fulssī* > (39.3) *fulsī* as well as **mergsī* > (13.6) **merksī* > (16.6) **merssī* > (39.3) *mersī*. The assimilations SCN 18.6 (k > t / _t) and 16.6 (k > s / _s) are usually not found in educated speech, but belong to the strata of common speech.

- **SCN 35 C > 0 / R_N   A stop is lost between a liquid and a nasal**

The word *pulmentum* {pulmentum} 'relish of meat' is derived from *pulpa* {pulpa} 'meat'. It goes back to **pulpmentum* and reveals that a stop was also lost between a liquid and a nasal: **pulpmentum* > (35.2) *pulmentum*. Another example is *tormentum* 'hurling engine', which is derived from the verb *torkueō* {torqueo} 'I turn' and goes back to **torkumentum* > (40.3) **torkmentum* > (35.6) *tormentum*. Also this sound change can be modeled as a deep structural assimilation with the subsequent simplification of the double consonant: **pulpmentum* > (14.1) **pulbmentum* > (17.1) **pulmmentum* > (39.5) *pulmentum*, as well as **torkmentom* > (14.7) **torgmentum* > (17.6) **tormmentum* > (39.5) *tormentum*.

Exercises

E1 Consonant loss in A1 and B1 and consonant assimilation in A2 and B2.

A1 {fulcio} *fulkiō* 'I support' :: **fulkmentom* > (35.3a) *_____ > (9.18) _____

{_____} 'column' **A2** {fulcio} *fulkiō* 'I support' :: **fulkmentom* > (14.7) *_____ >

(17.6) *_____ > (39.5) _____ > (9.18) _____ {_____} 'column'

B1 {sarpio} *sarpiō* 'I cut off' :: **sarpmentom* > (35.1a) *_____ > (9.18) _____ 'twig'

B2 {sarpio} *sarpiō* 'I cut off' :: **sarpmentom* > (14.1) *_____ > (17.1) *_____ >

(39.5) *_____ > (9.18) _____ 'twig'

E2 /k/ is lost between a liquid and a consonant.

A {ulciscor} *ulkiskor* 'I take revenge' :: **ulktus* > (34.2a) _____ {_____} 'revenge

taken' **B** {fulcio} *fulkiō* 'I support' :: PPP **fulktus* > (34.2a) _____ {_____}

'supported' **C** **Martikos* > (4.1) *_____ > (18.4) *_____ > (39.3) *_____

> (A: a > ā due to *Mārs*) **Mārkos* > (9.18) _____ {_____}

E3 Enjoy the espresso-rule with assimilations and vowel changes.

A {capio} *kapiō* 'I grasp' :: **súpskapiō* > (31.1a) *_____ > (8.1) *_____ > (8.3)

*_____ > (Ac1) _____ {_____} 'I undertake' **B** {luceo} *lūkeō* 'I light' ::

*inlūkstris > (31.3a) *_____ > (21.2) _____ {_____} 'noble' **C** {texo}

teksō 'I weave' :: **teksla* > (32.3a) *_____ > (15.3) *_____ > (2.2) _____

{_____} 'tissue' **D** {traho} *trahō* 'I carry' :: **tragsma* > (13.6) *_____ > (31.2a)

*_____ > (15.1) *_____ > (2.2) _____ {_____} 'a thin' **E** {luceo}

lūkeō 'I light' :: **lūksna* > (32.1a) *_____ > (15.2) *_____ > (2.2) _____

{_____} 'moon' **F** {spica} *spīka* 'ear of corn' :: **spīksna* > (32.1a) *_____ >

(15.2) *_____ > (2.2) _____ {_____} 'thorn' **G** {paciscor} *pakīskor* 'I

agree' :: **pakslos* > (32.3a) *_____ > (15.3) *_____ > (2.2) *_____ >

(9.18) _____ {_____} 'post'

31   The Semivowels /i̯/ and /u̯/

● **SCN 40.1**   i̯ > 0 / V_V   **Loss of intervocalic /i̯/**

The two semivowels /i̯/ and /u̯/ were only weakly articulated in Latin and vanished in many different positions. Even before the earliest attestation of Latin, /i̯/ had vanished between vowels. Preforms can therefore only be reconstructed on the basis of cognate forms in other IE languages. One example is the reconstruction and development of the cardinal number 'three': *trei̯es > (40.1) *trees > (3.1) trēs {tres}. The preform *trei̯es can be reconstructed by comparison with Sanskrit tráyas 'three'. Greek trēs shows exactly the same development.

● **SCN x11.1/x11.2**   (g,d) > i̯ / _i̯   **Intervocalic {i} was geminate /i̯i̯/**

The first syllable of ai̯i̯ō {aio} 'I say', mai̯i̯us {maius} 'bigger' and pei̯i̯or {peior} 'worse' always counts heavy in Latin poetry. This syllable length must have been a positional length because the root vowels of the forms are short. In Latin, intervocalic {i} was always geminate /i̯i̯/ because single /i̯/ was lost according to SCN 40.1. The assimilations SCN x11.1 and SCN x11.2, which describe the assimilation of /g/ or /d/ to /i̯/, were the main sources for the intervocalic double /i̯i̯/. Inscriptions like {cuiius} 'whose?', {eiius} 'his' or the acc. sg. {maiiorem} 'bigger' are examples for a more phonetic notation of the corresponding CL forms. According to the grammarian Quintilian, even Cicero preferred writing the phonetically more accurate {aiio} instead of {aio}.

● **SCN 40.2**   u̯ > 0 / V₁_V₁   **Loss of intervocalic /u̯/ between vowels**

The semivowel /u̯/ was lost between identical vowels if the syllable following the /u̯/ was not stressed. The loss of /u̯/ can be seen in the contracted perfect form audī́t for audī́u̯it 'he heard', in opposition to the preservation of /u̯/ in au̯ārus {auarus} 'greedy' and seu̯ērus {seuerus} 'harsh'. After the loss of intervocalic /u̯/ in audī́u̯it, the two vowels /ī/ and /i/ came into contact, and the long vowel was shortened before the two vowels contracted to form a long vowel: {audiuit} audī́u̯it > (40.2) *audī́it > (1.1) *audiit > (3.1) audī́t {audit}. Also the form dī́tior {ditior} 'richer' shows the same development because it goes back to dī́u̯itior {diuitior}. In common speech, /u̯/ was also lost between non-identical vowels and by the dissimilatory effect of a preceding labial sound, which can be seen in {fauilla} fau̯illa > (24.7) VL failla {failla} 'ashes' and {mouere} mou̯ēre > (24.7) VL moēre {moere} 'to move'.

● **SCN 40.5**   u̯ > 0 / _(o, ō, u, ū)   **Loss of /u̯/ before the phonetically similar vowels /o/, /ō/, /u/, /ū/**

The semivowel /u̯/ was also lost before the back vowels /o/, /ō/, /u/ and /ū/, which can be seen in the development of EL {suodales} su̯odālēs > (40.5) CL sodālēs {sodales} 'companions'. This sound change also affected the clusters /ku̯/ and /gu̯/ which originated out of PIE labiovelars (see unit 33). In sterku̯ilīnium {sterquilinium} 'dunghill', one sees the retention of /u̯/, whereas the related *sterku̯os > (40.5) *sterkos > (9.18) sterkus {stercus} 'dung' exhibits its loss. Quite often /u̯/ was reintroduced by analogy because the regular development would have yielded paradigms with too divergent forms. /u̯/ was lost regularly in *paru̯om > (40.5) *parom > (9.18) parum {parum} 'little', whereas the related adjective paru̯us {paruus} 'small' must have been remodeled in analogy to forms such as the gen. sg. paru̯ī {parui}. The regular outcome of the preform *paru̯os should have been *paru̯os > (40.5) paros* > (9.18) parus*. In common speech, however, one finds the regularly expected forms. The Appendix Probi, a grammatical glossary, has au̯s {aus} for au̯us {auus} 'grandfather' and flau̯s {flaus} for flau̯us {flauus} 'golden yellow'.

Exercises

E1 After the loss of a semivowel, the clashing vowels were contracted.

A {consueueram} *kōnsuēu̯eram* > (40.2) *_____ > (1.1) *_____ > (3.1)

_____ {_____} 'I was used to' **B** {lauo} *lau̯ō* 'I wash' :: *lau̯a-trīna* > (40.2)

*_____ > (3.1) _____ {_____} 'bath' **C** {uiuo} *u̯īu̯ō* 'I live' :: *u̯īu̯ita* >

(40.2) *_____ > (1.1) *_____ > (3.1) _____ {_____} 'life'

> **INFO** The abbreviation A in the SCN-rules means that the sound change did not happen according to regular sound laws but happened by analogy to another form. Analogy keeps morphologically related words together, by preventing that related forms become dissimilar due to regular sound laws. The next unit will take a closer look at analogical remodeling.

E2 Assimilation of /d/ and /g/ to following /i̯/.

A *magis* {magis} 'much' ::*magi̯ōs* > (x11.1) *_____ > (A: s > r by gen. *mai̯i̯ōrem*)

*_____ > (1.4) _____ {_____} 'bigger' **B** {adagium} *ad-ag-ium* 'pun' ::

agi̯ō > (x11.1) _____ {_____} 'I say' **C** *pedi̯ōs* > (x11.2) *_____ > (A:

s > r by gen. *pei̯i̯ōris*) *_____ > (1.4) _____ {_____} 'worse'

E3 The semivowel /u̯/ is lost before velar vowels.

A {loqui} *loku̯ī* 'to speak' :: *loku̯utus* > (40.5) *_____ > (A: u > ū caused by PPPs like

lau̯dātus or *au̯dītus*) _____ {_____} 'spoken' **B** {sequor} *seku̯or* 'I follow'

:: *seku̯utus* > (40.5) *_____ > (A: u > ū caused by PPPs like *lau̯dātus* or *au̯dītus*)

_____ {_____} 'followed' **C** {quinque}+{uncia} :: *ku̯īŋku̯-ūnk-s* > (40.5)

_____ {_____} 'five twelfths' **D** {sequor} *seku̯or* 'I follow' :: *seku̯ondos* > (9.18)

*_____ > (9.19) *_____ > (40.5) _____ {_____} 'the following'

32   Analogical Changes

● **Leveling of intraparadigmatic differences**

The nominative *hiems* 'winter' was not formed by regular sound changes, but was phonologically remodeled. The expected development is *hiems* > (19.9) *hiens** > (2.1) *hiēns**, which would have yielded the irregular paradigm nom. *hiēns**, gen. *hiemis*, dat. *hiemī*, etc. As the majority of forms shows a stem formant /m/, the /n/ of the expected regular nom. *hiēns** was thought to be irregular and changed to /m/, in opposition to the regular sound change m > (19.9) n / _s. The formation of a word due to a pattern found in another word is called analogy. This process is one of the main driving forces of language development. Analogical processes resolve variation between related forms by keeping them phonologically together. This prevents sound changes to create forms which are regarded unrelated by the speakers.

● **Modeling analogical changes**

The form *eiiusdem* {eiusdem} 'of the same (person)', which is the gen. of *īdem* {idem} 'the same', was not formed regularly according to Latin sound changes because in this case the expected development is *eiiusdem* > (15.5) *eiiuzdem** > (2.2) *eiiūdem**. Therefore, the form *eiiusdem* {eiusdem} has been remodeled in analogy to the nom. *eiius* {eius}. This development is written as *eiiūdem** > (A: *eiius*) *eiiusdem* and read as "*eiiūdem** has been remodeled to *eiiusdem* in analogy to *eiius*". The starting point of this analogical formation is clearly the nom. sg.

The paradigm of CL *honor, honōris* {honor, honoris} 'honor' looks like an r-stem but was originally an s-stem, as can be seen in OL *honōs* {honos}. In the oblique cases such as the gen. **honōs-is* > (15.6) **honōzis* > (26.1) *honōris*, the r-stem originated by rhotazism and was subsequently transferred to the nom. in order to level out the variation within the paradigm. This development is written as *honōs* > (A: gen. *honōris*) **honōr* > (1.4) *honor* and read as "the nom. of OL *honōs* was remodeled to **honōr* in analogy to the gen. *honōris*". The starting point of this analogical formation cannot be clearly seen in the gen. because also other case forms or the paradigm as a whole might have caused this analogical change.

● **Recomposition was the antagonist to vowel weakening**

The Romance languages witness that Vulgar Latin abolished almost completely the effects of vowel weakening by taking over the root vowel of non-compound verbs into compound verbs. Early writers sometimes use the 'regular' weakened forms, which appear only in their recomposed form in later writers. Plautus has the regular form *ēnikō* {enico} 'I torture to death', which is derived from *nekō* {neco} 'I kill', whereas later writers used *ēnekō* {eneco} with the root vowel of the base form. Cato has the form *praesikō* {praesico} 'I cut at the front side', which is built regularly from the base *sekō* {seco} 'I cut', whereas *praesikō* {praesico} was remodeled to *praesekō* {praeseco} in later times. In CL times already, the compound forms of *petō* {peto} 'I strive for', *tegō* {tego} 'I protect', *ụokō* {uoco} 'I call' regularly took over the root vowel of their base forms. The compound forms were not *appitō**, *dētigō** and *reụikō**, but *appetō* 'I strive after', *dētegō* 'I uncover' and *rēụokō* 'I call back' (cf. Niedermann 1953:32/33). On a case-by-case basis, it is, however, not possible to decide whether the forms originated by recomposition or after the end of the productive phase of vowel weakening.

Exercises

E1 Is *alaker, alakris* {alacer, alacris} 'lively' formed according to regular sound laws? Hint: You need vowel weakening (SCN 8) and vowel assimilation (SCN 6) for the answer.

_____

_____

E2 Is *integer, integris* {integer, integris} 'untouched' formed according to regular sound laws?

_____

_____

E3 Is *genitrīks* {genitrix} 'mother' the expected regular development from **genatrīks* ?

_____

_____

E4 Is the paradigma of *eku̯us, eku̯ī* {equus, equi} 'horse' formed according to regular sound laws?

_____

_____

E5 Is the paradigm of *arks, arkis* {arx, arcis} 'castle' formed according to regular sound laws?

_____

_____

E6 Are *ku̯ot* {quot} 'how many?' and *ku̯od* {quod} 'what?' regular forms?

_____

_____

33   The PIE Labiovelars in Latin

- **SCN x4.1** $k^w > k\underset{\circ}{u}$ **Velar sounds with labial coarticulation:** $*/k^w/$, $*/g^w/$, $*/g^{wh}/$

In consequence of the sound correspondences described in lines 45–58 of chapter 37, it is possible and necessary to reconstruct sounds for the PIE parent language, which are called labiovelars and resulted in Latin {qu} and {gu}. These PIE sounds were velar $*/k/$, $*/g/$ and $*/g^h/$ with the additional articulation of lip-rounding. Therefore, the labiovelars $*/k^w/$, $*/g^w/$ and $*/g^{wh}/$ are written in linguistic notation with superscript {^{w}} in order to say that these two sounds constitute one phoneme and not a sequence of two phonemes. Whether the Latin sounds must be regarded as one phoneme or as a sequence of two phonemes is, however, disputed. One the one hand, Latin {qu} almost never causes positional length of a preceding vowel and thus counted as a single consonant. On the other hand, there are only very few minimal pairs like *seku̯ī* {sequi} 'to follow' :: 1 sg. perf. *seku̯ī* {secui} 'I cut', which corroborate the status of a Latin phoneme /k^w/. Furthermore, these minimal pairs can also be regarded as examples of the opposition /u̯/ :: /u/. In this book, the Latin labiovelars are regarded as a sequence of two phonemes, which is described by SCN x4.

- **SCN 40.3/40.4** $\underset{\circ}{u} > 0 / (k,g)\_C$ **The labial element is lost before consonants**

The labial element of PIE labiovelars disappeared before consonants, which can be seen by the comparison of *ekstiṇguō* {extinguo} 'I extinguish' and *ekstiṇksī* {exstinxi} 'I extinguished'. The development of {extinxi} was: $*eks\text{-}stiṇg^wsī >$ (x2.2) $*eks\text{-}stiṇgu̯sī >$ (40.4) $*eks\text{-}stiṇgsī >$ (13.6) $*eks\text{-}stiṇksī >$ (39.2) *ekstiṇksī* {exstinxi}. This form also appears as *ekstīṇksī* with a long vowel in analogy to its PPP *ekstiṇktus >* (2.3/2.4) *ekstīṇktus*, which has regular vowel length according to Lachmann's law. Another example is *unguentum* {unguentum} 'perfume' in comparison to *ūṇktiō* {unctio} 'anointment'. In this case, the development was: $*uṇg^wtiō >$ (x2.2) $*uṇgu̯tiō >$ (40.4) $*uṇgtiō >$ (12.7) $*uṇktiō >$ (2.3/2.4) *ūṇktiō* {unctio}.

- **SCN 36.1** $g > 0 / V\_\underset{\circ}{u}V$ **/g/ is lost before /u̯/ in the initial and medial position**

Lines 49/50 of chapter 37 show that initial Latin /u̯/ can go back to an original PIE labiovelar if related languages show respective sound correspondences. Forms such as *u̯enio* {uenio} 'I come' and *u̯orō* {uoro} 'I devore' go back to former *gu̯enio* and *gu̯orō*, and further back to $*g^weniō$ and $*g^worō$. In the medial position between vowels, the cluster /gu̯/ was simplified to /u̯/ by SCN 36.1. The form *kōnīu̯eō* {coniueo} 'I close my eyes' can thus be traced to *kōnīgu̯eō* because the comparison with the perfect $*kōnīgu̯sī >$ (40.4) $*kōnīgsī >$ (13.6) *kōnīksī* {conixi} 'I closed my eyes' witnesses that there must have been a guttural element in the root. First, the labial element /u̯/ was lost before a following consonant (SCN 40.4), and then /g/ was subsequently devoiced to /k/ before /s/ (SCN 13.6). It was later on that a new perfect *kōnīu̯ī* {coniui} was built in analogy to the present form *kōnīu̯eō*.

The same development is found in *niks* {nix} 'snow' and *niṇguit* {ninguit} 'it snows'. By tracing *niks* back to the preform *nigu̯s*, the nominative can be brought into accordance with the seemingly irregular genitive *niu̯is* {niuis}. During the development of the nominative $*nigu̯s >$ (40.4) $*nigs >$ (13.6) *niks*, the labial element was lost before /s/, before /g/ was subsequently devoiced before the /s/. The development of the genitive $*nigu̯is >$ (36.1) *niu̯is* {niuis}, however, exhibits the simplification of the cluster /g^w/ to /u̯/ in the intervocalic position.

Exercises

E1 The labial element /u̯/ is lost before consonants.

A {assequor} *asseku̯or* 'I reach' :: **asseku̯la* > (40.3) _____ {_____} 'follower'

B {coquo} *koku̯ō* 'I cook' :: **kok^wtos* > (x4.1) *_____ > (40.3) *_____ > (9.18)

_____ {_____} 'cooked' **C** {delinquo} *dēliŋku̯ō* 'I fail' :: **dēliku̯tum* > (40.3)

_____ {_____} 'fault' **D** {sequor} *seku̯or* 'I accompany' :: **sek^wtor* > (x4.1)

*_____ > (40.3) _____ {_____} 'I accompany'. Intensive form of

seku̯or derived from the PPP **sektos*. **E** **g^wr̥Htos* > (x2.15) **g^wrātos* > (x4.2) *_____ >

(40.4) *_____ > (9.18) _____ {_____} 'thankful' **F** **g^wregs* > (13.6)

*_____ > (x4.2) *_____ > (40.4) _____ {_____} 'herd'

E2 /g/ is lost before /u̯/ in the initial position.

A **g^worāi̯ō* > (x4.2) *_____ > (40.1) *_____ > (1.1) *_____ > (3.4)

*_____ > (30.11) _____ {_____} 'I devour' **B** **g^wī̯u̯os* > (x4.2)

*_____ > (30.11) *_____ > (9.18) _____ {_____} 'alive'

E3 PIE */p/ assimilates to a non-adjacent labiovelar */k^w/.

A **pek^wō* > (x11.3) **k^wek^wō* > (x4.1) *_____ > (9.11) *_____ (This stage is proven

by Plautus 2. sg. *ku̯oku̯ās* {quoquas} 'you cook') > (40.5) *_____ {_____} 'I

cook'

These SCN-rules appear in the exercises		
SCN 1.1	$\bar{V} > V /\_V$	A vowel before a vowel is shortened.
SCN 3.4	$a + \bar{o} > \bar{o}$	/a/ and /ō/ contract to /ō/.
SCN 9.11	$e > o / u̯\_C(C)V$	This vowel assimilation is caused by velar vowels.
SCN 13.6	$g > k /\_s$	Voiced /g/ becomes voiceless /k/ before voiceless /s/.
SCN 30.11	$g > 0 / \#\_u̯$	/g/ is lost in the initial position before /u̯/.
SCN 40.5	$u̯ > 0 /\_(o, \bar{o}, u, \bar{u})$	/u̯/ is lost before the phonetically similar velar vowels /o/, /ō/, /u/, /ū/.
SCN x4.1	$*k^w > ku̯$	The PIE labiovelar */k^w/ becomes the biphonemic sequence /ku̯/.
SCN x4.2	$*g^w > gu̯$	The PIE labiovelar */g^w/ becomes the biphonemic sequence /gu̯/.
SCN x11.3	$*p > *k^w /\_ ...*k^w$	*/p/ becomes */k^w/ before non-adjacent */k^w/.

34   The Syllabic Resonants *[n̥], *[m̥], *[r̥], *[l̥]

● **Resonants as syllabic nuclei**

The nucleus of a syllable is defined as the peak of sonority which most often consists of a vowel (cf. unit 7). The syncope of a vowel (SCN 4.1) next to a resonant /n/, /n/, /r/, /l/, however, causes these resonants to slip into the nucleus position of the syllable. Then, they are called syllabic resonants and transcribed with a circle { ̥} at the bottom. It is a characteristic feature of syllabic resonants that anaptyctic vowels appear next to them to facilitate the pronunciation. Lines 12–15 of unit 37 exemplify the reconstruction of the PIE syllabic resonants *[n̥], *[m̥], *[r̥], *[l̥] and their reflexes in Sanskrit, Greek and Latin.

● **SCN x5.6   n̥ > en. SCN x5.7   m̥ > em   The reflexes of PIE *[n̥] and *[m̥] in Latin**

In contrast to *[r̥] and *[l̥], PIE *[n̥] and *[m̥] consistently became Latin /en/ and /em/. CL *kentum* {centum} 'hundred' can be traced back to *$\hat{k}$m̥tom* with a syllabic *[m̥], as described in line 42 of unit 37. After palatal */$\hat{k}$/ had become velar */k/, the preform *km̥tom* developed to *kemtom*, and subsequently by the assimilation SCN 19.7 (m > n >/ _t) to *kentom*, which became *kentum* {centum} by SCN 9.18 (o > u).

● **SCN x5.1   r̥ > or. SCN x7.4   l̥ > ol   The reflexes of PIE *[r̥] and *[l̥] in Latin**

The Latin reflexes of PIE *[r̥] and *[l̥] are not uniform (cf. Meiser 1998:63). The standard reflexes are r̥ > or, exemplified by *$\hat{k}$r̥d* > (x1.1) *kr̥d* > (x5.1) *kord* > (38.5) *kor* {cor} 'heart', as well as l̥ > ol, exemplified by *ml̥duis* > (x5.4) *molduis* > (22.4) *molluis* > (40.9) *mollis* 'soft'. There are, however, other examples that show the development r̥ > ur if *[r̥] was in contact with a labial sound such as /u/ or a labiovelar. Lat. *kurtus* {curtus} 'short' goes back to *kuurtos*, and further back to *kʷr̥tos*, and can be connected with Hittite *kuer-zi* 'he cuts'.

● **SCN 6.2   r̥ > er   The development of EL *sakros* {sakros} to CL *saker* {sacer}**

In the EL Forum inscription, one finds the word *sakros* 'sacred', which became CL *saker* {sacer} by a complex development. In a first step, the vowel /o/ in the second syllable was syncopated: EL *sakros* > (4.1) *sakrs*. This had the effect that /r/ was placed between two consonants and became the syllabic nucleus of the second syllable > *sakrs* > (6.1) *sakr̥s*. Next to this newly formed syllabic resonant, the anaptyctic vowel /e/ appeared, which resulted in *sakr̥s* > (6.2) *sakers*. Final /s/ was subsequently sonorized to [z], which assimilated to the preceding /r/ and produced the double consonant /rr/, which was afterwards simplified in the final position: EL {sakros} *sakros* > (4.3) *sakrs* > (6.1) *sakr̥s* > (6.2) *sakers* > (15.9) *sakerz* > (22.3) *sakerr* > (39.12) CL *saker* {sacer}.

● **SCN 6.4   n̥ > in   Syllabic *[n̥] formed withing Latin develops to /in/**

After the PIE syllabic resonants had developed into the sequences of a vowel plus a resonant, new syncopes brought about new syllabic resonants in the history of Latin. This happened when lo-diminutives were derived from no-formations e.g. in the form *púgnolos* 'small fist', which was derived from *pugnos*, which itself developed to CL *pugnus* 'fist'. The syncope of the medial syllable caused the nasal /n/ to slip into the nucleus position thus becoming a syllabic resonant: *púgnolos* > (4.1) *púgnlos* > (6.3) *púgn̥los*. Afterwards an anaptyctic /i/ emerged next to *[n̥]: *púgnlos* > *púginlos* before the consonant cluster /nl/ assimilated to /ll/ producing the form *púginlos* > (21.2) *púgillos*. In a final step, the initial stress accent changed to the rule of the penult: *púginlos* > (21.2) *púgillos* > (Ac1) *pugíllos* > (9.18) *pugillus* 'a handful'.

Exercises

E1 PIE *[n̩] and *[m̩] develop to Latin /en/ and /em/.

A *tn̩tos > (x5.6) *_____ > (9.18) _____ 'stretched' **B** acc. sg. *pedm̩ > (x5.7)

_____ 'foot' **C** *septm̩ > (x5.7) _____ 'seven' **D** *ḱm̩tom > (x1.1) *km̩tom > (x5.7)

*_____ > (19.7) *_____ > (9.18) _____ {_____} 'hundred'

E *deḱm̩ > (x1.1) *dekm̩ > (x5.7) _____ {_____} 'ten' **F** *gʷm̩tos > (x4.2)

*_____ > (x5.7) *_____ > (19.7) *_____ > (30.11) *_____ >

(9.18) _____ {_____} 'come'

E2 PIE *[r̩] becomes Latin /or/ or /ur/.

A *ḱr̩d > (x1.1) *kr̩d > (x5.1) *_____ > (38.5) _____ {_____} 'heart'

B *mr̩tis > (x5.1) *_____ > (4.2) *_____ > (16.4) *_____ > (39.7)

_____ {_____} 'death' **C** kʷr̩tos > (x4.1) *_____ > (x5.2) *_____

> (40.5) *_____ > (9.18) _____ {_____} 'short'

E3 Syllabic *[n̩], which originated by Latin syncope, becomes /in/; *[r̩] becomes /er/.

A {scamnum} *skamnum* 'bench' :: *skábnolom > (4.1) *_____ > (6.3) *_____ >

(6.4) *_____ > (Ac1) *_____ > (21.2) *_____ > (9.18) _____

{_____} 'small bench' **B** {tignum} *tīŋnum* 'piece of timber' :: *tígnolom > (4.1)

*_____ > (6.3) *_____ > (6.4) *_____ > (Ac1) *_____ >

(21.2) *_____ > (9.18) _____ 'small piece of timber' **C** *ager* 'field' :: *ágrolos

> (4.1) *_____ > (6.1)*_____ > (6.2) *_____ > (Ac1) *_____

> (21.3) *_____ > (9.18) _____ 'small field' **D** *liber* 'book' :: *líbrolos > (4.1)

*_____ > (6.1) *_____ > (6.2) *_____ > (Ac1) *_____ > (21.3)

*_____ > (9.18) _____ 'small book' **E** *imbris > (4.2) *_____ > (6.1)

*_____ > (6.2) *_____ > (15.9) *_____ > (22.3) *_____ >

(39.8) _____ 'rain'

SCN 21.2	**n > l / _l**	/n/ becomes /l/ before /l/.
SCN 21.3	**r > l / _l**	/r/ becomes /l/ before /l/.
SCN 30.11	**g > 0 / #_u̯**	/g/ is lost before /u̯/ in the initial position.
SCN 39.8	**r > 0 / r_#**	Double consonants are always simplified in the final position.

35

The Complex Development of the PIE Mediae Aspiratae (MA)

There are two different models that describe the development of the PIE voiced aspirated stops in Latin (cf. unit 37, lines 30–35). In Latin, the reflexes of the voiced aspirated stops, which are also called mediae aspiratae (MA), are voiceless in the initial position and voiced in the medial position, except for /h/. For this reason, the first model from **Ascoli** assumes that the PIE voiced aspirated stops became voiceless in all positions and then again voiced in the medial position. The first step is corroborated by Greek data where the reflexes of the PIE voiced aspirated stops are voiceless in all positions, too. In contrast to this, the model from Hartmann assumes that the PIE voiced aspirated stops became voiceless only in the initial position and their feature of [+voice] was retained in the medial position (cf. Meiser 1998:101). In this book, the model from Hartmann is applied and subdivided into four phases, which are presented in the table below.

- **Phase 1: SCN x6.1 $*b^h > *\beta$. SCN x6.2 $*d^h > *\delta$. SCN x6.3 $*g^h > *\gamma$.**

  The MA $*/b^h/$, $*/d^h/$, $*/g^h/$ ($*/\hat{g}^h/$ also goes back to $*/\hat{g}^h/$ and $*/g^h\underset{\sim}{u}/ <$ (x4.3) $*/g^{wh}/$) become the voiced fricatives $*/\beta/$, $*/\delta/$, $*/\gamma/$.

- **Phase 2: SCN x6.5 $*\beta > f$; SCN x6.6 $*\delta > *\theta$. SCN $*\gamma > *\chi$. SCN x6.7/8 $*\gamma > g$ / #_R.**

  In the initial position before /r/ and /l/, the fricative $*/\gamma/$ transformed into the stop /g/ (SCN x6.7/8). The other voiced fricatives $*/\beta/$, $*/\delta/$, $*/\gamma/$ were allophonically devoiced in the initial position and became the voiceless fricatives $*/\varphi/$, $*/\theta/$, $*/\chi/$. The sounds $*/\varphi/$ and $*/\chi/$ developed further to Latin /f/ and /h/. Due to these developments, a correlation of voiceless fricatives in the initial position and voiced fricatives in the medial position was established. One exception is the development of medial intervocalic $*/\gamma/$, which, if not in position before /R/, became -just like in the initial position- first $*/\chi/$ and then /h/, before it was lost completely in VL.

- **Phase 3: SCN x7.1 $*\theta > f$. SCN x7.3b-x7.7 $*\delta > *\beta$.**

  Dental and labial fricatives merged partially. The initial voiceless fricative $*/\theta/$ became /f/, as did initial /s/ before /r/ by SCN x7.2. The medial voiced fricative $*/\delta/$ became $*/\beta/$ next to /r/, /l/ or /$\underset{\sim}{u}$/.

- **Phase 4: SCN x8.1-x8.6 $*\beta > b$. SCN x8.7 $*\delta > *d$. SCN x8.8/9 $*\gamma > g$.**

  In the medial position, $*/\beta/$, $*/\delta/$ and partially $*/\gamma/$ transformed into the stops /b/, /d/ and /g/. These developments led to the synchronous phonological system of CL.

	PIE	Phase 1	Phase 2	Phase 3	Phase 4	CL
1	$*b^h r\bar{a}ter$	$*\beta r\bar{a}ter$	$*\varphi r\bar{a}ter > fr\bar{a}ter$	>	>	{frater}
2	$*neb^h el\bar{a}$	$*ne\beta ela$	>	>	$*nebela$	{nebula}
3	$*d^h\bar{u}mos$	$*\delta\bar{u}mos$	$*\theta\bar{u}mos$	$*f\bar{u}mos$	>	{fumus}
4	$*\underset{\sim}{u}id^h e\underset{\sim}{u}\bar{a}$	$*\underset{\sim}{u}i\delta e\underset{\sim}{u}\bar{a}$	>	>	$*\underset{\sim}{u}ide\underset{\sim}{u}\bar{a}$	{uiduua}
5	$*\underset{\sim}{u}erd^h om$	$*\underset{\sim}{u}er\delta om$	>	$*\underset{\sim}{u}er\beta om$	$*\underset{\sim}{u}erbom$	{uerbum}
6	$*\hat{g}^h elos$	$*\gamma elos$	$*\chi elos > helos$	>	>	{helus}
7	$*\underset{\sim}{u}e\hat{g}^h\bar{o}$	$*\underset{\sim}{u}e\gamma\bar{o}$	$*\underset{\sim}{u}e\chi\bar{o} > \underset{\sim}{u}eh\bar{o}$	>		{ueho}
8	$*g^h lad^h ros$	$*\gamma la\delta ros$	$*gla\delta ros$	$*gla\beta ros$	$*glabros$	{glabrus}

Exercises

INFO The Greek letters /β/, /δ/, /γ/ and /φ/, /θ/, /χ/ are graphemes for voiced and voiceless fricatives.	Place of Articulation		
	Labial	Interdental	Velar
Fricatives	φ β	θ δ	χ γ

E1 Voiced fricatives become voiceless in the initial position.

A *$b^herō$ > (x6.1) *_____ > (x6.5a) *_____ > (x6.5b) _____

{_____} 'I carry' **B** *$b^héh_2meh_2$ > (x2.3) *$b^hah_2mah_2$ > (x2.9) *$b^hāmā$ > (x6.1)

*_____ > (x6.5a) *_____ > (x6.5b) *_____ > (1.6) _____

{_____} 'gossip' **C** *$d^hūmos$ > (x6.2) *_____ > (x6.6) *_____ > (x7.1)

*_____ > (9.18) _____ {_____} 'smoke' **D** *$ĝ^helh_3os$ > (x1.3) *g^helh_3os

> (x2.7) *g^helos > (x6.3) *_____ > (x6.9a) *_____ > (x6.9b) *_____ >

(28.3) *_____ > (9.9) *_____ > (9.18) _____ {_____} 'green

vegetables'

E2 Voiced fricatives become stop consonants in the medial position.

A *neb^heleh_2 > (x2.3) *neb^helah_2 > (x2.9) *$neb^helā$ > (x6.1) *_____ > (1.6) *_____

> (x8.1) *_____ > (28.3) *_____ > (8.8) *_____ > (8.10) *_____

{_____} 'cloud' **B** *alb^hos > (x6.1) *_____ > (x8.2) _____ > (9.18)

_____ {_____} 'white' **C** *$u̯id^heu̯eh_2$ > (x2.3) *$u̯id^heu̯ah_2$ > (x2.9)*$u̯id^heu̯ā$ >

(x6.2) *_____ > (x8.7) *_____ > (1.6) *_____ > (8.9) *_____ >

(8.11) _____ {_____} 'widow' **D** *$u̯eĝ^hō$ > (x1.3) *$u̯eg^hō$ > (x6.3) *_____

> (x8.12a) *_____ > (x8.12b) _____ {ueho} 'I drive'

E3 Dental fricatives merge with labial fricatives in the medial position.

A *$u̯erd^hom$ > (x6.2) *_____ > (x7.4) *_____ > (x8.5) *_____ >

(9.18) _____ {_____} 'word' **B** *rud^hros > (x6.2) *_____ > (x7.3b)

*_____ > (x8.4) *_____ > (4.2) *_____ > (6.1) *_____ >

(6.2) *_____ > (15.9) *_____ > (22.3) *_____ > (39.8) _____

{_____} 'red'

36

Sound correspondences as well as linguistic arguments make it possible to reconstruct the three laryngeals */h$_1$/, */h$_2$/, */h$_3$/ for PIE (cf. unit 37, lines 59–67), although their exact phonetic value is unknown. The special thing about these sounds was the 'coloring' of */e/ to /a/ next to adjacent */h$_2$/, as well as the 'coloring' of */e/ to /o/ next to adjacent */h$_3$/. After these sound changes, the laryngeals disappeared completely before 'colored' or 'uncolored' vowels. If placed behind a vowel, the laryngeals disappeared as well, but caused a compensatory lengthening of the preceding vowel. The cover symbol /H/ is used for whatever laryngeal if it is not possible to determine exactly the number of the laryngeal.

- **SCN x2.5 *h$_1$ > 0 / _V**   Laryngeal */h$_1$/ is lost before a vowel
  *h$_1$ed-ō > (x2.5) edō {edo} 'I eat'

- **SCN x2.8 *eh$_1$ > ē**
  Laryngeal */h$_1$/ is lost after a vowel with compensatory lengthening
  *u̯eh$_1$ros > (x2.8) *u̯ēros > (9.18) u̯ērus {uerus} 'true'

- **SCN x2.1 *e > a / *h$_2$ _**   Laryngeal */h$_2$/ colors */e/ to /a/ and is lost before a vowel
  *h$_2$eĝō > (x1.2) *h$_2$egō > (x2.1) *h$_2$agō > (x2.6) agō {ago} 'I drive'

- **SCN x2.3 *e > a / _*h$_2$**
  Laryngeal */h$_2$/ colors */e/ to /a/ and is lost with compensatory lengthening
  *keh$_2$ros > (x2.3) *kah$_2$ros > (x2.9) *kāros > (9.18) kārus {carus} 'dear'

- **SCN x2.2 *e > o / *h$_3$ _**
  Laryngeal */h$_3$/ colors */e/ to /o/ and is lost before a vowel
  *h$_3$ektoh$_1$ > (x2.2) *h$_3$oktoh$_1$ > (x2.7) *oktoh$_1$ > (x2.8) oktō {octo} 'eight'

- **SCN x2.4 *e > o / _*h$_3$**
  Laryngeal */h$_3$/ colors */e/ to /o/ and is lost with compensatory lengthening
  *peh$_3$tos > (x2.4) *poh$_3$tos > (x2.10) *pōtos > (9.18) pōtus {potus} 'drink'

- **SCN x2.13 *H > 0 / #_C**
  Laryngeals are lost in the initial position before a consonant
  *h$_3$miĝʰō > (x1.3) *h$_3$mingʰō > (x2.13) *mingʰō > (x6.3) *miŋγō > (x8.9) miŋgō {mingo} 'I piss'

- **SCN x2.14 *H > a / C_C**   Laryngeals between consonants are vocalized to /a/
  *sth̥$_2$tos > (x2.14) *statos > (9.18) status {status} 'state'

- **SCN x2.15-7 *R̥H > Rā**
  A syllabic resonant plus a laryngeal result in a resonant plus long /ā/

  PIE sound cluster like /R̥H/, which consisted of a syllabic resonant plus a laryngeal, developed in Latin into the sequence of a resonant plus a long /ā/. CL nātus {natus} 'born' can be traced via OL gnātus back to *ĝn̥h$_1$tos. The palatal */ĝ/ became velar /g/, and the sequence */n̥h$_1$/ became /nā/. The development was: *ĝn̥h$_1$tos > (x1.2) *gn̥h$_1$tos > (2.17) OL gnātos > (30.2) *nātos > (9.18) CL nātus {natus} 'born'.

Exercises

E1 Laryngeal */h₁/ is lost without a trace before a vowel and with compensatory lengthening after a vowel.

A *h₁eu̯sō > (x2.5) *_____ > (9.10) *_____ > (15.6) *_____ >

(26.1) *_____ > (10.3) *_____ > (10.4) _____ {_____} 'I

burn' **B** *i̯eh₁-k-ai̯ > (x2.8) *_____ > (8.1) *_____ > (10.8) *_____

> (10.9) *_____ {_____} 'I threw' **C** *ĝenh₁os > (x1.2) *_____ >

(x2.5) *_____ > (9.18) _____ {_____} 'race' **D** *pleh₁nos > (x2.8)

*_____ > (9.18) _____ {_____} 'full'

E2 Laryngeal */h₂/ and */h₃/ color */e/ to /a/ and */e/ to /o/ before they are lost before the vowel.

A *h₂eĝ-s-i-s > (x1.2) *h₂egsis > (13.6) *h₂eksis > (x2.1) *_____ > (x2.6) _____

{_____} 'axis' **B** *h₂eu̯som > (x2.1) *_____ > (x2.6) *_____ > (15.6)

*_____ > (26.1) *_____ > (9.18) _____ {_____} 'gold' **C**

*h₂eu̯is > (x2.1) *_____ > (x2.6) *_____ {_____} 'bird' **D** *h₂eu̯sōsā >

(x2.1) *_____ > (x2.6) *_____ > (1.6) *_____ > (15.6) *_____

> (26.1) *_____ {_____} 'dawn'

E3 Laryngeal */h₂/ is lost after a colored vowel with compensatory lengthening of the vowel.

A *steh₂-se > (x2.3) *_____ > (x2.9) *_____ > (15.6) *_____ >

(26.1) _____ {_____} 'to stand' **B** *bʰeh₂ĝos > (x2.3) *_____ > (x2.9)

*_____ > (x6.1) *βāgos > (x6.5a) *φāgos > (x6.5b) *fāgos > (9.18) fāgus {fagus} 'beech-

tree' **C** *ĝleh₂m > (x1.1) *kleh₂m > (x2.3) *_____ > (x2.9) *_____ > (1.4) klam

{clam} 'secretly' derived from kelō {celo} 'I hide' **D** *gʷih₃u̯os > (x2.11) *_____ > (x4.2)

*_____ > (30.11) *u̯īu̯os > (9.18) u̯īu̯us {uiuus} 'alive'

E4 Laryngeal */h₃/ is lost after a colored vowel with compensatory lengthening of the vowel.

A *h₃neh₃mn̥ > (x2.13) *_____ > (x2.4) *_____ > (x2.10) *_____ >

(x5.6) _____ {_____} 'name' **B** *bʰleh₃ros > (x2.4) *_____ > (x2.10)

*_____ > (x6.1) *_____ > (x6.5a) *_____ > (x6.5b) *_____ >

(9.18) _____ {_____} 'reddish-yellow'

Reconstruction of PIE Phonemes

● **Systematic similarities and correspondences hint to a genetic language relationship**

If different languages exhibit systematic correspondences regarding their vocabulary and grammar, and the frequency of these correspondences is so high that it cannot be attributed to mere chance, it is possible to posit a genetic relationship between these languages and reconstruct a common ancestor or proto-language. Latin *tremō* and Greek *trémō*, which both mean 'I shiver', enable the reconstruction of a common preform **trémō*, out of which the two language forms originated without any changes. The comparison of Lat. *serpō* and Gr. *hérpō*, which both mean 'I creep', furthermore shows that these two forms are not identical, but that Lat. /s/ corresponds to Gr. /h/. One could thus posit **sérpō* as the preform and derive Gr. *hérpō* by the sound change s > h / #_V, or posit **hérpō* as the preform and explain the Lat. form via the sound change h > s / #_V. If one additionally takes into account Skr. *sárpā-mi* 'I creep' (*-mi* is the extended ending of the 1. ps. sg.), the first solution is corroborated because two languages have /s/ in the initial position. Nonetheless, **hérpō* could still be the preform of all the forms, in which case Latin and Sanskrit would exhibit a parallel development. But regarding the majority of IE languages, in which /s/ corresponds to Lat. and Skr. /s/, as well as to Gr. /h/, the preform **serpō* with initial */s/ is reconstructed. This accords to the linguistic principle of majority and simplicity. The sound, which is exhibited by most languages and which takes the fewest intermediate steps from the preform to the attested language form, can be most often reconstructed for the preform.

● **Phonological correspondences between Sanskrit, Greek and Latin**

The following charts are examples for etymological word correspondences between Sanskrit, Greek and Latin on the left side, the PIE preform and its meaning in the middle and the sound correspondences illustrated by the examples on the right side. One example often furnishes results for more than one sound. The sound, which is being compared in a line, is printed in **bold**. The following description serves as an introduction to the comparative method and does not exhaustively present and explain all the correspondences and irregularities of the given words. Usually, the meanings of the attested forms and the meaning of the preform are the same. Otherwise, they will be mentioned in the commentary. The abbreviation **L** stands for line.

● **1. Short vowels**

	Compared Languages			Preform and Meaning		Sound Correspondences			
	Sanskrit	**Greek**	**Latin**	**PIE**	**Meaning**	**Skr.**	**Gr.**	**Lat.**	**PIE**
1	*sal-ilám*	*hál-s* (nom.)	*sal-is* (gen.)	**sal-*	'salt'	/a/	/a/	/a/	**/**a**/
2	*saptá*	*heptá*	*septem*	**septm̥*	'seven'	/a/	/e/	/e/	**/**e**/
3	*dviṣ*	*dís*	*bis*	**du̯is*	'twice'	/i/	/i/	/i/	**/**i**/
4	*aṣṭáu*	*oktṓ*	*oktō*	**oḱtṓ*	'eight'	/a/	/o/	/o/	**/**o**/
5	*jā́nu*	*gónu*	*(genu)*	**ǵo/enu*	'knee'	/ā/	/o/	(/e/)	**/**o**/
6	*śrutás*	*klutós*	*in-klutus*	**ḱlutós*	'famous'	/u/	/u/	/u/	**/**u**/

L1: All languages have an /a/, and therefore */a/ is reconstructed for the parent language. The phoneme */a/ is, however, rare in PIE words. Skr. *salilám* has the meaning 'ocean' in the sense of 'salt water'. Gr. *háls* 'salt' can also be used in the figurative sense of 'ocean'. Lat. *sāl* has a long vowel in contrast to the oblique cases. Cf. L25 for Gr. /h/ from */s/. **L2**: Lat. and Gr. /e/ always correspond to Skr. /a/. Cf. L12 for the development of final syllabic *[m̥]. **L3**: Skr. almost completely conserves the PIE form. The so called RUKI-rule states that Skr. /s/ becomes retroflex /ṣ/ after /r/, /u/, /k/ and /i/. In retroflex sounds, the tongue is bent upwards. In Latin, the cluster /du̯/ became /b/ by SCN 40.11. In Greek, the initial consonant cluster was simplified to /d/ by the loss of /u̯/. **L4**: Lat. and Gr. /o/ correspond to Skr. /a/. In Sanskrit, the medial consonant cluster */k̂t/ is continued by /ṣṭ/. The word is enlarged by a particle *-u*. **L5**: Lat. and Gr. /e/ and /o/ usually correspond to Skr. /a/ (cf. L2/ L4). In open syllables before /r/, /l/, /n/ or /m/, however, the vowel /a/ was sometimes lengthened according to "Brugmann's law". The Lat. form is put into parenthesis because in this case Latin /e/ is not an example for a sound correspondence but for the phenomenon of ablaut, which is a morphological vowel change (cf. appendix 1). **L6**: Cf. L41/42 for Skr. /ʃ/ {ś}. Lat. /u/ from /o/ by SCN 9.18.

2. Long vowels

By the comparison of the IE languages, it is possible to reconstruct a series of long vowels for the parent language. In most cases, however, these long vowels can be traced back to a combination of a short vowel plus a laryngeal.

	Compared Languages			Preform and Meaning		Sound Correspondences			
	Sanskrit	**Greek**	**Latin**	**PIE**	**Meaning**	**Skr.**	**Gr.**	**Lat.**	**PIE**
7	*mātā́*	*mā́tēr*	*māter*	**mātēr*	'mother'	/ā/	/ā/	/ā/	**/ā/*
8	*rājā*	*(orégō)*	*rēks*	**h₃rēĝ-s*	'king'	/ā/	/ē/	/ē/	**/ē/*
9	*jīvás*	*(bíos)*	*u̯īu̯us*	**gʷīu̯os*	'alive'	/ī/	/ī/	/ī/	**/ī/*
10	*dā́nam*	*dõron*	*dōnum*	**dōnom*	'gift'	/ā/	/ō/	/ō/	**/ō/*
11	*yū́ṣ*	*zdū́-mē*	*i̯ūs*	**i̯ūs*	'broth'	/ū/	/ū/	/ū/	**/ū/*

L7: Just as for short */a/, also for long */ā/ only very few examples can be found. Skr. exhibits the loss of the final /r/ after a long vowel. The Gr. word is Doric and has /ā/ instead of Ion-Att. /ē/. In Latin, the final long vowel was shortened by SCN 1.4. **L8**: Also long */ē/ is rare and can be reconstructed in the word for 'king', which does not have a direct cognate in Gr. where the root is continued in *orégo* 'I reach out'. Cf. L43/44 for Skr. /ʤ/ {j} from */ĝ/. For */h₃/ cf. L67. **L9**: Gr. *bíos* 'life' exhibits the loss of /u̯/, which is illustrated in L24. For the development of the labiovelar */gʷ/ cf. L49–54. **L10**: Gr. *dõron* does not go back directly to PIE **dō-no-m*, but is derived from **dō-ro-m* with a different suffix. Final */m/ became Gr. /n/. **L11**: Gr. *zdū́mē* 'leaven' is enlarged by the suffix *-mē*. For Gr. /zd/ from */i̯/ cf. L22. Skr. /ṣ/ according to the RUKI-rule (cf. L3).

3. Syllabic resonants

If placed between consonants, the nasals */n/, */m/ and the liquids */r/, */l/ have allophonic syllabic variants, which are called syllabic resonants and written as *[n̥], *[m̥], *[r̥], *[l̥].

	Compared Languages			Preform and Meaning		Sound Correspondences			
	Sanskrit	Greek	Latin	PIE	Meaning	Skr.	Gr.	Lat.	PIE
12	saptá	heptá	septem	*septm̥	'seven'	/a/	/a/	/em/	*[m̥]
13	tatás	tatós	in-tentus	*tn̥tós	'stretched'	/a/	/a/	/en/	*[n̥]
14	hr̥d	kradíē	kor(dis)	*k̂r̥d-	'heart'	/r̥/	/ra/ /ar/	/or/	*[r̥]
15	mr̥dús	bladús	mollis	*ml̥du-	'soft'	/r̥/	/la/ /al/	/ol/	*[l̥]

L12: For Lat. /em/ from PIE *[m̥], the other languages regularly have /a/. Cf. L25 for Gr. /h/ from */s/. **L13**: For Lat. /en/ from PIE *[n̥], the other languages regularly have /a/. **L14/15**: The development of Skr. /h/ from PIE */k̂/ is irregular and unexplained. Cf. L41/42 for the normal development, which is seen in the etymologically related Skr. śrad- < *k̂red- in śrad-dʰā 'trust'. This word matches Lat. kredere {credere} and originally meant 'to put your heart in sb.' in the sense of 'trust'. **L15**: The representation of PIE *[r̥] and *[l̥] in Lat. is usually /or/ and /ol/, but the further development to /ur/ and /ul/ is common, too. Cf. SCN x5. In Greek, *[r̥] is continued by /ar/ and /ra/, and *[l̥] is continued by /al/ and /la/. In Sanskrit, the syllabic resonants are preserved. The form is an example of the development *[l̥] to *[r̥], which can be also seen in L20 for */l/ and */r/. Unit 34 presents more details about this process. Gr. /b/ from */m/ originated by a process similar to SCN x9.1.

4. Non-syllabic resonants, semivowels and the fricative */s/

The nasals /m/, /n/ and liquids /r/, /l/, which are discussed in L16–20, undergo only little changes, whereas the semivowels */i̯/, */u̯/ of L21–24 tend to be lost or changed in Lat. and Gr.

	Compared Languages			Preform and Meaning		Sound Correspondences			
	Sanskrit	Greek	Latin	PIE	Meaning	Skr.	Gr.	Lat.	PIE
16	mātā́	mā́tēr	māter	*mātēr	'mother'	/m/	/m/	/m/	*/m/
17	návas	néos	noṷus	*néu̯os	'new'	/n/	/n/	/n/	*/n/
18	sarpā-mi	hérpō	serpō	*serpō	'I creep'	/r/	/r/	/r/	*/r/
19	lubʰati	-	lubet	*lubʰeti	~ 'likes'	/l/	/l/	/l/	*/l/
20	śrutás	klutós	in-klutus	*k̂lutós	'famous'	/r/	/l/	/l/	*/l/
21	yakr̥-t	hẽpar	i̯ekur	*Hi̯ē/ek^wr̥	'liver'	/i̯/ {y}	/h/	/i̯/	*/Hi̯/
22	yugám	zdugón	i̯ugum	*i̯ugóm	'joke'	/i̯/ {y}	/zd/	/i̯/	*/i̯/
23	tráyas	trḗs	trēs	*trei̯es	'three'	/i̯/{y}	0	0	*/i̯/
24	návas	néos	noṷus	*néu̯os	'new'	/u̯/ {v}	0	/u̯/	*/u̯/
25	saptá	heptá	séptem	*septm̥	'seven'	/s/	/h/	/s/	*/s/

L16: Lines 16–19 present exact correspondences for nasals and liquids, thus these sounds are reconstructed for PIE as well. **L17**: For the intervocalic loss of /u̯/ in Gr. *néos* cf. L24. Lat. *nou̯us* is not regular but analogically formed to the gen. *nou̯ī*, because the loss of intervocalic /u̯/ by SCN 40.5 is expected, just as in Gr. **L18**: Skr. *-mi* is the ending of the 1. ps. sg. **L19**: The Lat. variant {lubet} besides {libet} hints to a pronunciation *lybet*, according to SCN 9.23. Skr. *lubʰati* means 'he desires'. **L20**: For Skr. /r/ from */l/ cf. L15. For Skr. /ʃ/ {ś} from */k̂/ cf. L41/42. **L21**: The ablaut grade */e/ of the preform *Hi̯ek̯ʷr̥* resulted in Skr *yakr̥-t* and Lat. *i̯ekur*, whereas the long vowel in Gr. *hē̃par* either stems from the ablaut grade */ē/ of the preform *Hi̯ēk̯ʷr̥* or it is secondary. In Skr., the word is enlarged by an extension *-t*. Initial */Hi̯/ results in Greek /h/. **L22**: Initial */i̯/ gives /zd/ in Greek. **L23**: In the medial position, Gr. */i̯/ was lost as in Lat. (SCN 40.1). Subsequently, the vowels were contracted. **L24**: Cf. L17. **L25**: For initial Gr. /h/ from */s/ cf. L1 and L18. For *[m̥] cf. L12.

5. Labial and dental stops

Exact matches can be found for labial and dental stops; examples for */b/, however, are very rare. The examples for */g/ and */k/ are discussed from L36 on, together with the other dorsal stops.

	Compared Languages			Preform and Meaning		Sound Correspondences			
	Sanskrit	**Greek**	**Latin**	**PIE**	**Meaning**	**Skr.**	**Gr.**	**Lat.**	**PIE**
26	*bálam*	*beltíōn*	*dē-bilis*	**bel-*	~ 'strong'	/b/	/b/	/b/	**/b/*
27	*pád-am*	*pód-a*	*ped-em*	**ped-m̥*	'foot' acc. sg.	/p/	/p/	/p/	**/p/*
28	*ád-mi*	*éd-o-mai*	*edō*	**h₁éd-ō*	'I eat'	/d/	/d/	/d/	**/d/*
29	*ás-ti*	*es-ti*	*es-t*	**h₁és-ti*	'is'	/t/	/t/	/t/	**/t/*

L26: Skr. *bálam* 'force'; Gr. *beltíōn* 'better'; Lat. *dēbilis* 'weak' with vowel weakening according to SCN 8.3. **L27**: The different vowels Gr. /o/ and Lat. /e/ are due to ablaut (cf. appendix A1). The Skr. form was remarked by /m/. **L28**: The verbal forms have different endings. The phoneme */h₁/ of the reconstructed form *h₁éd-ō* is a laryngeal and is dealt with from L59 on. **L29**: In Latin, final */i/ of the ending of the 3. sg. was lost due to apocope (SCN 4.3).

6. The voiced aspirated stops (mediae aspiratae)

Due to the following correspondences, it is possible to reconstruct PIE voiced stops which differed from the 'normal' voiced stops by the additional feature of aspiration. Sounds like these can be found e.g. in the Indic language Hindi. This additional phonological feature is noted by a superscript {ʰ}.

	Compared Languages			Preform and Meaning		Sound Correspondences			
	Sansrit	**Greek**	**Latin**	**PIE**	**Meaning**	**Skr.**	**Gr.**	**Lat.**	**PIE**
30	*bʰárā(mi)*	*pʰérō*	*ferō*	**bʰérō*	'I carry'	/bʰ/	/pʰ/	/f/	**/bʰ/*
31	*~ nabʰas*	*nepʰélē*	*nébula*	**nebʰeleh₂*	'dust'	/bʰ/	/pʰ/	/b/	**/bʰ/*
32	*dʰū́mas*	*tʰūmós*	*fūmus*	**dʰū́mos*	'smoke'	/dʰ/	/tʰ/	/f/	**/dʰ/*
33	*mádʰyas*	*més(s)os*	*medius*	**médʰi̯os*	'middle'	/dʰ/	*/tʰ/	/d/	**/dʰ/*
34	*rudʰirás*	*erutʰrós*	*ruber*	**(h₁)rudʰrós*	'red'	/dʰ/	/tʰ/	/b/	**/dʰ/*
35	*vah-ati*	*~ ókʰos*	*u̯ehit*	**u̯eĝʰeti*	'goes'	/h/	/kʰ/	/h/	**/ĝʰ/*

The PIE voiced aspirated stops are preserved in Skr. and correspond to voiceless aspirated stops in Greek. The Gr. graphemes {φ}, {θ}, {χ} originally represented the stops /pʰ/, /tʰ/, /kʰ/. Even after their change to the fricatives /φ/, /θ/ and /χ/, these graphemes were retained. Latin has devoiced reflexes in the initial position and voiced reflexes in the medial position. Dental */dʰ/ is continued as labiodental /f/. The developments in Latin are discussed in more detail in unit 35. **L31**: Gr. presents a development of the meaning 'dust' > 'cloud'. **L32**: Gr. presents a development of the meaning 'smoke' > 'disposition of mind'. Cf. the German way of saying 'the head smokes' for strong mental activity. In Lat., the reflexes of */bʰ/ and */dʰ/ merge in /f/ (SCN x6.5/x7.2). **L33**: Gr. *més(s)os* goes back to *métʰios*. The cluster */tʰi̯/ became */ss/ and was further simplified to /s/. In Lat., */i̯/ became a vowel by SCN 27.1. /o/ is raised to /u/ by SCN 19.8. **L34**: The initial Gr. /e/ may continue an initial laryngeal (cf. L65) or it is a prothetic vowel. In the medial position next to /r/, /l/ or /u/, the reflex of */dʰ/ merges with the reflex of */bʰ/. **L35**: Gr. *ókʰos* 'chart' goes back to the nominal form PIE *u̯óǵʰos. Skr. /h/ is the palatalized reflex of expected /gʰ/.

● **7.1 The dorsal stops**

The velar stops of L36–40, the palatal stops of L35 and L41–44, and the labiovelar stops of L45–58 are also called gutturals, dorsals or tectals.

	Compared languages			Preform and Meaning		Sound Correspondences			
	Sanskrit	Greek	Latin	PIE	Meaning	Skr.	Gr.	Lat.	PIE
36	*krūrás*	*kruerós*	*kruor*	**kruh₂-*	'meat, raw'	/k/	/k/	/k/	*/k/
37	*kaniṣṭʰás*	*kainós*	*re-kēns*	**ken- / *kn̥-*	'new, fresh'	/k/	/k/	/k/	*/k/
38	*rōcás*	*leu̯kós*	*lūkus*	**léu̯kos*	'bright'	/t͡ʃ/ {c}	/k/	/k/	*/k/
39	*yugám*	*dzugón*	*i̯úgum*	**i̯ugóm*	'joke'	/g/	/g/	/g/	*/g/
40	*yójanam*	-	-	**i̯éu̯genom*	'team of oxen'	/d͡ʒ/ {j}	-	-	*/g/
41	*dáśa*	*déka*	*dékem*	**dékm̥*	'ten'	/ʃ/ {ś}	/k/	/k/	*/k̂/
42	*śatám*	*he-katón*	*kéntum*	**k̂m̥tóm*	'hundred'	/ʃ/ {ś}	/k/	/k/	*/k̂/
43	*jā́nu*	*gónu*	*genu*	**ĝo/enu*	'knee'	/d͡ʒ/ {j}	/g/	/g/	*/ĝ/
44	*jánas*	*génos*	*genus*	**ĝenh₁os*	'race'	/d͡ʒ/ {j}	/g/	/g/	*/ĝ/

L36/37: If all languages have a /k/, PIE velar */k/ is reconstructed. **L38**: In Skr., velar */k/ was subject to a secondary palatalization before /e/ and /i/ and developed to an affricate /t͡ʃ/, which is pronounced like {tch} in *switch*. An affricate is a stop immediately followed by a fricative. The /ō/ in Skr. *rōcás* originated out of the monophthongization of */au̯/ from PIE */eu̯/ (similar to SCN 10.1). Skr. *rōcás* cannot go back to PIE *leu̯kos directly because */k/ did not become Skr. {c} before /o/. The sound {c} originated in the gen. *leu̯kesos, which developed regularly to Skr. *rocasas*, and then spread analogically over the complete paradigm. Lat. *lūkus* has the meaning 'grove'. **L39**: If all languages have a /g/, PIE velar */g/ is reconstructed. Cf. L22 for Gr. /zd/ in the initial position. Final */m/ became /n/ in Gr. **L40**: Just like */k/ (see L38), also */g/ was subject to a secondary palatalization and developed to an affricate /d͡ʒ/, which is pronounced like {j} in *jungle*. **L41/42**: If Skr. /ʃ/, which is pronounced like {sh} in shine, corresponds to Lat. and Gr. /k/, PIE palatal */k̂/ is reconstructed. Cf. L12 for *[m̥]. The Gr. word for hundred is prefixed by a particle *he-*. **L43/44**: If Lat. and Gr. /g/ correspond to Skr. /d͡ʒ/, PIE palatal */ĝ/ is reconstructed. For Skr. /ā/ from */o/ cf. L5.

7.2 Labiovelars

Sometimes, Greek exhibits an alternation of dental and labial stops in words which are derived from the same root. The distribution of these stops depends on the following vowel. Normally, the labial stops /pʰ/, /p/, /b/ are found before /a/ and /o/, and the dental stops /tʰ/, /t/, /d/ are found before /e/ and /i/, but there my be dialectal variation to this pattern. If the respective words are compared to their Skr. counterparts, one finds that the Gr. sounds correspond to the dorsal stops /k/, /g/, /gʰ/, as well as to their palatalized variants /tʃ/ {c}, /dʒ/ {j}, /h/. Latin /ku̯/ corresponds to voiceless sounds, Latin /u̯/ corresponds to voiced sounds in the initial position before a vowel, Latin /g/ corresponds to the respective sounds in the initial position before /r/, and Latin /g/ corresponds in the medial position after nasal. An example are the Gr. interrogative pronouns *tís* 'who?' and *tí* 'what?' with the dental stop /t/, which corresponds directly to Latin /ku̯/ in *ku̯is* {quis} and *ku̯id* {quid}. In Gr. *póteros* 'who of two?', the initial /p/ corresponds to /k/ in Skr. *katarás* 'who of two?'. The Skr. pronoun *kás* 'who?' corresponds to Gr. *tís* and has a /k/. Hittite *ku̯is* 'who?' has a /k/ with a /u̯/ following. These sound correspondences can be traced back to original labiovelars. A labiovelar is a velar stop immediately followed by /u̯/. Thus one can reconstruct: **1.** **kʷis* > het. *ku̯is*, Lat. *ku̯is*, Gr. *tís* and **2.** **kʷos* > Skr. *kás* and **3.** **kʷoteros* > Gr. *póteros*, Skr. *katarás*.

	Compared languages			Preform and Meaning		Sound Correspondences			
	Sanskrit	Greek	Latin	PIE	Meaning	Skr.	Gr.	Lat.	PIE
45	*ka-*	*po-*	*ku̯o-d*	**kʷo-d*	'what?'	/k/	/p/	/ku̯/	**/kʷ/*
46	*sác-(ati)*	*hép-o-*	*seku̯-or*	**sekʷ-e/o-*	~'to follow'	/tʃ/ {c}	/p/	/ku̯/	**/kʷ/*
47	*cid*	*tí*	*ku̯id*	**kʷid*	'what?'	/tʃ/ {c}	/t/	/ku̯/	**/kʷ/*
48	*ca*	*te*	*ku̯e*	**kʷe-*	~ 'and'	/tʃ/ {c}	/t/	/ku̯/	**/kʷ/*
49	*gam-ati*	*baínō*	*u̯eniō*	**gʷm̥-(i̯ō)*	'come/goes'	/g/	/b/	/u̯/	**/gʷ/*
50	*garás*	*boró̄*	*u̯orō*	**gʷorh₃-*	'to devore'	/g/	/b/	/u̯/	**/gʷ/*
51	*gurús*	*barús*	*grau̯is*	**gʷr̥Hús*	'heavy'	/g/	/b/	/g/	**/gʷ/*
52	*gāu̯s*	*boũs*	~ *bōs*	**gʷous*	'cow'	/g/	/b/	(/b/)	**/gʷ/*
53	*gárbʰas*	*delpʰús*	-	**gʷelbʰo/us*	'foetus'	/g/	/d/	-	**/gʷ/*
54	-	*adḗn*	*inguen*	**n̥gʷēn*	'groin'	-	/d/	/gu/	**/gʷ/*
55	*gʰarmás*	*tʰermós*	*formus*	**gʷʰormos*	'heat/hot'	/gʰ/	/tʰ/	/f/	**/gʷʰ/*
56	*gʰnanti / hanti*	*tʰḗnō*	*dē-fendō*	**gʷʰen-i̯ō*	'to hit'	/gʰ/ /h/	/tʰ/	/f/	**/gʷʰ/*
57	*snih-(ati)*	~*nipʰás*	*ninguit*	**(s)neigʷʰ-*	~ 'to snow'	/h/	/pʰ/	/gu/	**/gʷʰ/*
58	*dáh-ati*	~*tépʰra*	*fou̯-eō*	**dʰegʷʰ-*	'to burn'	/h/	/pʰ/	/u̯/	**/gʷʰ/*

L45: Gr. has /p/ before /o/. **L46:** Skr. has a secondarily palatalized variant /tʃ/ {c} before palatal /e/. Cf. L38. **L47/L48:** The Skr. particle *cid* emphasises a preceding word. Gr. has /t/ before /i/ and /e/, corresponding to Skr. /tʃ/ {c}. **L49/L50:** The next examples illustrate correspondences of the voiced stop **/gʷ/*. Skr. /g/ corresponds to Gr. /b/ before /a/ and /o/. Lat. /u̯/ stands in the initial position because the preceding /g/ had been lost according to SCN 30.11. Gr. *borā́* 'food' and Skr. *garás* 'devouring' are nominal forms. **L51:** Lat. has /g/ because /u̯/ is lost between consonants according to SCN 40.4. The vowel shortening of the expected **grāu̯is* > *grau̯is* is unexplained. **L52:** Latin

R E C O N S T R U C T I O N

bōs must be a loanword from a Sabellic dialect, which exhibits the development **gʷ > b*, because the expected Latin reflex would have been something like *u̯ūs**, according to SCN 30.11 and 10.4 (cf. L69). **L53**: Gr. /d/ before /e/ corresponds to Skr. /g/. There is no reflex of this word in Latin. **L54**: The Latin reflex of PIE */gʷ/ after a nasal is /gu/ (cf. L57). No word corresponds to Gr. *adén* 'gland'. **L55/56**: The next examples illustrate correspondences of the voiced aspirated stop */gʷʰ/. Gr. /tʰ/ corresponds to Skr. /gʰ/ or its palatalized variant /h/, as seen in L56. Latin has /f/ in the initial position. **L57**: Skr. /h/ corresponds to Gr. /pʰ/ before /a/. Lat. preserves the labiovelar as /gu/ after a nasal. **L58**: Lat. has intervocalic /u̯/ according to SCN x8.10.

7.3 Centum-languages and satem-languages

Due to the word correspondences of L36, L41 and L45, three series of dorsal stops must be reconstructed for PIE: velar, palatal and labiovelar stops. Otherwise, it is not possible to connect all the correspondences.

36	*krūrás*	*kruerós*	*kruor*	**kruh₂-*	'meat, raw'	/k/	/k/	/k/	*/k/
41	*dáśa*	*déka*	*dekem*	**dékm̥*	'ten'	/ʃ/	/k/	/k/	*/k̂/
45	*ka-*	*po-(teros)*	*ku̯o-d*	**kʷo-d*	'what?'	/k/	/p/	/ku̯/	*/kʷ/

The individual IE languages, however, always have only two series of dorsal stops. The so called centum-languages share the same reflex of the velar and palatal series (cf. SCN x1), whereas the so called satem-languages share the same reflex of the velar and labiovelar series, due to the loss of the labial element of the labiovelars. In the satem-languages, the palatal series develops further to s-like sibilants (cf. L41/42) or affricates (cf. L38/40/43/44), although divergences to this pattern are found in Slavic and Baltic. The Anatolian language Luwian, which normally would be expected to be classified as a centum-language, even seems to have reflexes of all three series of stops. The examples used for the argumentation are, however, disputed because of alternative etymologies or scant attestation of the words.

8 The laryngeals

The Anatolian language Hittite is attested from 1700 BC on and is therefore the oldest attested IE language. In some positions, Hittite has an aspirate sound /h/ which the other IE languages do not have anymore. Therefore, one can assume at least one phoneme in an older state of language, which was lost on the way to the other languages Sanskrit, Greek and Latin. Due to different structural arguments, historical linguistics nowadays normally assumes three of those phonemes, which are called laryngeals and reconstructed for PIE. The exact phonetic value of these laryngeals is unknown. The next two tables present correspondences, which are most relevant for this issue. Unit 36 presents an overview of the Latin reflexes of the PIE laryngeals.

	Compared languages				Preform and Meaning		Sound Correspondences				
	Hit.	Skr.	Gr.	Lat.	PIE	Meaning	Hit.	Skr.	Gr.	Lat.	PIE
59	*hant-*	*anti*	*antí*	*ante*	**h₂énti*	'frontside'	/ha/	/a/	/a/	/a/	*/h₂e/
60	*pahs-*	*pā-*	-	*pāstor*	**peh₂-(s)-*	'to protect'	/ah/	/ā/	-	/ā/	*/eh₂/
61	*hau̯i*	*ávis*	*óis*	*ou̯is*	**h₂óu̯is*	'sheep'	/ha/	/a/	/o/	/o/	*/h₂o/

L59: The Hittite words means 'frontside' and reveals the other language forms to be an old locative with the meaning 'at the frontside', which semantically developed to 'in front of'. PIE */h₂/ caused the 'coloring' of PIE */e/ to */a/. The laryngeal, which can be still seen in Hittite, was lost afterwards. Lat. /e/ from */i/ by SCN 9.14a. **L60**: PIE */h₂/ caused the 'coloring' of */e/ to */a/. The larygeal was lost afterwards and caused a compensatory lengthening of the preceding vowel. **L61**: */h₂/ did not alter */o/ because the laryngeals only affected PIE */e/. Intervocalic /u̯/ was lost in Greek. The development was: *h₃éu̯is > (x2.2) *h₃óu̯is > (x2.7) *óu̯is > Gr. óis.

	Compared languages			Preform and Meaning		Sound Correspondences			
	Sanskrit	**Greek**	**Latin**	**PIE**	**Meaning**	**Skr.**	**Gr.**	**Lat.**	**PIE**
62	*dʰíṣnyas*	*tʰés-pʰatos*	*fānum*	*$dʰh_1s$-*	'holy'	/i/	/e/	/a/	*/h₁/
63	*pitā́*	*patḗr*	*pater*	*$ph_2tḗr$*	'father'	/i/	/a/	/a/	*/h₂/
64	*dítis*	*dósis*	*datiō*	*dh_3ti-*	'gift'	/i/	/o/	/a/	*/h₃/
65	*rájas*	*érebos*	-	*$h_1regʷos$*	'darkness'	0	/e/	-	*/h₁/
66	*náras*	*anḗr*	*Nerō*	*h_2ners*	'man'	0	/a/	0	*/h₂/
67	*bʰrū́*	*opʰrŭ̃s*	-	*$h_3bʰruH$-*	'eye-brow'	0	/o/	-	*/h₃/

L62–64 Skr. /i/ corresponds to Lat. /a/. In Gr., one finds different vowels depending on which laryngeal had been in the word. Gr. /e/ stems from */h₁/, Gr. /a/ from */h₂/, and Gr. /o/ from */h₃/. **L62**: Lat. *fānum* goes back to *fasnom*, which first became *faznom* by SCN 15.2, then *fānom* by SCN 2.2, and finally *fānum* by SCN 9.18. **L63**: Skr. /r/ is lost after a long vowel (cf. L7). **L64**: The Latin form was remodeled to an n-stem. **L65–67**: Initial Greek vowels, which are not present in other languages, can usually be traced back to laryngeals. The Greek vowel color is determined by the PIE laryngeal.

Latin and the Sabellic Languages
Oscan and Umbrian

Latin is more closely related to the other Italic languages, which consist mainly of the Sabellic languages Oscan and Umbrian, than it is to non-Italic languages such as Sanskrit or Greek. Therefore, it is necessary to posit an intermediate step between PIE and Latin which includes all the criteria in which the Italic languages differ from the other IE languages. An overview of the IE and Italic languages can be found in appendix 5. Unfortunately, most Italic languages are attested only by some small inscriptions which do not permit to reconstruct their complete phonological and morphological system, in contrast to Sanskrit and Greek, of which numerous texts and inscriptions supply all necessary linguistic information. The following Oscan and Umbrian examples give a short but not exhaustive overview of some characteristic sound changes of the Sabellic languages. The longest Oscan inscriptions are the **Tabula Bantina** and the **Cippus Abellanus**, the longest Umbrian inscription is known as the **Iguvine Tablets**. For better legibility, Oscan and Umbrian words are transcribed according to the transcription system used in this book.

- ### Main differences of consonantism between Latin and the Sabellic languages

The PIE labiovelars */kʷ/ and */gʷ/ became the labial stops /p/ and /b/ (L68–69). There was no development of medial fricatives to stops (SCN x8.1-x8.9), which happened in Latin (L71). The Latin merger of labial and dental fricatives, which happened in the initial position (SCN x7.1/2) and before /r/, /l/ and /u/ (SCN x7.3-x7.7), was extended to all contexts in Sabellic (L71). Umbrian exhibits the development of PIT *k > ʃ {ś} before palatal vowels (L72/73) as well as the development of velar [ɫ] to /u̯/, which is not listed in the following table. Intervocalic /d/ developed to [δ], which probably was a fricativised /r/ or a retroflex dental fricative (L78).

- ### Main vowel differences between Latin and Sabellic

In the Sabellic languages, short /i/ merged with long /ē/ to become /ẹ/ (L68/73/75), and short /u/ and long /ō/ merged to become /ọ/ (L77). The same development is found in VL. The PIT diphthongs are preserved in Oscan (L70), in contrast to Latin, where they were monophthongized according to SCN 10, and in contrast to Umbrian, where monophthongizations are common already in the oldest texts. Latin vowel raising of monophthongized /ẹ/ to /ī/ (SCN 10.8) and /ọ/ to /ū/ (SCN 10.4) did not happen in Umbrian. Furthermore, Umbrian shares with VL a strong tendency of syncopation. Non-initial long vowels were probably shortened in the Sabellic languages but the evidence is scarce because vowel length was spelled only rarely by writing a double vowel.

- ### Comparison of the Italic languages Latin, Oscan and Umbrian with intermediate proto-languages

	PIE	PIT	Proto-Sab.	Osc.	Umb.	OL	CL
68	*kʷis	*kʷis	*pis	pẹs	pẹs	ku̯is	ku̯is
69	*gʷōu̯s	*gʷou̯s	*bou̯s	-	bōs	u̯ou̯s*	u̯ūs*
70	*se-bʰei̯	*seβei̯	*seβei̯	sẹβei̯	-	sibei̯	sibī
71	*medʰi̯eh₂	*meδi̯ā	*meβi̯ā	meβi̯o*	-	*media	media
72	*dʰh₁kii̯āt	*fakii̯āt	*fakii̯ād	fakii̯ad	faśii̯a	*fakii̯at	fakii̯at
73	*takeh₁tos	*takētos	*takētos	-	taśẹts	*takitos	takitus
74	*n̥bʰri-bʰos	*n̥βriβos	*anβriβs	anaβrẹss	-	*imbribos	imbribus

75	*skriptos	*skriptos	*skriftos	skrẹfts*	skrẹts*	*skrīptos	skrīptus
76	-	*rektēd	*rektēd	-	rētẹ	rēktēd	rēkte
77	*aĝetōd	*agetōd	*agtōd	aktọd	aịtọ?	*agitōd	agitō
78	*me/odos	*medos	*medos	-	meðs	*modos	modus
79	-	*deịu̯īnaịs	-	deịu̯inaịs	-	*deịu̯īnīs	dīu̯īnīs

L68: The PIE labiovelar */kʷ/ became PIT */p/. Oscan and Umbrian both share this sound change, which is also found in Greek (cf. L45, L46, L49–52). PIT */kʷ/ became Latin /ku̯/ by SCN x4. PIT */i/ was lowered to */ẹ/ already in Proto-Sabellic because Oscan und Umbrian both share this sound change. **L69:** The PIE labiovelar */gʷ/ became PIT */b/ exemplified by Umbrian *bōs* 'cow', which was borrowed from Latin. The regular outcome of PIE *gʷōu̯s* in Latin would have been *u̯ūs*. **L70:** In Sabellic, the PIT voiced fricatives were continued by /β/, which was spelled {f}. In Latin, the PIT voiced fricatives became stops in the medial position by SCN x8. Diphthongs normally remained in Oscan, in contrast to Latin where they were monophthongized by SCN 10.8/10.9. **L71:** In Sabellic, dental and labial fricatives merged and became /β/. Non-initial long syllables were probably shortened. In Latin, dental and labial fricatives merged only in the initial position (SCN x7.1) and in the medial position next to /r/, /l/ and /u/ (SCN x7.3-x7.7). In Oscan, final /ā/ was raised to /ō/ and shortened to /o/. In Latin, final /ā/ was shortened to /a/ by SCN 1.6. **L72:** A special feature of Umbrian is the palatalization of /k/ to /ʃ/ {ś} before palatal vowels. This sound change is similar to the Old Indic development described in L41/42. In Umbrian, final consonants were lost after a long vowel (cf. SCN 38.3). **L73:** In Sabellic, the last syllable of words ending in *-tos* was regularly syncopated to *-ts*. Palatalization of of /k/ to /ʃ/ {ś} in Umbrian (cf. L72). Latin *takitus* does not go back directly to *takētos* but to *taketos* with a short vowel because otherwise it would not have undergone vowel weakening by SCN 8.3. **Z74:** The syllabic resonants must have been still intact in PIT because Latin and Sabellic have different reflexes of *[m̥] and *[n̥]. After the development of PIE */bʰ/ to */β/, syllabic *[n̥] developed to /an/ in Sabellic and remained unchanged due to the following anaptyxis. The final syllable was syncopated and the resulting cluster */βs/ developed first to */fs/ and then to /ss/. In Latin *imbribus*, the PIT fricative */β/ developed to /b/ in the medial position after a nasal. Subsequently, the place of articulation of the nasal /n/ assimilated to /m/ before /b/. **L75:** PIT */pt/ became */ft/ in Proto-Sabellic and remained unchanged in Oscan, whereas in Umbrian it was changed to /ht/ before the /h/ was lost with compensatory lengthening of the preceding vowel. **L76:** PIT /kt/ in the medial position developed to Umbrian /ht/ before /h/ was lost. Umbrian and Latin lost the final consonant. **L77:** Vowel weakening (SCN 8.3) and the loss of final /d/ (38.3) took place in Latin. In Oscan and Umbrian, /g/ became /k/ before /t/ by SCN 12.7 after the syncope of the medial short vowel. Final /d/ was lost in Umrian. **L78:** The vowel variation of Oscan *medos* and Latin *modus* < OL *modos* is due to ablaut (cf. appendix 1). After the change of d > δ, the final vowel was syncopated in Umbrian. The development was: *medos* > *meðos* > *meðs*. Umbrian *meðs* and Oscan *medos* both mean 'law' and correspond to Latin *i̯ūs* {ius}. Latin *i̯ūdeks* {iudex} 'judge' corresponds to Oscan *meddiss* < *medo-diks* 'law-speaker', which shows the syncope of the medial syllable as well as the assimilation k > s / _s (SCN 16.6). **L79:** In Oscan and Old Latin, PIT diphthongs were preserved.

Key to Exercises

Unit 2: Spelling and Pronunciation

E1. {carpo} *karpō* 'I pluck' {tracto} *traktō* 'I drag' {deleo} *dēleō* 'I destroy'

{rego} *regō* 'I govern' {exerceo} *eks-erkeō* 'I work' {arceo} *arkeō* 'I enclose'

E2. {ualide} *ualidē* 'very' {oblitus} *oblītus* 'forgotten' {uerto} *u̯ertō* 'I turn'

{quid} *ku̯id* 'what?' {coquo} *koku̯ō* 'I cook' {uiuus} *u̯īu̯us* 'alive'

{quippe} *ku̯ippe* 'of course' {dexter} *dekster* 'right' {obliuiscor} *oblīu̯īskor* 'I forget'

E3. {exilium} *eksilium* 'exil' :: {exulare} *eksulāre* 'to be banished'

{simul} *simul* 'at once' :: {similis} *similis* 'similar'

{familia} *familia* 'family' :: {famulus} *famulus* 'servant'

{sepelio} *sepeliō* 'I bury' :: {sepultus} *sepultus* 'buried'

E4. {iungo} *i̯uŋgō* 'I join' {tango} *taŋgō* 'I touch' {frango} *fraŋgō* 'I break'

E5. OL {sibei} *sibei̯* '-self' {iuuenis} *i̯uu̯enis* 'young' {laudare} *lau̯dāre* 'to praise'

Ü6. {cuius} *ku̯ii̯us* 'whose?' {peior} *pei̯i̯or* 'worse' {maior} *mai̯i̯or* 'bigger'

{aio} *ai̯i̯ō* 'I say'

Unit 4: Phonemes, Phones and Allophones

Opposition	Minimal Pair
s :: t	*serō* :: *terō*
s :: n	*sīdus* :: *nīdus*
u̯ :: u	*seku̯ī* {sequi} :: *sekuī* {secui}
l :: t	*lōtus* :: *tōtus*
n :: l	*nūmen* :: *lūmen*
n :: t	*nam* :: *tam*
l :: r	*lēks* {lex} :: *rēks* {rex}
p :: h	*portō* :: *hortō*
n :: p	*niger* :: *piger*
h :: 0	*hortus* :: *ortus*
d :: m	*dōs* :: *mōs*
r :: k {c}	*rapiō* :: *kapiō* {capio}
f :: t	*ferō* :: *terō*
p : m	*pōns* :: *mōns*
k :: f	*kūr* {cur} :: *fūr* {fur}
n :: ŋ	*annus* :: *aŋnus* {agnus}
b :: m	*sub* :: *sum*
u̯ :: s	*u̯īu̯us* :: *u̯īsus*
i̯ :: t	*i̯am* {iam} :: *tam*

Unit 5: Feature Structures of Latin Consonants

E1. b [+labial, +stop, +voiced] p [+labial, +stop]

d [+dental, +stop, +voiced] t [+dental, +stop]

r [+alveolar, +continuant, +voiced, +trill] n [+dental, +nasal, + continuant, +voiced]

E2. i̯ [+palatal, + continuant, +voiced, +approximant] u̯ [+labial, + continuant, +voiced, +approximant, +velarized]

h [+glottal, +fricative] f [+labiodental, + continuant, +fricative]

E3. 1. [n] and [ŋ] differ in their place of articulation.

2. [l] and [ł] differ in their place of articulation.

Unit 6: Latin Vowels and Diphthongs

Opposition	Example 1	Example 2	Example 3
a :: ā	*malus* :: *mālus*	*latus* :: *lātus*	*plaga* :: *plāga*
e :: ē	*es* :: *ēs*	*regeris* :: *regēris*	*leu̯is* :: *lēu̯is*
i :: ī	*datis* :: *datīs*	*turris* :: *turrīs*	*liber* :: *līber*
o :: ō	*os* :: *ōs*	*populus* :: *pōpulus*	*solum* :: *sōlum*
u :: ū	*domus* :: *domūs*	*lustrum* :: *lūstrum*	*fugit* :: *fūgit*

Unit 7: Syllabification of Latin Words

E1. 1. {factus} :: *faktus* :: *fak.tus* 2. {aedes} :: *aedēs* :: *ae.dēs* 3. {confectus} :: *kōnfektus* :: *kōn.fek.tus*

4. {laudare} :: *lau̯dāre* :: *lau̯.dā.re* 5. {gaudia} :: *gau̯dia* :: *gau̯.di.a* 6. {uirtutem} :: *u̯irtūtem* :: *u̯ir.tū.tem*

7. {mulierem} :: *mulierem* :: *mu.li.e.rem* 8. {filiolus} :: *filiolus* :: *fī.li.o.lus* 9. {ornamentum} :: *ōrnāmentum* :: *ōr.nā.men.tum*

10. {attingo} :: *attiŋgō* :: *at.tiŋ.gō*

E2.

Initial syllable			Final syllable		
Onset	Nucleus	Offset	Onset	Nucleus	Offset
f	*a*	*k*	*t*	*u*	*s*
	a	*ę*	*d*	*ē*	*s*

Initial syllable			Medial syllable			Final syllable		
Onset	Nucleus	Offset	Onset	Nucleus	Offset	Onset	Nucleus	Offset
k	*ō*	*n*	*f*	*e*	*k*	*t*	*u*	*s*
l	*a*	*u̯*	*d*	*ā*		*r*	*e*	
g	*a*	*u̯*	*d*	*i*			*a*	
u̯	*i*	*r*	*t*	*ū*		*t*	*e*	*m*
	a	*t*	*t*	*i*	*ŋ*	*g*	*ō*	

Initial syllable			Medial syllable			Medial syllable			Final syllable		
Onset	Nucleus	Offset	Onset	Nucleus	Offset	Onset	Nucleus	Offset	Onset	Nucleus	Offset
m	*u*		*l*	*i*			*e*		*r*	*e*	*m*
f	*ī*		*l*	*i*			*o*		*l*	*u*	*s*
	ō	*r*	*n*	*ā*		*m*	*e*	*n*	*t*	*u*	*m*

Unit 8: Accentuation of Latin Words

E1. **A** {nostras} *nostrás* **B** {samnis} *Samnís* **C** {illic} *illík* **D** {posthac} *posthák* **E** {fumat} *fūmát*

E2. **A** {arceo} *arkeō* 'I repel' :: *éks-arkeō > (8.1) *éks-erkeō* > (Ac1) *eks-érkeō* {exerceo} 'I exercise'

    B {carpo} *karpō* 'I pluck' :: *dískarpō > (8.1) *dískerpō > (Ac1) *diskérpō* {discerpo} 'I tear into pieces'

    C {tracto} *traktō* 'I drag' :: *détraktō > (8.1) *détrektō > (Ac1) *dētréktō* {detrecto} 'I refuse'

E3. **A** CL {colubra} *kó.lu.bra* > (Ac2) VL *ko.lúb.ra*

    B CL {integrum} *ín.te.grum* > (Ac2) VL *in.tég.rum*

    C CL {tenebras} *té.ne.brās* > (Ac2) VL *te.néb.ras*

Unit 9: Modeling Sound Changes

E1.

SCN	Formula	Description
16.1	p > f / _ f	/p/ becomes /f/ before /f/.
16.2	p > s / _ s	/p/ becomes /s/ before /s/.
30.6	d > 0 / # _ i̯	/d/ is lost in the initial position before /i̯/.
27.2	u̯ > u / C _ C	/u̯/ becomes /u/ between consonants.
28.2	l > ł / V _ #	/l/ becomes velar [ł] in the final position after a vowel.
29.2	0 > p / m _ l	An epenthetic /p/ is inserted between /m/ and /l/.
35.1	b > 0 / r _ m	/b/ is lost between /r/ and /m/.
30.9	p > 0 / # _ s	/p/ is lost in the initial position before /s/.
40.5	u̯ > 0 / _ (o, ō, u, ū)	/u̯/ is lost before /o/, /ō/, /u/, /ū/.
9.15	o > e / # u̯ _ (s, t, rC)	/o/ becomes /e/ between initial /u̯/ and /s/, /t/ or /r/+consonant.
8.15	i > [y] {u/i} / _ (f, m, b)	/i/ becomes [y] before /f/, /m/ or /b/. This sound was written {u} or {i}.
34.1	k {c} > 0 / r _ t	/k/ written {c} was lost between /r/ and /t/.
x9.2	m > b / # _ r	/m/ becomes /b/ in the initial position before /r/.
x8.12c	h > 0 / V _ V	/h/ is lost between vowels.

Unit 10: Vowel Shortening

E1. The exceptions are: a) The gen. sg. *-īus* of the pronominal adjectives b) *ē* after *i* in the gen. sg. of the 5. declension of *diēs, diēī* in contrast to *rēs, reī* c) The vowel before the contracted vocative *-ī* of the 2. declension in words such as *Gāī, Pompēī* d) The 1. ps. sg. prs. *fīō*, which is derived from *fierī* 'to become'.

E2.

SCN	Old Latin	Classical Latin	Spelling
1.1	*fūimus*	*fuimus*	{fuimus}
1.4	*ūtār*	*ūtar*	{utar}
1.1	*īerō*	*ierō*	{iero}
1.4	*tenēt*	*tenet*	{tenet}
1.4	*u̯elīt*	*u̯elit*	{uelit}
1.1	*fūisset*	*fuisset*	{fuisset}
1.1	*adnūit*	*adnuit*	{adnuit}
1.1	*fidēī*	*fideī*	{fidei}
1.4	*seru̯āt*	*seru̯at*	{seruat}
1.4	*memorāt*	*memorat*	{memorat}
1.1	*fūerim*	*fuerim*	{fuerim}
1.4	*tinnīt*	*tinnit*	{tinnit}

E3. A {domi} *domī* > (1.3) *domi* 'at home' **B** **benē* > (1.3) *bene* {bene} 'well' **C** **modōd* > (38.3) **modō* > (1.3) *modo* {modo} 'only' **D** OL {sibei} *sibei̯* > (10.8/9) **sibī* > (1.3) *sibi* {sibi} 'oneself' **E** {mihi} *mihī* > (1.3) *mihi* {mihi} 'me' **F** {tibi} *tibī* > (1.3) *tibi* {tibi} 'you' **G** {ibi} *ibī* > (1.3) *ibi* {ibi} 'there' **H** {puta} *putā* 'think!' > (1.3) *puta* {puta} 'for example'

Unit 11: Vowel Lengthening

E1. A {consol} *konsoł* > (2.1) *kōnsoł* > (9.18) *kōnsuł* {consul} 'consul' **B** {contuli} *kon-tulī* 'I collected' :: **konferre* > (2.1) *kōnferre* {conferre} 'to collect' **C** **insīdiaę* > (2.1) *īnsīdiaę* {insidiae} 'snare, trap' **D** {maneo} *maneō* 'I stay' :: *mansī* > (2.1) *mānsī* {mansi} 'I stayed'

E2. A {aes} *aes* 'ore' :: **aesnos* > (15.2) **aeznos* > (2.2) **aēnos* > (9.18) *aēnus* {aenus} 'of copper, of bronze' **B** {cascus} *kaskus* 'very old' :: **kasnos* > (15.2) **kaznos* > (2.2) **kānos* > (9.18) *kānus* {canus} 'grey' **C** {fas} *fās* 'divine law' :: **fasnom* > (15.2) **faznom* > (2.2) **fānom* > (9.18) *fānum* {fanum} 'sanctuary' **D** **nisdos* > (15.5)**nizdos* > (2.2) **nīdos* > (9.18) *nīdus* {nidus} 'nest' **E** {sedo} *sedō* 'I sit' :: **si-sd-ō* > (15.5) **si-zd-ō* > (2.2) *sīdō* {sido} 'I settle' **F** *is* 'this' :: {isdem} *isdem* > (15.5) **izdem* > (2.2) *īdem* {idem} 'the same' **G** **i̯ūzdeks* > (15.5) **i̯uzdeks* > (2.2) *iūdeks* {iudex} 'judge'

E3. A {lego} *legō* 'I read' :: PPP **legtus* > (2.3) **lēgtus* > (12.7) *lēktus* {lectus} 'read' **B** {iungo} *i̯uŋgō* 'I join' :: PPP **i̯uŋgtus* > (2.3/2.4) **i̯ūŋgtus* > (12.7) *i̯ūŋktus* {iunctus} 'joined' **C** {fungo} *fuŋgō* 'I perform' :: PPP **fuŋgtus* > (2.3/2.4) **fūŋgtus* > (12.7) *fūŋktus* {functus} 'performed' **D** {frango} *fraŋgō* 'I break' :: PPP **fragtus* > (2.3) **frāgtus* > (12.7) *frāktus* {fractus} 'broken' **E** {sancio} *saŋki̯ō* 'I sanctify' :: PPP **saŋktus* > (2.4) *sāŋktus* {sanctus} 'sanctified' **F** {uincio} *u̯iŋki̯ō* 'I chain' :: PPP **u̯iŋktus* > (2.4) *u̯īŋktus* {uinctus} 'chained'

Unit 12: Vowel Contraction

E1. A {ire} *īre* 'to go' :: inf. perf. *i-isse* > (3.1) *īsse* {isse} 'having gone' **B** {alo} *alō* 'I nourish' :: **prō-olēs* > (1.1) **pro-olēs* > (3.1) *prōlēs* {proles} 'descendants' **C** {lauo} *lau̯ō* 'I wash' :: perf. **lau̯ā-u̯ī* > (40.2) **lau̯āu̯ī* > (3.1) *lāu̯ī* {laui} 'I washed' **D** {hortor} *hortor* 'I urge' :: *ko-hors* > (x8.12c) **ko-ors* > (3.1) *kōrs* {cors} 'cohort' **E** {os} *ōs, ōris* 'face' :: **ko-ōram* > (3.1) *kōram* {coram} 'publicly' **F** {diues} *dīu̯es* 'rich' :: gen. sg. *dīu̯itis* > (40.2) **dīitis* > (1.1) **diitis* > (3.1) *dītis* {ditis} **G** {obliuiscor} *oblīu̯īskor* 'I forget' :: PPP **oblīu̯itus* > (40.2) **oblīitus* > (1.1) **obliitus* > (3.1) *oblītus* {oblitus} 'forgotten'

E2. A *hiems* 'winter' :: **bi-himos* > (x8.12c) **biimos* > (3.1) **bīmos* > (9.18) *bīmus* {bimus} 'of two winters' **B** {si uis} *sī u̯īs* > *sīu̯īs* > (40.2) **sūīs* > (1.1) **siīs* > (3.1) *sīs* 'if you like' **C** {uiuus} *u̯īu̯us* 'alive' :: **u̯īu̯ita* > (40.2) **u̯īita* > (1.1) **u̯iita* > (3.1) *u̯īta* {uita} 'life' **D** **trei̯es* > (40.1) **trees* > (3.1) *trēs* {tres} 'three' **E** {homo} *homō* 'human being' :: **ne-hemō* > (x8.12c) **neemō* > (3.1) *nēmō* {nemo} 'nobody' **F** {deleo} *dēleō* 'I destroy' :: *dēlēu̯eram* > (40.2) **dēlēeram* > (1.1) **dēleeram* > (3.1) *dēlēram* {deleram} 'I had destroyed'

Unit 13: Syncope and Apocope

E1. A {positus} *positus* > *po.si.tus* > (4.1) *postus* {postus} 'placed' **B** {aliter} *aliter* > *a.li.ter* > (4.1) *alter* {alter} 'one of two' **C** {calidus} *kalidus* > *ka.li.dus* > (4.1) *kaldus* {caldus} 'hot' **D** {ualide} *u̯alidē* > *u̯a.li.dē* > (4.1) *u̯aldē* {ualde} 'much' **E** {auis} *au̯is* 'bird' :: **au̯ispeks* > (4.1) *au̯speks* {auspex} 'augur'

E2. A {nauis} *nāu̯is* 'ship' :: {nauita} *nāu̯ita* > (4.1) **nāu̯ta* > (1.2) *nau̯ta* {nauta} 'sailor' **B** {gauisus} *gāu̯isus* 'happy' :: **gāu̯ideō* > (4.1) **gāu̯deō* > (1.2) *gau̯deō* {gaudeo} 'I am happy' **C** {rauis} *rāu̯is* 'hoarseness' :: **rāu̯ikos* > (4.1) **rāu̯kos* > (1.2) **rau̯kos* > (9.18) *rau̯kus* {raucus} 'hoarse' **D** {rego} *regō* 'I erect' :: abl. sg. **ēregō* > (4.1) **ērgō* > (1.2) *ergō* {ergo} 'in consequence of'

E3. A {date} *date* 'give!' :: **ke-date* > (4.1) **kedte* > (12.5) *kette* {cette} 'look!' **B** {sitis} *sitis* 'thirst' :: **sitikos* > (4.1) **sitkos* > (18.4) **sikkos* > (9.18) *sikkus* {siccus} 'dry' **C** {dico} *dikō* 'I speak' :: **práę̄dikō* > (4.1) **práę̄dkō* > (12.6) **práę̄tkō* > (18.4) **práę̄kkō* > (39.1) *práę̄kō* {praeco} 'herald' **D** {rego} *regō* 'I erect' :: **perregō* > (4.1) **perrgō* > (39.2) *pergō* {pergo} 'I go on' **E** {positus} *positus* 'placed' :: **po-sinō* > (4.1) **posnō* > (15.2) **poznō* > (2.2) *pōnō* {pono} 'I place'

Unit 14: Vowel Weakening I

E1. A {annus} *annus* 'year' :: **bí-annium* > (8.1) **bíennium* > (Ac1) *biénnium* {biennium} 'time of two years' **B** {arma} *arma* 'weapons' :: **ín-armis* > (8.1) **ínermis* > (Ac1) *inérmis* {inermis} 'unarmed' **C** {carpo} *karpō* 'I plug' :: **éks-karpō* > (8.1) **ékskerpō* > (Ac1) *ekskérpō* {excerpo} 'I discard'

E2. A {placet} *plaket* 'it is pleasing' :: **dísplaket* > (8.1) **displeket* > (8.3) *díspliket* {displicet} 'it is not pleasing' **B** {medius} *medius* 'medial' :: **dímedios* > (8.3) **dímidios* > (Ac1) *dímídios* > (9.18) *dīmidius* {dimidius} 'by half' **C** {rego} *regō* 'I govern' :: **díregō* > (8.3) *dīrigō* {dirigo} 'I straighten' **D** {peto} *petō* 'I strive for' :: **kompetum* > (8.3) *kompitum* {compitum} 'crossroads' **E** {lego} *legō* 'I read' :: **élegō* > (8.3) *éligō* {eligo} 'I choose' **F** {statuo} *statuō* 'I put up' :: **réstatuō* > (8.1) **réstetuō* > (8.3) **réstituō* > (Ac1) *restítuō* {restituo} 'I restore' **G** {cornu} *kornu* 'horn' :: **kornu-ger* > (8.4) *korniger* {corniger} 'having horns' **H** {manus} *manus* 'hand' :: **manuka* > (8.4) *manika* {manica} 'sleeve'

E3. A {manus} *manus* 'hand' :: **mánu-pułus* > (8.6) **mánypułus* > (Ac1) *manýpułus* {manipulus} 'handful' **B** **opos* 'work' > (9.18) *opus* {opus} + *fakiō* :: **opo-fak-s* > (8.1) **opofeks* > (8.2) **opefeks* > (8.3) **opifeks* > (8.5) *opyfeks* {opifex} 'craftsman' **C** {ars} *ars* 'art' + *fakiō* :: **arti-faks* > (8.1) **artifeks* > (8.5) *artyfeks* {artifex} 'artist' **D** **optemos* > (8.3) **optimos* > (8.5) **optymos* > (9.18) *optymus* {optimus} 'the best'

Unit 15: Vowel Weakening II

E1. A {frango} *fraŋgō* 'I break' ::*kṓnfraŋgō* > (8.1) **kṓnfreŋgō* > (8.7) **kṓnfriŋgō* > (Ac1) *kōnfríŋgō* {confringo} 'I break into pieces'
   B {pango} *paŋgō* 'I fix' :: *súbpaŋgō* > (12.1) **súppaŋgō* > (8.1) *súppeŋgō* > (8.7) *súppiŋgō* > (Ac1) *suppíŋgō* {suppingo} 'I fix below'

E2. A {lauo} *lau̯ō* 'I wash' :: **ablau̯ō* > (8.1) **ableu̯ō* > (8.9) **ablou̯ō* > (8.11) *abluu̯ō* {abluo / abluuo} 'I wash off' **B** {pauio} *pau̯i̯ō* 'I hit'
   :: **dḗpau̯i̯ō* > (8.1) **dḗpeu̯i̯ō* > (8.9) **dḗpou̯i̯ō* > (8.11) **dḗpuu̯i̯ō* > (Ac1) *dēpúu̯i̯ō* {depuio/depuuio} 'I cudgel' **C** **nou̯os* > (9.18) *nou̯us*
   {nouus} 'new' :: *dē-nou̯ōd* > (8.11) **dēnuu̯ōd* > (38.3) *dēnuu̯ō* {denuo} 'anew' **D** **sēd-dolōd* > (39.1) **sēdolōd* > (8.10) **sēdulōd* >
   (38.3)*sēdulō* {sedulo} 'zealous' **E** {sicilia} *Sikilia* 'Sicily' :: **Sikelos* > (8.8) **Sikolos* > (8.10) **Sikulos* > (9.18) *Sikulus* {siculus} 'Sicilian'

E3. A {remus} *rēmus* 'oar of a ship' + *agō* ::*rēm-ag-s* > (13.6) **rēm-aks* > (8.1) *rēmeks* {remex} 'rower' **B** {primus} *prīmus* 'first' + *kaput*
   'head' :: *prīmo-kaps* > (4.1) **prīmkaps* > (19.11) **prīŋkaps* > (8.1) *prīŋkeps* {princeps} 'leading person'

Unit 16: The Sound Changes e > i and i > e

E1. A {decus} *dekus* 'honor' :: **deknos* > (14.5) **degnos* > (17.5) **deŋnos* > (9.6) **diŋnos* > (2.5) **dīŋnos* > (9.18) *dīŋnus* {dignus} 'worthy'
   B {lego} *legō* 'I collect' ::*legnom* > (17.5) **leŋnom* > (9.6) **liŋnom* > **līŋnom* > (9.18) *līŋnum* {lignum} 'firewood' **C** {tego} *tegō* 'I
   cover' :: **tegnom* > (17.5) **teŋnom* > (9.6) *tiŋnom* > (2.5) **tīŋnom* > (9.18) *tīŋnum* {tignum} 'piece of lumber'

E3. A **sedīli* > (9.14a) *sedīle* {sedile} 'chair' **B** **breu̯i* > (9.14a) *breu̯e* {breue} 'short' **C** **forti* > (9.14a) *forte* 'brave' **D** **anti* > (9.14a) *ante*
   {ante} 'before' **E** {heri} *herī* > (1.3) **heri* > (9.14a) *here* {here} 'yesterday'

E1. A {commercium} *kommerkium* > (9.4) *kommirkium* {commircium} 'commerce' **B** {stercus} *sterkus* > (9.4) *stirkus* {stircus} 'manure'
   C {Mercurius} *Merkurius* > (9.4) *Mirkurius* {Mircurius} 'God of commerce' **D** *penna* > (9.3) *pinna* 'feather' **E** {uellus} *u̯ellus* > (9.3)
   u̯illus {uillus} 'wool' **F** {uetulus} *u̯etulus* > (9.3) *u̯itulus* {uitulus} 'elderly' **G** {uespillo} *u̯espillō* > (9.3) *u̯ispillō* {uispillo} 'undertaker'

Unit 17: The Sound Change e > o

E1. A {uelle} *u̯elle* 'to want' :: **u̯eltis* > (28.1) **u̯eltis* > (9.9) *u̯oltis* > (9.19) *u̯u̯ltis* {uultis} 'you want' **B** **ku̯elō* > (28.3) **ku̯elō* > (9.9) **ku̯olō*
   > (40.5) *kolō* {colo} 'I cultivate' **C** **helos* > (28.3) **helos* > (9.9) *holos* > (9.18) *holus* {holus} 'green vegetables'

E2. A **su̯epnos* > (9.11) **su̯opnos* > (40.5) **sopnos* > (14.2) **sobnos* > (17.2) **somnos* > (9.18) *somnus* {somnus} 'sleep' **B** **ku̯eku̯ō* > (9.11)
   *ku̯oku̯ō > (40.5) *koku̯ō* {coquo} 'I cook' **C** **su̯esōr* > (9.11) **su̯osōr* > (40.5) **sosōr* > (15.6) **sozōr* > (26.1) **sorōr* > (1.4) *soror* {soror}
   'sister' **D** **su̯ekrūs* > (9.11) **su̯okrūs* > (40.5) **sokrūs* > (A: ū > u) *sokrus* {socrus} 'mother-in-law' **E** **su̯e-kord-s* > (9.11) **su̯o-kord-s* >
   (40.5) **sokords* > (13.4) **sokorts* > (16.4) **sokorss* > (39.7) *sokors* {socors} 'sorrowless' **F** **u̯emō* > (9.11) *u̯omō* {uomo} 'I vomit'

Unit 18: The Sound Changes o > e and o > u

E1. A OL {diuortium} *dīu̯ortium* > (9.15) *dīu̯ertium* {diuertium} 'divorce' **B** OL {uortex} *u̯orteks* > (9.15) *u̯erteks* {uertex} 'whirl' **C** OL
   {uorro} *u̯orrō* > (9.15) *u̯errō* {uerro} 'I sweep' **D** OL {aruorsum} *ar-u̯orsum* > (9.15) *ad-u̯ersum* {aduersum} 'against' **E** OL {uorto} *u̯ortō*
   > (9.15) *u̯ertō* {uerto} 'I turn' **F** OL {reuortus} *reu̯ortus* > (9.15) *reu̯ertus* {reuertus} 'come back'

E2. A {uelle} *u̯elle* 'want' :: **u̯eltis* > (28.1) **u̯eltis* > (9.9) *u̯oltis* > (9.21) *u̯u̯ltis* {uultis} 'you want' **B** *polenta* 'peeled barley' :: **pols* > (28.1)
   *pols > (9.21) *puls* {puls} 'pap' **C** *pollen* 'fine flour' :: **polu̯is* > (28.1) **polu̯is* > (9.21) *pulu̯is* {puluis} 'dust' **D** {consol} *kōnsol* > (28.2)
   kōnsol > (9.18) *kōnsul* {consul} 'consul'

E3. A {sequontur} *seku̯ontur* > (9.19) *seku̯untur* {sequuntur} 'they follow' **B** {probaueront} *probāu̯ēront* > (9.18) *probāu̯ērunt* {probauerunt}
   'they approved' **C** *suom* > (9.18) *suum* 'his own' **D** {honc} *hoŋk* > (9.16) *huŋk* {hunc} 'this' **E** {donom} *dōnom* > (9.18) *dōnum* {donum}
   'gift' **F** {auonculus} *au̯oŋkulus* > (9.16/9.19) *au̯uŋkulus* {auunculus} 'oncle' **G** {uolnus} *u̯olnus* > (28.1) *u̯olnus* > (9.21/9.19) *u̯u̯lnus*
   {uulnus} 'wound' **H** {uolgus} **u̯olgus* > (28.1) *u̯olgus* > (9.21/9.19) *u̯u̯lgus* {uulgus} 'ordinary people' **I** {uolua} **u̯olu̯a* > (28.1) *u̯olu̯a* >
   (9.21/9.19) *u̯u̯lu̯a* {uulua} 'womb'

Unit 19: Monophthongizations in Final and Medial Syllables

E1. A **ai̯stimō* 'I estimate' (10.6) > *ae̯stimō* {aestimo} :: **éks-ai̯stimō* > (8.1) **eks-ei̯stimō* > (Ac1) *eks-éi̯stimō* > (10.8) *eks-ē̜stimō* > (10.9)
   eks-īstimō {existimo} 'I estimate' **B** **lai̯dō* > (10.6) *lae̯dō* {laedo} 'I injure' :: **ád-lai̯dō* > (20.4) **állai̯dō* > (8.1) **álleí̯dō* > (Ac1) **alléi̯dō*
   > (10.8) **allē̜dō* > (10.9) *allīdō* {allido} 'I bump at' **C** **ólai̯u̯a* > (8.1) **óleiu̯a* > (Ac1) *oléi̯u̯a* > (10.8) *olē̜u̯a* > (10.9) *olī̯u̯a* {oliua} 'olive
   tree' **D** {aequus} *ae̯ku̯us* 'even' :: **ín-ai̯ku̯os* > (8.1) **ín-ei̯ku̯os* > (Ac1) *in-éi̯ku̯os* > (10.8) *inē̜ku̯os* > (10.9) **inīku̯os* > (9.18) *inīku̯us*
   {iniquus} 'uneven' **E** {taedet} *tae̯det* 'he is tired of' :: **dís-tai̯d-to-m* > (12.5) **distai̯ttom* > (x3) **dístai̯ssom* > (8.1) **distei̯ssom* > (Ac1)
   *distéi̯ssom > (10.8) *distē̜ssom* > (10.9) *distīssom* > (39.1) **distīsom* > (9.18) *distīsum* {distisum} 'he is strongly tired of' **F** **kai̯dō* >
   (10.6) *kae̯dō* {caedo} 'I chop' :: **ké-kai̯dai̯* > (8.1) **ké-kei̯d-ei̯* > (Ac1) **kekéi̯dei̯* > (10.8) **kekē̜dē̜* > (10.9) *kekīdī* {cecidi} 'I chopped'

E2. A {causa} *kau̯sa* 'cause' :: **éks-kau̯ssō* > (8.1) **eks-keu̯ssō* > (8.9) **eks-kou̯ssō* > (Ac1) *eks-kóu̯ssō* > (10.3) **eks-kō̜ssō* > (10.4) **eks-
   kūssō* > (39.1) *ekskūsō* {excuso} 'I apologize' **B** {fraudo} *frau̯dō* 'I betray' :: *dḗ-frau̯dō* > (8.1) **dḗfreu̯dō* > (8.9) **dḗfrou̯dō* > (Ac1)
   *dēfróu̯dō > (10.3)**dēfrō̜dō* > (10.4) *dēfrūdō* {defrudo} 'I betray' **C** {claudo} *klau̯dō* 'I close' :: **ín-klau̯dō* > (8.1) **ín-kleu̯dō* > (8.9)
   *ín-klou̯dō > (Ac1) **inklóu̯dō* > (10.3) **in-klō̜dō* > (10.4) *inklūdō* {includo} 'I enclose'

K E Y

Unit 20: Monophthongizations in Initial Syllables

E1. A *laureola* > (10.1) VL *lōreola* 'little victory' **B** *aurikula* > (10.1) VL *ōrikula* 'earlobe' **C** *Aulus* > (10.1) VL *Ōlus* 'a name' **D** *plaudere* > (10.1) VL *plōdere* 'to applaud' **E** *plaustrum* > (10.1) VL *plōstrum* 'wagon'

E2. A {deus} *deus* 'god' :: *deiuos* > (10.8) *dēuos* > (10.9) *dīuos* > (9.18) *dīuus* {diuus} 'divine' **B** *deikō* > (10.8) *dēkō* > (10.9) *dīkō* {dico} 'I say' **C** {feido} *feidō* > (10.8) *fēdō* > (10.9) *fīdō* {fido} 'I believe' **D** OL {sei} *sei* > (10.8) *sē* > (10.9) *sī* {si} 'if' **F** OL {sibei} *sibei* > (10.8) *sibē* > (10.9) *sibī* > (1.3) *sibi* {sibi} 'oneself' **G** {abeis} *ab-eis* > (10.8) *abēs* > (10.9) *abīs* {abis} 'you go away' **H** {ceiuis} *keiuis* > (10.8) *kēuis* > (10.9) *kīuis* {ciuis} 'citizen' **I** {uirtutei} *uirtūtei* > (10.8) *uirtūtē* > (10.9) *uirtūtī* {uirtuti} dat. sg. 'virtue'

E3. A OL {loidos} *loidos* > (10.10) *loedos* > (10.11) *lōdos* > (10.4) *lūdos* > (9.18) *lūdus* {ludus} 'game' **B** {coiraueront} *koirāuēront* > (10.10) *koerāuēront* > (10.11) *kōrāuēront* > (10.4) *kūrāuēront* > (9.18) *kūrāuērunt* {curauerunt} 'they cared for' **C** OL {moerum} *moerom* > (10.11) *mōrom* > (10.4) *mūrom* > (9.18) *mūrum* {murum} 'wall' **D** OL {moinicipiom} *moinikipiom* > (10.10) *moenikipiom* > (10.11) *mōnikipiom* > (10.4) *mūnikipiom* > (9.18) *mūnikipium* {municipium} 'town' **E** OL {oetantur} *oetantur* > (10.11) *ōtantur* > (10.4) *ūtantur* {utantur} 'they use' **F** *foidos* > (10.10) *foedos* > (9.18) *foedus* {foedus} 'contract'

Unit 21: Anaptyxis and Vowel Assimilation

E1. A *poplus* > (5.2) *populus* {populus} 'people' **B** *pōtlom* > (28.4) *pōkłom* > (5.2) *pōkułom* > (9.18) *pōkulum* {poculum} 'drinking cup' **C** {piaclum} *piākłum* > (5.2) *piākułum* {piaculum} 'sin offering' **D** {uinclum} *uiŋkłum* > (5.2) *uiŋkułum* {uinculum} 'binding rope' **E** *stabłum* > (5.2) *stabułum* {stabulum} 'stable' **F** *stablis* > (5.1) *stabilis* {stabilis} 'solid' **G** {iuglans} *iūgłāns* > (5.2) *iūgułāns* {iugulans} 'walnut' **H** *faklis* > (5.1) *fakilis* {facilis} 'easy' **I** {extemplo} *ekstempłō* > (5.2) *ekstempułō* {extempulo} 'instantly'

E2. A *kouos* > (9.22) *kauos* > (9.18) *kauus* {cauus} 'hollow' **B** *foueō* > (9.22) *faueō* {faueo} 'I favor'

E3. A {semper} *sem-per* 'always' :: *semlis* > (5.1) *semilis* > (7.1) *similis* {similis} 'similar' **B** *ne-sī* > (7.1) *nisī* {nisi} 'if not' **C** {hilum} *hīlum* 'shred' :: *ne-hīl* > (7.1) *ni-hīl* > (x8.12c) *nīīl* > (3.1) *nīl* {nil} 'nothing' **D** *ne-mios* > (7.1) *nimios* > (9.18) *nimius* 'too much' **E** *meliom* > (7.1) *miliom* > (9.18) *milium* 'millet'

E4. A {passer} *passer* > (7.3) VL *passar* {passar} 'sparrow' **B** {farferus} *farferus* > (7.3) VL *farfarus* {farfarus} 'horsefoot'

Unit 22: Assimilation of Consonants I

E1. A {loquor} *lokuor* 'I speak' :: *adlokuor* > (20.4) *allokuor* {alloquor} 'I speak to' **B** {lustro} *lūstrō* 'I illuminate' :: *inlūstris* > (21.2) *illūstris* {illustris} 'illuminated' **C** {moueo} *moueō* 'I move' :: *admoueō* > (17.3) *anmoueō* > (19.3) *ammoueō* {ammoueo} 'I move to' **D** {rado} *rādō* 'I scrape' :: *rādlom* > (20.4) *rāllom* > (9.18) *rāllum* {rallum} 'scraping knife'

E2. A {facilis} *fakilis* 'easy' :: superlative *fakil-simus* > (15.7) *fakil-zimus* > (22.1) *fakillimus* {facillimus} 'very easy' **B** {acer} *aker* 'sharp' :: superlative *aker-simus* > (15.8) *aker-zimus* > (22.2) *akerrimus* {acerrimus} 'very sharp' **C** {uelim} *uelim* 1. sg. subj. prs. :: prs. inf. *uel-se* (-se is the ending of the infinitive as in *es-se*) > (15.7) *uelze* > (22.1) *uelle* {uelle} 'want'

E3. A {scribo} *skrībō* 'I write' :: *skrib-tus* > (2.3) *skrībtus* > (12.2) *skrīptus* {scriptus} 'written' **B** {rego} *regō* 'I govern' :: *reg-tus* > (2.3) *rēgtus* > (12.7) *rēktus* {rectus} 'governed' **C** {ago} *agō* 'I drive' :: *agtus* > (2.3) *āgtus* > (12.7) *āktus* {actus} 'driven'

Unit 23: Assimilation of Consonants II

E1. A {eum} *eum* 'him' :: *eum-dem* > (19.8) *eundem* {eundem} 'the same' **B** {tam} *tam* 'there' :: *tam-dem* > (19.8) *tandem* {tandem} 'finally' **C** {quam} *kuam* 'how?' :: *kuam-dō* > (19.8) *kuandō* {quando} 'when?' **D** {clam} *klam* 'secretly' :: *klam-kułum* > (19.11) *klaŋkułum* {clanculum} 'secretly'

E2. A {daps} *daps* 'meal' :: *dapnom* > (14.2) *dabnom* > (17.2) *damnom* > (9.18) *damnum* {damnum} 'loss' **B** {scabillum} *skabillum* 'small chair' :: *skabnom* > (17.2) *skamnom* > (9.18) *skamnum* {scamnum} 'stool' **C** {sopor} *sopor* 'deep sleep' :: *suepnos* > (9.11) *suopnos* > (40.5) *sopnos* > (14.2) *sobnos* > (17.2) *somnos* > (9.18) *somnus* {somnus} 'sleep' **D** *seknom* > (14.5) *segnom* > (17.5) *seŋnom* > (9.6) *siŋnom* > (2.5) *sīŋnom* > (9.18) *sīŋnum* {signum} 'sign'

E3. A {artis} *artis* gen. sg. 'of the art' :: nom. sg. *artis* > (4.2) *arts* > (16.4) *arss* > (39.7) *ars* {ars} 'art' **B** {montis} *montis* gen. sg. 'of the mountain' :: nom. sg. *montis* > (4.2) *monts* > (16.4) *monss* > (39.7) *mons* > (2.1) *mōns* {mons} 'mountain' **C** {do} *dō* 'I give' :: nom. sg. *dōtis* > (4.2) *dōts* > (16.4) *dōss* > (39.7) *dōs* {dos} 'gift' **D** {damno} *damnō* 'I condemn' :: *damnātos* > (4.2) *damnāts* > (16.4) *damnāss* > (39.7) *damnās* {damnas} 'condemned'

Unit 24: Assimilation of Consonants III

E1. A {sum} *sum* 'I am' :: *adsum* > (13.4) *atsum* > (16.4) *assum* {assum} 'I am there' **B** {pedis} *pēdis* 'of the foot' :: nom. sg. *pēds* > (13.4) *pēts* > (16.4) *pēss* > (39.7) *pēs* {pes} 'foot' **C** *hod-ke* > (12.6) *hotke* > (18.4) *hokke* > (4.3) *hokk* > (39.6) *hok* {hoc} 'this' **D** {quid} *kuid* 'what?' :: *kuid-kuam* > (12.6) *kuit-kuam* > (18.4) *kuikkuam* {quicquam} 'anything' **E** {quid} *kuid* 'what?' :: *kuid-pe* > (12.4) *kuitpe* > (18.3) *kuippe* {quippe} 'of course' **F** {idcirco} *idkirkō* > (12.6) *itkirkō* > (18.4) *ikkirkō* {iccirco} 'that is why' **G** {sequor} *sekuor* 'I follow' :: *adsekuor* > (13.4) *atsekuor* > (16.4) *assekuor* {assequor} 'I reach'

E2. A {fero} *ferō* 'I carry' :: *ad-ferō* > (13.3) *at-ferō* > (16.3) *af-ferō* {affero} 'I bring' **B** gen. sg. {uirtutis} *uirtūtis* 'of the virtue' :: *uirtūt-s* > (16.4) *uirtūss* > (39.7) *uirtūs* 'virtue' **C** gen. sg. {noctis} *noktis* 'of the night' :: *nokts* > (16.4) *nokss* > (39.7) *noks* {nox} 'night' **D** {laudo} *laudō* 'I praise' :: *laud-s* > (13.4) *lauts* > (16.4) *lauss* > (39.7) *laus* {laus} 'praise' **E** {sedeo} *sedeō* 'I sit' :: *dēseds* >

(13.4) *dēsets > (16.4) *dēsess > (39.7) dēses, -idis {deses} 'sitting aside' **F** {supra} suprā 'above' :: *supmos > (14.1) *submos > (17.1) *summos > (9.18) summus {summus} 'the highest' **G** {globo} glūbō 'I peel' :: *glūbma > (17.1) *glūmma > (39.1) glūma {gluma} 'hull'

Unit 25: Dissimilation / Dissimilatory Deletion / Haplology

E1. **A** {caelum} kaẹlum 'sky' :: *kaẹluleụs > (23.1) kaẹruleụs {caeruleus} 'blue' **B** {pales} Palēs 'goddess of shepherds' :: Palīlia > (23.1) Parīlia {parilia} 'celebration for the goddess Palēs' **C** {flagellum} flagellum > (23.1) VL fragellum {fragellum} 'whip' **D** {lunalis} *lūnālis > (23.9) lūnāris {lunaris} 'moonly' **E** *mīlitālis > (23.9) mīlitāris {militaris} 'of a soldier' **F** *singulālis > (23.9) singulāris {singularis} 'singular' **G** {monimentum} monimentum > (23.6) VL molimentum {monimentum} 'monument'

E2. **A** {flagellum} flagellum 'whip' :: *flaglom > (23.9) *flagrom > (9.18) flagrum {flagrum} 'whip' **B** {scalpo} skalpō 'I scrape' :: *skalplom > (23.9) *skalprom > (9.18) skalprum {scalprum} 'chisel' **C** {premo} premō 'I press' :: *presrom > (23.10) *preslom > (15.3) *prezlom > (2.2) *prēlom > (9.18) prēlum {prelum} 'press, winepress' **D** {rado} rādō 'I scrape' :: *rādrom > (23.10) *rādlom > (20.4) *rāllom > (9.18) rāllum {rallum} 'scraping knife'

E3. **A** {culter} kulter 'knife' :: VL *kultellus > (l…l > n…l) kuntellus {cuntellus} 'small knife' **B** {peregrinus} peregrīnus > (r…r > l…r) VL pelegrīnus {pelegrinus} 'foreign' **C** {meretrix} meretrīks > (r…r > n…r) menétrīks {menetrix} 'prostitute' **D** {fragrare} fragrāre > (r…r > l…r) VL flagrāre {flagrare} 'to smell' **E** {genui} genuī 'I brought forth' :: *genmen > (n…n > r…n) germen {germen} 'sprout'

E4. **A** {caluor} kalụor 'I play a trick' :: *kalụilla > (l…l > 0…l) kaụilla {cauilla} 'trick' **B** {trabs} traps 'beam' :: *traberna > (r…r > 0…r) taberna {taberna} 'hut'

Unit 26: Double Consonants

E1. **A** bāka {baca} :: bakka {bacca} 'berry' **B** mūkus {mucus} :: mukkus {muccus} 'snot' **C** sūkus {sucus} :: sukkus {succus} 'juice' **D** kīpus {cipus} :: kippus {cippus} 'pale, stake, post' **E** kūpa {cupa} 'barrel' :: kuppa {cuppa} 'cup' **F** stlāta {stlata} :: stlatta {stlatta} 'merchant vessel' **G** lītus {litus} :: littus {littus} 'beach'

E2. **A** {paro} parō 'I provide' :: *sēdparō > (12.4) *sētparō > (18.3) sēpparō > (39.1) sēparō {separo} 'I separate' **B** {pono} pōnō 'I put' :: *sēdpōnō > (12.4) *sētpōnō > (18.3) *sēppōnō > (39.1) sēpōnō {sepono} 'I set aside' **C** {praedico} praẹdikō 'I declare' :: *praẹdikō > (4.1) *praẹdkō > (12.6) *praẹtkō > (18.4) *praẹkkō > (39.1) praẹkō {praeco} 'herald' **D** {accusso} akkūssō > (39.1) akkūsō {accuso} 'I accuse' **E** {quaesso} kụaẹssō > (39.1) kụaẹsō {quaeso} 'I ask for' **F** {claudo} klaụdō 'I close' :: *klaụd-to-s > (12.5) *klaụttos > (x3) *klaụssos > (39.1) *klaụsos > (9.18) klaụsus {clausus} 'closed' **G** {haussi} haụssī > (39.1) haụsī {hausi} 'I drew up'

E3. **A** *ad-spīrō > (13.4) *at-spīrō > (16.4) asspīrō > (39.2) aspīrō {aspiro} 'I breathe' **B** *adstō > (13.4) *atstō > (16.4) *asstō > (39.2) astō {asto} 'I stand at' **C** *disstō > (39.2) distō {disto} 'I am distant'

E4. **A** {canna} kanna 'reed' :: *kannālis > (39.5) kanālis {canalis} 'channel' **B** {currus} kurrus 'chariot' :: *kurrūlis > (39.5) kurūlis {curulis} 'of a chariot' **C** {far} far 'spelt' :: *farrīna > (39.5) farīna {farina} 'flour'

Unit 27: The Fricative /s/ and Its Allophone [z]

E1. 1. Loss of nasal before fricative by SCN x10.1 trāns- > *trās-. 2. Sonorization of /s/ to [z] before voiced sounds by SCN 15 *trās- > *trāz-. 3. Loss of [z] by SCN 2.2. Since the preceding vowel was long, no compensatory lengthening took place: *trāz > trā.

E2. 1. *ges-ō > (15.6) *gezō > (26.1) gerō. 2. ges-s-ī > (no change) gessī.

E3. The preform *hes- plus the old ending of the locative -ī became herī by rhotazism. No change of *hes- occurred before /t/ of the suffix -ternus.

E4. **A** {dumetum} dūmētum 'undergrowth' :: *dusmos > (15.1) *duzmos > (2.2) *dūmos > (9.18) dūmus {dumus} 'undergrowth' **B** {positus} positus 'placed' :: *posinō > (4.1) *posnō > (15.2) *poznō > (2.2) pōnō {pono} 'I put' **C** {gusto} gustō 'I taste' :: *dēgusnō > (15.2) *dēguznō > (2.2) dēgūnō {deguno} 'I taste' **D** {egestas} egestās 'indigence' :: *egesnos > (15.2) *egeznos > (2.2) *egēnos > (9.18) egēnus {egenus} 'indigent' **E** {premo} premō 'I press' :: *preslom > (15.3) *prezlom > (2.2) *prēlom > (9.18) prēlum {prelum} 'press, wine press' **F** {quasillum} kụasillum 'small basket' :: *kụaslom > (15.3) *kụazlom > (2.2) *kụālom > (9.18) kụālum {qualum} 'basket'

Unit 28: Loss of Initial Consonants

E1. **A** OL {gnatus} gnātus > (30.2a) *ŋnātus > (30.2b) nātus {natus} 'born' **B** OL {gnotus} gnōtus > (30.2a) *ŋnōtos > (30.2b) nōtus {notus} 'known' **C** OL {gnauus} gnāụus > (30.2a) *ŋnāụus > (30.2b) nāụus {nauus} 'busy' **D** *stlātos > (37.2) *slātos > (30.12) *lātos > (9.18) lātus {latus} 'broad' **E** {tollo} tollō 'I bear' :: *stlātos > (37.2) *slātos > (30.12) *lātos > (9.18) lātus {latus} 'carried'

E2. **A** EL {duenos} dụenos > (9.11) *dụonos > (40.11) *bonos > (9.18) bonus {bonus} 'good' **B** OL {duonorom} *dụonōrom > (40.11) bonōrum {bonorum} **C** *dụenēd > (40.11) *benēd > (38.3) *benē > (1.3) bene {bene} 'well' **D** {duellom} dụellom > (40.11) *bellom > (9.18) bellum {bellum} 'war' **E** {duo} duō 'two' :: dụis > (40.11) bis {bis} 'twice' **F** {duidens} dụidēns > (40.11) bidēns {bidens} 'having two teeth'

E3. **A** *snō > (30.12) nō {no} 'I swim' **B** *ụlōrum > (40.7) lōrum {lorum} 'reigns' **C** *ụrādiks > (40.7) rādiks {radix} 'root' **D** *ksentos > (30.8) *sentos > (9.18) sentus {sentus} 'tangled' **E** *ksnéụātlā > (30.8) *snéụātlā > (30.12) *néụātlā > (1.6) *néụātla > (9.10) *nóụātla > (28.3) *nóụātla > (28.4) *nóụākla > (Ac1) *noụákła > (5.2) noụākuła {nouacula} 'clipping blade' **F** *psternuō > (30.7) sternuō {sternuo} 'I sneeze' **G** *psablom > (30.7) *sablom > (28.3) *sabłom > (5.2) *sabułom > (9.18) sabułum 'sand' **H** *dlongos > (30.5) *longos > (9.18)

K
E
Y

longus 'long' **I** **knīdōs* > (30.1) **gnīdōs* > (30.2a) **ŋnīdōs* > (30.2b) **nīdōs* > (A: gen. *nidōris*) **nīdōr* > (1.4) *nīdor* {nidor} 'steam' **J** **slūbrikus* > (30.12) *lūbrikus* {lubricus} 'lubricious'

Unit 29: Loss of Final Consonants

E1. **A** OL {magistratud} *magistrātūd* > (38.3) *magistrātū* {magistratu} **B** OL {datod} *datōd* > (38.3) *datō* {dato} 'he shall give' **C** OL {suntod} *suntōd* > (38.3) *suntō* {sunto} 'he shall be' **D** OL {sententiad} *sententiād* > (38.3) *sententiā* {sententia} **E** OL {uiolatod} *ųiolātōd* > (38.3) *ųiolātō* {uiolato} 'he shall violate' **F** OL {licetod} *likētōd* > (38.3) *likētō* {liceto} 'it shall be permissible'

E2. **A** **mīlets* > (16.4) **mīless* > (39.7) *mīles* {miles} 'soldier' **B** **kustōds* > (13.4) **kustōts* > (16.4) **kustōss* > (39.7) *kustōs* {custos} 'gardien' **C** EL *sakros* > (4.2) >**sakrs* > (6.1) **sakr̥s* > (6.2) **sakers* > (15.9) **sakerz* > (22.3) **sakerr* > (39.8) *saker* {sacer} 'holy' **D** **ākris* > (4.2) **ākrs* > (6.1) **ākr̥s* > (6.2) **ākers* > (15.9) **ākerz* > (22.3) **ākerr* > (39.8) *āker* {acer} 'sharp' **E** **hodke* > (12.6) **hotke* > (18.4) **hokke* > (4.3) **hokk* > (39.6) *hok* {hoc} 'this'

E3. **A** {ossis} *ossis* 'of the bone' :: nom. sg. **oss* > (39.7) *os* {os} 'bone' **B** {cordis} *kordis* 'of the heart' :: nom. sg. **kord* > (38.5) *kor* {cor} 'heart' **C** {lactis} *laktis* 'of the milk' :: nom. sg. **lakt* > (38.4) *lak* {lac} 'milk'

Unit 30: Simplification of Medial Consonant Clusters

E1. **A1** {fulcio} *fulkiō* 'I support' :: **fulkmentom* > (35.3a) **fulmentom* > (9.18) *fulmentum* {fulmentum} 'column' **A2** {fulcio} *fulkiō* 'I support' :: **fulkmentom* > (14.7) **fulgmentom* > (17.6) **fulmmentom* > (39.5) *fulmentom* > (9.18) *fulmentum* {fulmentum} 'column' **B1** {sarpio} *sarpiō* 'I cut off' :: **sarpmentom* > (35.1a) **sarmentom* > (9.18) *sarmentum* 'twig' **B2** {sarpio} *sarpiō* 'I cut off' :: **sarpmentom* > (14.1) **sarbmentom* > (17.1) **sarmmentom* > (39.5) **sarmentom* > (9.18) *sarmentum* 'twig'

E2. **A** {ulciscor} *ulkiskor* 'I take revenge' :: **ulktus* > (34.2a) *ultus* {ultus} 'revenge taken' **B** {fulcio} *fulkiō* 'I support' :: PPP **fulktus* > (34.2a) *fultus* {fultus} 'supported' **C** **Martikos* > (4.1) **Martkos* > (18.4) **Markkos* > (39.3) **Markos* > (A: ā from Mārs) **Mārkos* > (9.18) *Mārkus* {Marcus}

E3. **A** {capio} *kapiō* 'I grasp' :: **súpskapiō* > (31.1a) **súskapiō* > (8.1) **súskepiō* > (8.3) **súskipiō* > (Ac1) *suskípiō* {suscipio} 'I undertake' **B** {luceo} *lūkeō* 'I light' :: **in-lūkstris* > (31.3a) **inlūstris* > (21.2) *illūstris* {illustris} 'noble' **C** {texo} *teksō* 'I weave' :: **teksla* > (32.3a) **tesla* > (15.3) **tezla* > (2.2) *tēla* {tela} 'tissue' **D** {traho} *trahō* 'I carry' :: **tragsma* > (13.6) **traksma* > (31.2a) **trasma* > (15.1) **trazma* > (2.2) *trāma* {trama} 'thin' **E** {luceo} *lūkeō* 'I light' :: **lūksna* > (32.1a) **lūsna* > (15.2) **lūzna* > (2.2) *lūna* {luna} 'moon' **F** {spica} *spīka* 'ear of corn' :: **spīksna* > (32.1a) **spīsna* > (15.2) **spīzna* > (2.2) *spīna* {spina} 'thorn' **G** {paciscor} *pakīskor* 'I agree' :: **pakslos* > (32.3a) **paslos* > (15.3) **pazlos* > (2.2) **pālos* > (9.18) *pālus* {palus} 'post'

Unit 31 : The Semivowels /i̯/ and /u̯/

E1. **A** {consueueram} *kōnsuēu̯eram* > (40.2) **kōnsuēeram* > (1.1) **kōnsueeram* > (3.1) *kōnsuēram* {consueram} 'I was used to' **B** {lauo} *lau̯ō* 'I wash' :: **lau̯a-trīna* > (40.2) **laa-trīna* > (3.1) *lātrīna* {latrina} 'latrine' **C** {uiuo} *u̯īu̯ō* 'I live' :: **u̯īu̯ita* > (40.2) **u̯īita* > (1.1) **u̯iita* > (3.1) *u̯īta* {uita} 'life'

E2. **A** *magis* {magis} 'much' :: **magi̯ōs* > (x11.1) **mai̯i̯ōs* > (A: s>r by gen. *mai̯i̯ōrem*) **mai̯i̯ōr* > (1.4) *mai̯i̯or* {maior} 'bigger' **B** {adagium} *ad-ag-ium* 'pun' :: **agi̯ō* > (x11.1) *ai̯i̯ō* {aio} 'I say' **C** **pedi̯ōs* > (x11.2) **pei̯i̯ōs* > (A: s>r by gen. *pei̯i̯ōris*) **pei̯i̯ōr* > (1.4) *pei̯i̯or* {peior} 'worse'

E3. **A** {loqui} *loku̯ī* 'to speak' :: **loku̯utus* > (40.5) **lokutus* > (A: u>ū caused by PPPs such as *lau̯dātus* or *au̯dītus*) *lokūtus* {locutus} 'spoken' **B** {sequor} *seku̯or* 'I follow' :: **seku̯utus* > (40.5) **sekutus* > (A: u>ū caused by PPPs such as *lau̯dātus* or *au̯dītus*) > *sekūtus* {secutus} 'followed' **C** {quinque}+{uncia} :: **ku̯īŋku̯-ūnk-s* > (40.5) *ku̯īŋkūŋks* {quincunx} 'five twelfths' **D** {sequor} *seku̯or* 'I follow' :: **seku̯ondos* > (9.18) **seku̯ondus* > (9.19) **seku̯undus* > (40.5) *sekundus* {secundus} 'the following'

Unit 32: Analogical Changes

E1. The expected regular development is **alaker* > (8.1) **aleker* > (8.3) *aliker**, and *alakris* > (8.1) *alekris**. Vowel assimilation took place in the nom. *aliker** > (7.2) *alaker*, before /a/ was analogically transferred into the oblique cases: *alekris** > (A: nom. *alaker*) *alakris*.

E2. The gen. is formed regularly. The expected regular development of the nom. is **integer* > (8.3) *intiger**. In this case, the vowel of the oblique cases was transferred into the nominative *intiger** > (A: gen. *integris*) nom. *integer*.

E3. The expected regular development is **genatrīks* > (8.1) *genetrīks** because /a/ is weakened to /e/ instead of /i/ in closed syllables. The word *genitrīks* was analogically formed according to *genitor* 'father':: **genatrīks* > (A: *genitor*) *genitrīks* {genitrix}

E4. The expected regular development of the nom. is **eku̯os* > (40.5) *ekos** > (9.18) *ekus**. This form is attested in inscriptions. The paradigm *ekus**, *eku̯ī* was analogically remodeled because it was too irregular: *ekus** > (A: *eku̯ī*) *eku̯us*.

E5. The expected regular development of the nom. is *arks* > (34.4) *ars** > (15.9) *arz** > (22.3) *arr** > (39.8) *ar**. The paradigm *ar**, *arkis* was analogically remodeled because the nom. and the gen. differed too much from each other. The same is true for *kalks, kalkis* {calx, calcis} 'hoof' and *merks, merkis* {merx, mercis} 'ware'.

E6. /u̯/ should have been lost before /o/. The expected regular forms are *kot** and *kod**. In these cases, /u̯/ was restored in analogy to forms like *ku̯ī* {qui}, *ku̯ae̯* {quae}, in which /u̯/ remained.

Unit 33: PIE Labiovelars in Latin

E1. **A** {assequor} *assekŭor* 'I reach' :: **assekŭla* > (40.3) *assekla* {assecla} 'follower' **B** {coquo} *kokŭō* 'I cook' :: **kokʷtos* > (x4.1) **kokŭtos* > (40.3) **koktos* > (9.18) *koktus* {coctus} 'cooked' **C** {delinquo} *dēliŋkŭō* 'I fail' :: **dēlikŭtum* > (40.3) *dēliktum* {delictum} 'fault' **D** {sequor} *sekŭor* 'I accompany' :: **sekʷtor* > (x4.1) *sekŭtor* > (40.3) *sektor* {sector} 'I accompany'. **E** **gʷr̥Htos* > (x2.15) **gʷrātos* > (x4.2) **gŭrātos* > (40.4) **grātos* > (9.18) *grātus* {gratus} 'thankful' **F** **gʷregs* > (13.6) **gʷreks* > (x4.2) **gŭreks* > (40.4) *greks* {grex} 'herd'

E2. **A** **gʷorāi̯ō* > (x4.2) **gŭorāi̯ō* > (40.1) **gŭorāō* > (1.1) **gŭoraō* > (3.4) **gŭorō* > (30.11) *ŭorō* {uoro} 'I devour' **B** **gʷīŭos* > (x4.2) **gŭīŭos* > (30.11) **ŭīŭos* > (9.18) *ŭīŭus* {uiuus} 'alive'

E3. **A** **pekʷō* > (x11.3) **kʷekʷō* > (x4.1) **kŭekŭō* > (9.11) **kŭokŭō* > (40.5) **kokŭō* {coquo} 'I cook'

Unit 34: The Syllabic Resonants *[n̥], *[m̥], *[r̥], *[l̥]

E1. **A** **tn̥tos* > (x5.6) **tentos* > (9.18) *tentus* 'stretched' **B** acc.sg. **pedm̥* > (x5.7) *pedem* 'foot' **C** **septm̥* > (x5.7) *septem* 'seven' **D** **k̂m̥tom* > (x1.1) **km̥tom* > (x5.7) **kemtom* > (19.7) **kentom* > (9.18) *kentum* {centum} 'hundred' **E** **dek̂m̥* > (x1.1) **dekm̥* > (x5.7) *dekem* {decem} 'ten' **F** **gʷm̥tos* > (x4.2) **gŭm̥tos* > (x5.7) **gŭemtos* > (19.7) **gŭentos* > (30.11) **ŭentos* > (9.18) *ŭentus* {uentus} 'come'

E2. **A** **k̂r̥d* > (x1.1) **kr̥d* > (x5.1) **kord* > (38.5) *kor* {cor} 'heart' **B** **mr̥tis* > (x5.1) **mortis* > (4.2) **morts* > (16.4) **morss* > (39.7) *mors* {mors} 'death' **C** *kʷr̥tos* > (x4.1) **kŭr̥tos* > (x5.2) **kŭurtos* > (40.5) **kurtos* > (9.18) *kurtus* {curtus} 'short'

E3. **A** {scamnum} *skamnum* 'bench' :: **skábnolom* > (4.1) **skábnlom* > (6.3)**skábn̥lom* > (6.4) **skábinlom* > (Ac1) **skabínlom* > (21.2) **skabillom* > (9.18) *skabillum* {scabillum} 'small bench' **B** {tignum} *tīŋnum* 'piece of timber' :: **tígnolom* > (4.1)**tígnlom* > (6.3) **tígn̥lom* > (6.4) **tíginlom* > (Ac1) **tigínlom* > (21.2) **tigillom* > (9.18) *tigillum* 'small piece of timber' **C** *ager* 'field' :: **ágrolos* > (4.1)**ágrlos* > (6.1)**ágr̥los* > (6.2) **ágerlos* > (Ac1)**agérlos* > (21.3) **agellos* > (9.18) *agellus* 'small field' **D** *liber* 'book' :: **librolos* > (4.1)**librlos* > (6.1)**libr̥los* > (6.2) **líberlos* > (Ac1) **libérlos* > (21.3) **libellos* > (9.18) *libellus* 'small book' **E** **imbris* > (4.2) **imbrs* > (6.1) **imbr̥s* > (6.2) **imbers* > (15.9) **imberz* > (22.3) **imberr* > (39.8) *imber* 'rain'

Unit 35: The Complex Development of the PIE Mediae Aspiratae

E1. **A** **bʰerō* > (x6.1) **βerō* > (x6.5a) **φerō* > (x6.5b) *ferō* {fero} 'I carry' **B** **bʰéh₂meh₂* > (x2.3) **bʰah₂mah₂* > (x2.9) **bʰāmā* > (x6.1) **βāmā* > (x6.5a) **φāmā* > (x6.5b) *fāmā* > (1.6) *fāma* {fama} 'gossip' **C** **dʰūmos* > (x6.2) **δūmos* > (x6.6) **θūmos* > (x7.1) **fūmos* > (9.18) *fūmus* {fumus} 'smoke' **D** **ĝʰelh₃os* > (x1.3)**gʰelh₃os* > (x2.7) **gʰelos* > (x6.3) **γelos* > (x6.9a) **χelos* > (x6.9b) **helos* > (28.3) **hełos* > (9.9) **holos* > (9.18) *hołus* {holus} 'green vegetables'

E2. **A** **nebʰeleh₂* > (x2.3) **nebʰelah₂* > (x2.9) **nebʰelā* > (x6.1) **neβelā* > (1.6) **neβela* > (x8.1) **nebela* > (28.3) **nebeła* > (8.8) **neboła* > (8.10) **nebuła* {nebula} 'cloud' **B** **albʰos* > (x6.1) **alβos* > (x8.2) *albos* > (9.18) *albus* {albus} 'white' **C** **ŭidʰeŭeh₂* > (x2.3) **ŭidʰeŭah₂* > (x2.9)**ŭidʰeŭā* > (x6.2) **ŭiδeŭā* > (x8.7) **ŭideŭā* > (1.6) **ŭideŭa* > (8.9) **ŭidoŭa* > (8.11) *ŭiduŭa* {uidua} 'widow' **D** **ŭeĝʰō* > (x1.3) **ŭegʰō* > (x6.3) **ŭeγō* > (x8.12a) **ŭeχō* > (x8.12b) *ŭehō* {ueho} 'I drive'

E3. **A** **ŭerdʰom* > (x6.2) **ŭerδom* > (x7.4) **ŭerβom* > (x8.5) **ŭerbom* > (9.18) *ŭerbum* {uerbum} 'word' **B** **rudʰros* > (x6.2) **ruδros* > (x7.3b) **ruβros* > (x8.4) **rubros* > (4.2) **rubrs* > (6.1) **rubr̥s* > (6.2) **rubers* > (15.9) **ruberz* > (22.3) **ruberr* > (39.8) *ruber* {ruber} 'red'

Unit 36: The PIE Laryngeals in Latin

E1. **A** **h₁eŭsō* > (x2.5) **eŭsō* > (9.10) **oŭsō* > (15.6) **oŭzō* > (26.1) **oŭrō* > (10.3) **ṓrō* > (10.4) *ūrō* {uro} 'I burn' **B** **i̯eh₁-k-ai̯* > (x2.8) **i̯ēkai̯* > (8.1) **i̯ēkei̯* > (10.8) **i̯ēkē* > (10.9) **i̯ēkī* {ieci} 'I threw' **C** **ĝenh₁os* > (x1.2) **genh₁os* > (x2.5) **genos* > (9.18) *genus* {genus} 'race' **D** **pleh₁nos* > (x2.8) **plēnos* > (9.18) *plēnus* {plenus} 'full'

E2. **A** **h₂eĝ-s-i-s* > (x1.2) **h₂egsis* > (13.6) **h₂eksis* > (x2.1) **h₂aksis* > (x2.6) *aksis* {axis} 'axis' **B** **h₂eŭsom* > (x2.1)**h₂aŭsom* > (x2.6) **aŭsom* > (15.6) **aŭzom* > (26.1) **aŭrom* > (9.18) *aŭrum* {aurum} 'gold' **C** **h₂eŭis* > (x2.1) **h₂aŭis* > (x2.6) **aŭis* {auis} 'bird' **D** **h₂eŭsōsā* > (x2.1) **h₂aŭsōsā* > (x2.6) **aŭsōsā* > (1.6) **aŭsōsa* > (15.6) **aŭzōza* > (26.1) **aŭrōra* {aurora} 'dawn'

E3. **A** **steh₂-se* > (x2.3) **stah₂se* > (x2.9) **stāse* > (15.6) **stāze* > (26.1) *stāre* {stare} 'to stand' **B** **bʰeh₂ĝos* > (x2.3) **bʰah₂gos* > (x2.9) **bʰāgos* > (x6.1) **βāgos* > (x6.5a) **φāgos* > (x6.5b) **fāgos* > (9.18)*fāgus* {fagus} 'beech tree' **C** **k̂leh₂m̥* > (x1.1) **kleh₂m̥* > (x2.3) **klah₂m̥* > (x2.9) **klām* > (1.4) *klam* {clam} 'secretly' **D** **gʷih₂ŭos* > (x2.11) **gʷīŭos* > (x4.2) **gŭīŭos* > (30.11) **ŭīŭos* > (9.18) *ŭīŭus* {uiuus} 'alive'

E4. **A** **h₃neh₃mn̥* > (x2.13) **neh₃mn̥* > (x2.4) **noh₃mn̥* > (x2.10) **nōmn̥* > (x5.6) *nōmen* {nomen} 'name' **B** **bʰleh₃ros* > (x2.4) **bʰloh₃ros* > (x2.10) **bʰlōros* > (x6.1) **βlōros* > (x6.5a) **φlōros* > (x6.5b) **flōros* > (9.18) *flōrus* {florus} 'reddish-yellow'

KEY

Overview of the SCN-Rules

Vowels

    Quantitative Vowel Changes

        1   Vowel Weakening

        2   Vowel Lengthening

        3   Vowel Contraction

        4   Syncope and Apocope

        5   Anaptyxis

        6   Emergence of Anaptyctic Vowels next to Syllabic *[r̥] and *[n̥] after Syncope

    Qualitative Vowel Changes

        7   Vowel Assimilation

        8   Vowel Weakening in Medial Syllables

           Results of Vowel Weakening in Medial Syllables in CL Sorted by Vowels

           Vowel Weakening of Diphthongs with Subsequent Monophthongization

        9.1–9.27   Developments of Short Vowels

        9.28–9.32 Developments of Long Vowels

        10 Developments of Diphthongs

        11 Deep Structure of Monophthongization Processes

Consonants

    Assimilation / Dissimilation

        12–17   Assimilation of Manner of Articulation

        18–19   Assimilation of Place of Articulation

        20–22   Assimilation of Manner and Place of Articulation

        23 Dissimilation

        24 Dissimilatory Deletion of Sounds / Metathesis

    Various Sound Changes

        25 The Sporadic Changes d > r and d > l

        26 The Change z > r

        27 Semivowels Become Vowels: i̯ > i and u̯ > u

        28 Velar [ɫ]

    Emergence of Sounds

        Emergence of Epenthetic Consonants

    Deletion of sounds

        30 Simplification in the Initial Position

        31–37   Simplification in the Medial Position

        38 Simplification in the Final Position

        39 Simplification of Double Consonants

        40 The Semivowels /i̯/ and /u̯/

From PIE to Latin

    Consonants

        x1   PIE Palatal and Velar Stops Merge

        x2   Development of PIE Laryngeals

        x3   PIE */tt/ Transforms into Latin /ss/.

        x4   The Monophonematic Labiovelars become a Sequence of Two Phonemes

        x5   Anaptyctic Vowels next to Syllabic Resonants

        x6–x8   Development of PIE Mediae Aspiratae

        x9   Change of /m/ to /b/ before a Liquid

        x10 Weakening of Nasals before a Fricative

        x11 Assimilation of /d/ and /g/ to /i̯/ following

Ac0-Ac2 Accent rules

Quantitative Vowel Changes

Vowel Shortening

SCN	Rule	Example	Short description
1.1	$\bar{V} > V \,/\, \_V$	*fŭit > fuit*	Vocalis ante vocalem corripitur: 'a long vowel before a vowel is shortened'. In Plautus, /ū/ and /ī/ are preserved as long vowels before a vowel. Other longs vowels had been shortened in this position in prehistoric times.
1.2	$\bar{V} > V \,/\, \_RC$	**u̯ēntus > u̯entus*	Osthoff's law: A long vowel is shortened before a resonant plus a consonant. This rule was active in Proto-Italic and Latin.
1.3	$\breve{V}C\bar{V} > \breve{V}CV$	*egō >ego*	Correptio iambica: A disyllabic iambic word was shortened on the second syllable.
1.4	$\bar{V} > V \,/\, \_C\#$ (C = s)	*laŭdāt > laŭdat*	Long vowels in final long syllables were shortened except before final /s/.
1.5	$\bar{V}C_1 > VC_1C_1$	*līttera > littera*	The littera-rule: A long high vowel /ī/ or /ū/ plus a single voiceless consonant was replaced by a short vowel plus a double consonant.[1] Cf. SCN 39 for the simplification of double consonants.
1.6	$\bar{a} > a \,/\, \_\#$	**terrā > terra*	The nom. sg. of the a-declension originally ended with a long vowel /ā/, as evidenced by other PIE languages.[2]

Vowel Lengthening

SCN	Rule	Example	Short description
2.1	$V > \bar{V} \,/\, \_n(f, s)$	**mansī > mānsī*	Every CL vowel is lengthened before /nf/ and /ns/. Cf. SCN 2.4 and SCN x10.
2.2	$z > 0 \,/\, \_G$ +compensatory lengthening	> (15.1) **kozmis > *kōmis* {comis}	Voiced [z] was lost with compensatory lengthening of the preceding vowel. This happened also in secondary groups in which a voiced consonant had been lost before /s/.
2.3	$V > \bar{V} \,/\, \_Dtus$ D = (d, g)	*agō :: *agtos > *āgtos > (12.7) *āktos > (9.18)*	Lachmann's law: The PPP of some verbal roots that end in a voiced stop exhibit a lengthening of the root vowel.[3]
2.4	$V > \bar{V} \,/\, \_ŋkt$	**saŋktus > sāŋktus* {sanctus}	This lengthening is attested in inscriptions. It is identical to SCN 2.1 if /k/ in the cluster /kt/ developed into a fricative /χ/, just as in Umbrian. There is an overlap with SCN 2.3 in forms such as *i̯ūŋktus* {iunctus} and *frāktus* {fractus} from *i̯uŋgō* {iungo} and *fraŋgō* {frango}. Cf. SCN x10.2.
2.5	$i > \bar{i} \,/\, \_ŋn$	> (9.6) **siŋnum >* CL *sīŋnum*	Sporadic inscriptional attestations. The Romance languages do not show vowel lengthening in this position.
2.6	$V > \bar{V} \,/\, \_rC$	*forma > fôrma*	This sporadic sound change is attested in inscriptions as well as by reflexes in the Romance languages.

Vowel Contraction

SCN	Rule	Example	Short description
3.1	$V+V > \bar{V}$	(40.1) > **trees > trēs*	Vowels of the same quality contract to a long vowel of the same quality.
3.2	$a+e > \bar{a}$[4]	**laŭdāi̯es > (40.1) *laŭdāes > (1.1) *laŭdaes > laŭdās*	/a/ prevails before short /e/.
3.3	$a+\bar{e} > \bar{e}$	**laŭdāi̯ēs > (40.1) *laŭdāēs > (1.1) *laŭdaēs > laŭdēs*	/a/ does not prevail before long /ē/.

---

1   Cf. Michael Weiss in *http://conf.ling.cornell.edu/weiss/Observations_on_the_littera_rule.pdf*.

2   This shortening is usually considered to be an analogical takeover of the vocative form into the nominative (cf. Weiss 2009:232 or Meiser 1998:132). In disyllabic words like **fugā > fuga* 'escape', there is an overlap with the correptio iambica SCN 1.3.

3   The exact process is much more complicated. The assimilation of voice is expected at an early PIE stage, which would have eliminated the reason for the vowel lengthening. For further information cf. Jasanoff, Jay (2004). "Plus ça change... Lachmann's Law in Latin" in J.H.W. Penney, *Indo-European Perspectives: Studies in Honour of Anna Morpurgo Davies*. Oxford, 405–416.

4   I posit that this vowel contraction took place after SCN 1.1. It is, however, also possible to assume a direct contraction of the short and long vowel.

3.4	a+ō > ō	*laudā i̯ō > (40.1) laudāō > (1.1) *lau̯aō > lau̯dō	/a/ does not prevail before long /ō/.
3.5	o+a > ō	*ko-agō > kōgō {cogo}	/o/ prevails before /a/.
3.6	o+e > ō	*ko-emō > kōmō {como}	/o/ prevails before /e/.
3.7	e+a > ē	dē-agō > (1.1) de-agō > dēgō	/ē/ prevails before /a/.
3.8	ae̯+V > ae̯	prae̯-itor > prae̯tor {praetor}	/ae̯/ {ae} prevails before any vowel.

Syncope and Apocope

SCN	Rule	Example	Short description
4.1	V > 0 / C_C	*deksiter > dekster {dexter}	**Syncope in medial syllables**: A short vowel is lost between two consonants. Syncope is the counterpart to anaptyxis.
4.2	V > 0 / C_s#	sakros > sakr̥s > (6.1)	**Syncope in final syllables**: The oldest Latin inscriptions present unsyncopated forms such as sakros 'holy', which developed to CL saker {sacer}.[5]
4.3	e > 0 / C_#	{face} fake > fak {fac}	**Apocope**: A final short vowel is deleted. Examples are furnished by the short imperative forms dīk {dic} 'say!', dūk {duc} 'lead!', fak {fac} 'do!', fer {fer} 'carry!'.

Anaptyxis

SCN	Rule	Example	Short description
5.1	0 > i / C_l	*faklis > fakilis {facilis}	**Anaptyxis**: Consonant clusters are broken up to facilitate their pronunciation. The quality of the anaptyctic vowel depends on the quality of the sound following. /i/ is inserted before palatal /l/, and /u/ is inserted before velar [ł]. Anaptyxis is the counterpart to syncope.
5.2	0 > u / C_ł	{extemplo} > ekstempło > ekstempuło {extempulo}	

Anaptyctic Vowels Next to Syllabic *[r̥] and *[n̥] after Latin Syncope

SCN	Rule	Examples	Short description
6.1	r > r̥ / C_C[6]	(4.2) > *sakrs > *sakr̥s > (6.2)	Anaptyctic vowels emerge next to newly formed syllabic resonants after Latin syncope. Cf. SCN x5.
6.2	r̥ > er	(6.1) > *sakr̥s > *sakers > (15.9)	
6.3	n > n̥ / C_C	*skábnolom > *skábn̥lom > (6.4)	
6.4	n̥ > in	(6.3) > *skábn̥lom > *skábinlom > (21.2)	

Qualitative Vowel Changes

Vowel Assimilation

SCN	Rule	Example	Short description
7.1	e...i > i...i	*nesī > nisī > (1.3)	In regressive assimilations, the quality of a vowel assimilates to the quality of a vowel following.
7.2	a...i > a...a	*kalimitās > kalamitās	In progressive assimilations, the quality of a vowel assimilates to the quality of a preceding vowel.
7.3	a...e > a...a	karker > VL karkar	
7.4	e ...o > o ...o	> (x11.3) *ku̯eku̯ō > *ku̯oku̯ō > (40.5)	= SCN 9.11. The 'o-umlaut' is a vowel assimilation caused by a non-adjacent velar vowel.

---

5   Final -ros like in sakros was most often syncopated. The nominative of the ti-stems such as mors < *mortis and dōs < *dōtis was also subject to syncope, and damnā́s < *damnā́tos shows that to-formations were subject to syncope as well. This mean that nominative forms such as the PPP -tus < *-tos are alltogether analogically restituted forms (Cf. Meiser 1998:73).

6   This step is the immediate consequence of the preceding syncope. Both developments habe been separated only for didactic reasons.

Vowel Weakening in Medial Syllables in Chronological Order

LWP	Phase 1	Example	Short description
8.1	a > e	*ákkapiō > *akkepiō > (8.3)	/a/ is raised to /e/ in all syllables.
8.2	o > e / _C[7] (C ≠ ł)	*sókiotās > *sókietās	/o/ is fronted to /e/ in open syllables except before [ł]. It remains after /i/.
8.3	e > i / _C	*ákkepiō > *ákkipiō > (Ac1)	/e/ is raised to /i/ in open syllables.
8.4	u > i / _C	*káputes > *kápites > (9.8)	/u/ is fronted to /i/.
8.5	i > y / _P	*árripiō > *árrypiō > (Ac1)	Allophonic rounding of /i/ to [y] before labial sounds.
8.6	u > y / _P	*ób-stupēskō > *óbstypēskō	Allophonic rounding of /u/ to [y] before labial sounds.
	Phase 2		
8.7	e > i / _ŋ	*átteŋgō > áttiŋgō > (Ac1)	/e/ is raised to /i/ in closed syllables before [ŋ]. Cf. 9.6.
8.8	e > o / _ł[8]	*ókkełō > *ókkołō > (8.10)	/e/ is backed to /o/ before [ł]. Cf. 9.9.
8.9	e > o / _u̯[9]	*ábleu̯ō > *áblou̯ō > (8.11)	/e/ is backed to /o/ before /u̯/. Cf. 9.10 and 10.2.
8.10	o > u / _ł	*ókkołō > ókkułō	/o/ is raised to /u/ before [ł]. Cf 9.21.
8.11	o > u / _u̯	*áblou̯ō > ábluu̯ō	/o/ is raised to /u/ before /u̯/.
8.12	o > u / _CC	*prómonturium > prómunt...	/o/ is raised to /u/ in closed syllables.

CL Results of Vowel Weakening in Medial Syllables

/a/	a > i / _C	*ádrapiō > (8.1) *ádrepiō > (8.3) > *ádripiō > (Ac1) adrípiō
	a > e / _CC	*ádraptus > (8.1) *ádreptus > (Ac1) adréptus
	a > e / _r	pario 'I bring forth' :: perf. *péparī > (8.1) péperī
	a > e / _i̯	*kón-i̯akiant > (8.1) *kón-i̯ekiant > (Ac1) kon-i̯ékiant {conieciant}
	a > u / _ł	*dḗsaltor > (8.1) *dḗseltor > (8.7) *dḗsoltor > (8.10) *dḗsultor > (Ac1)
	a > u / _u̯	*áblau̯ō > (8.1) *ábleu̯ō > (8.8) *áblou̯ō > (8.11) ábluu̯ō {abluo}
	a > y {u/i} / _(f, m, b)	*kón-tabernālis > (8.1) *kónteber... > (8.3) *kóntiber... > (8.5) kóntyber...
/e/	e > i / _C	élegō > (8.3) éligō {eligo}
	e > i / _V[10]	lankea > (8.3) VL *lankia > (9.13) *lanki̯a > Italian lancia
	e > u / _ł	*ókkełō > (8.7) *ókkołō > (8.10) ókkułō {occulo}
	e > y {u/i} / _(f, m, b)	*éks-premō > (8.1) *éks-primō > éks-prymō {exprimo}
/i/	i > u / _u̯	*trídiu̯om > tríduu̯om {triduum}
	i > y {u/i} / _(f, m, b)	póntifeks > (8.5) póntyfeks {pontifex}
/o/	o > i / _C	*kúpido-tās > (8.2) *kúpide-tās > (8.3) kúpidi-tās > (Ac1) kupíditās
	o > e / _r and _C#	*lū́kifor > (8.2) lū́kifer {lucifer}
	o > e / _i̯	*pi̯otās > pi̯etās {pietas}
	o > u / _CC (C≠ r)	*prṓ-montōrium > (8.12) *prṓ-muntōrium > (Ac1) prō-muntṓrium
	o > u / _ł (≠ i, e, u̯_)	*sḗdolōd > (8.10) *sḗdulōd > (38.3) sḗdułō {sedulo}
	o > u / _u̯	*kṓn-flou̯ō > (8.11) kṓn-fluu̯ō {confluo}
	o > y {i, u} / _(f, m, b)	*áu̯rofaks > (8.2) *áu̯refeks > (8.3) *áu̯rifeks > (8.5) áu̯ryfeks {aurifex}

---

7   This development is attested in the inscription {apolenei}, cf. Weiss 2009:120.

8   This is not really a 'weakening' process because the vowel was not raised to /i/ but backed to /o/.

9   This rule had already been active in Proto-Italic times in stressed initial syllables (cf. SCN 9.10). It is thus a 'persistent' sound change which happens again and again and cannot be chronologically classified. It seems to have been caused by the inherent phonological structure of Latin.

10   A VL development which is the intermediate step of the following consonantification of /i/ to /i̯/.

INDEX

	u > i /_C	*káputis > kápitis {capitis}
/u/	? u > e /_r	*sokur > (A: gener) soker {socer}
	u > y {u/i} /_(f, m, b)	stupeō :: *ob-stupēskō > ob-stypēskō {obstupesco}

Vowel Weakening of Diphthongs with Subsequent Monophthongization

	ai̯ > ei̯	*kai̯dō > kae̯dō {caedo} :: *ínkai̯dō > (8.1) *ínkei̯dō > (Ac1)
/ai̯/	ei̯ > ę̄	> (8.1) *ínkei̯dō > (Ac1) *inkéi̯dō > (10.8) *inkę̄́dō > (10.9)
	ę̄ > ī	> (10.8) *inkę̄́dō > (10.9) inkī́dō {incido}
	au̯ > eu̯	klau̯dō {claudo} :: *ínklau̯dō > (8.1) *ínkleu̯dō > (8.9)
/au̯/	eu̯ > ou̯	> (8.1) *ínkleu̯dō > (8.9) *ínklou̯dō > (10.3)
	ou̯ > ǭ	> (8.9) *ínklou̯dō > (Ac1) *inklóu̯dō > (10.3) *inklǭ́dō > (10.4)
	ǭ > ū	(10.3) *inklǭ́dō > (10.4) inklū́dō {includo}
/oi̯/[11]	oi̯ > ei̯	*póst-moi̯riom > (8.2) *póstmei̯riom > (37.3) *pósmei̯riom > (15.1) *pózmei̯riom > (2.2)
	ei̯ > ę̄	(15.1) *pózmei̯riom > (2.2+Ac1) *pōméi̯riom > (10.8) *pōmę̄́riom > (9.18) pōmę̄́rium

Developments of Short /a/

SCN	Rule	Example	Short description
9.1	a > e /_i̯_i̯	OL {iaiento} i̯ai̯entō > i̯ei̯entō {ieiento}	/a/ is raised to /e/ between palatal /i̯/.
9.2	a > o /_u̯_	u̯akuus :: {uaciuos} u̯akī́u̯os > u̯okī́u̯os {uociuos}	/a/ is raised to /e/ after velar /u̯/. Cf. 9.22.

Developments of Short /e/

SCN	Rule	Example	Short description
9.3	e > i	penna > VL pinna	Dialectal tendency to raise /e/ to /i/.
9.4	e > i /_rk	sterkus > VL stirkus	Dialectal tendency to raise /e/ to /i/.
9.5	e > i /_mb	*ember > imber	/e/ is raised to /i/ before /mb/. Cf. 9.6, 9.7, 9.16, 9.17.
9.6	e > i /_ŋ	(17.5) > *seŋnom > *siŋnom > (2.5)	/e/ is closed to /i/ before [ŋ]. Vowel lengthening according to SCN 2.5 in CL.
9.7	e > i / m_nV[12]	*meneru̯a > mineru̯a	There are very few examples for this SC.
9.8	e > i /_C#	i̯ūnōnes > i̯ūnōnis	Highly frequent SC. Symmetrical to 9.18.
9.9	e > o /_ł	*u̯elō > u̯olō	/e/ is backed to /o/ before [ł]. Cf. 8.8.
9.10	e > o /_u̯	*breu̯ma > *brou̯ma > (10.3)	= 10.2. This SC operated in PIT and Latin. Cf. 8.9 for the unstressed position.
9.11	e > o / u̯_C(C)V (V =a, o, u)	du̯enos > *du̯onos > (40.11)	The 'o-umlaut' is a vowel assimilation due to a velar vowel following (cf. SCN 7.4).

---

11   The reflex of /oi̯/ in medial syllables is unclear due to ambiguous evidence.

   12   Formulation of the rule according to Weiss 2009:137.

Developments of Short /i/

SCN	Rule	Example	Short description
9.12a	i > y {y} / #(f, u̯, m)_r	u̯ir > VL u̯yr {uyr} firmus > VL fyrmus {fyrmus}	Rare allophonic rounding of /i/ to [y] between a labial sound and /r/. Cf. 9.20 and 9.29.
9.12b	y > i	*optymus > optimus	Derounding of [y] to /i/. The Romance languages do not preserve any trace of a rounded [y].
9.13	i > i̯ / C_V	gau̯dia > gau̯di̯a	Consonantification of /i/ to the corresponding semivowel /i̯/, which is already found in Ennius. This sound change is very common in VL.
9.14a	i > e / _#	*mari > mare	/i/ is lowered to /e/ in the final position.
9.14b	i > e / _r	*sisō > (15.6) > *sizō > (26.1) > *sirō > serō	/i/ is lowered to /e/ before /r/. Cf. the results of syllable weakening SCN 8 before /r/.

Developments of Short /o/

SCN	Rule	Example	Short description
9.15	o > e / #u̯_ (s,t,rC)	u̯oster > u̯ester	Dissimilation of /o/ to /e/ next to /u̯/.
9.16	o > u / _ŋ	{honc} hoŋk > huŋk {hunc}	/o/ is raised to /u/ before [ŋ]. Cf SCN 9.6.
9.17	o > u / _m	*homos > *humos > (9.18)	Sporadic SC. Not as frequent as 9.16.
9.18	o > u / _C(C)#	> (x2.10) *dōnom > dōnum	/o/ is raised to /u/ in closed final syllables. Symmetrical to SCN 9.8.
9.19	o > u / u̯_ [13]	seku̯ontur > seku̯untur {sequuntur}	/o/ is raised to /u/ after /u̯/.
9.20	o > u / f_r ? o > y / f_r	formika > furmika {furmica}	/o/ is raised to /u/ between a labial sound and /r/. Cf. 9.12a. Maybe rounding to [y].
9.21	o > u / _ɫC	*koɫpa > kuɫpa {culpa}	/o/ is raised to /u/ before [ɫ].
9.22	o > a / _u̯	*lou̯ō > lau̯ō {lauo}	Rule of Thurneysen and Havet.

Developments of Short /u/

SCN	Rule	Example	Short description
9.23	u > y {i, u, y} / l_P	lubet > lybet {libet} klupeus > klypeus {klipeus}	Allophonic rounding of /u/ to [y] between /l/ and a labial sound. Cf. 9.12a, 9.20.
9.24	u > u̯ / C_V	u̯idua > *u̯idu̯a {uidua}	/u/ becomes the semivowel /u̯/.
9.25	u > u̯ / VR_V	soɫuō > soɫu̯ō {soluo}	Special case of 9.24 after a resonant.
9.26	? u > o / _#	(38.2) > *Tereboniu > Terebonio	/u/ is lowered to /o/ in the final position.
9.27	u > o / _r	*fusē > (15.6) *fuzē > (26.1) > *furē > (1.3) > *fure > fore	Very rare SC. Cf 9.14b.

Developments of the Long Vowels

SCN	Rule	Example	Short description
9.28	ā > ē / i̯_	{ianua} i̯ānua > i̯ēnua {ienua}	Few examples in imperial times.
9.29	ō > ū / P_r	ferre :: *fōr > fūr {fur}	Only in monosyllabic words. Cf. 9.20, 9.27.

---

13   The sound change o > u was delayed after /u̯/ and carried through fully about 50 BC.

INDEX

SCN	Rule	Example	Short description
9.30	ō > ā / _u̯	{octo} oktṓ :: *oktṓu̯us > oktáu̯us {octauus}	Cf. 9.22.
9.31	ū > ī / _i̯V	*pū́i̯os > pī́i̯os > (40.1) *pī́os > (1.1) *pios > (9.18) pius	The Pius-Rule. Assimilation of /ū/ to a /i̯/ following.
9.32	ē > ī /…i	*subtḗlis > subtī́lis dēlḗniō > dēlī́niō	/ē/ is raised to /ī/ in case of an /i/ in the next syllable.

Developments of the Diphthongs

SCN	Rule	Example	Short description
10.1	au̯ > ǭ[14]	lau̯tus > VL lṓtus	The pronunciation /ǭ/ for /au̯/ was regarded as vulgar.
10.2	eu̯ > ou̯	*neu̯os > *nou̯os > (9.18)	This sound change was already active in PIT and remained active in Latin, too. Cf. SCN 8.9 and SCN 9.10.
10.3	ou̯ > ǭ	> (15.2) *lou̯zna > *lǭzna > (10.4)	Monophthongization of /ou̯/ to /ǭ/ before it was raised to /ū/.
10.4	ǭ > ū	> (10.3) *lǭzna > (2.2) lǫ́na > lū́na {luna}	/ǭ/ is raised to /ū/ as a final step in the process of the monophthongization of /ou̯/ to /ū/.
10.5	ou̯ > *oi̯ / #l_P	*lou̯ber > *loi̯ber > (10.13)	This dissimilation of labial /u̯/ to /i̯/ before a labial sound is seen only in very few examples.
10.6	ai̯ > ae̯	{aidem} ai̯dem > ae̯dem > (10.7)	The lowering i̯ > e̯ of the second element of the diphthong was the first step of its further monophthongization to long open /ẹ̄/, which was avoided in CL, but was very common in VL and rural areas in CL times already.
10.7	ae̯ > VL ē̜	> (10.6) ae̯dem > VL *ē̜dem	Monophthongization of /ae̯/ to /ē̜/ in VL.
10.8	ei̯ > ẹ̄	*dei̯u̯os > *dẹ̄u̯os > (10.9)	The diphthong /ei̯/ was monophthongized to /ẹ̄/ before it was raised to /ī/ by SCN 10.9. In rural areas, this sound change halted at the stage /ẹ̄/, analogous to SCN 10.3.[15]
10.9	ẹ̄ > ī	> (10.8) *dẹ̄u̯os > *dī́u̯os > (9.18)	The monophthongization of /ei̯/ yielded the intermediate step /ẹ̄/, which was raised to /ī/ in CL. The monophthongizations ei̯ > ī and ou̯ > ū are parallel processes and proceeded via the intermediate steps /ẹ̄/ and /ǭ/.
10.10	oi̯ > oe̯	oi̯nos > *oe̯nos > (10.11)	Analogous to SCN 10.6. After the lowering i̯ > e̯ of the second element of the diphthong, /oi̯/ remained in the initial position after /p/ or /f/, as seen in *poi̯na > poe̯na, if there was no /i/ in the next syllable. In this case, it developed further via SCN 10.11.[16]
10.11	oe̯ > ǭ	> (10.10) *oe̯nos > *ǭnos > (10.4) > *ūnos > (9.18) ūnus {unus}	Monophthongization of /oe̯/ to /ǭ/, which shares the same later evolution as /ǭ/ which had originated out of /ou̯/. Subsequent raising to /ū/.
10.12	oi̯ > ei̯ / #u̯_	*u̯oi̯kos > *u̯ei̯kos > (10.8) *u̯ẹ̄kos > (10.9) *u̯īkos > (9.18) u̯īkus {uicus}	After initial /u̯/, the diphthong /oi̯/ became /ei̯/, which joined the further development of original /ei̯/ by SCN 10.8, and was raised via /ẹ̄/ to /ī/.
10.13	oi̯ > ei̯ / l_P	> (10.5) *loi̯ber > *lei̯ber > (10.8) *lẹ̄ber > (10.9) līber	Subsequent development of SCN 10.5. This rule is necessary to explain the long /ī/ in līber {liber}, which is normally suspected only in the context of SCN 10.12.

---

14 Analogous to the development ai̯ > ae̯ and *oi̯ > oe̯, in which the monophthongization was preceded by the lowering of the second element, one can pose the pronunciation /aǭ/ for {au}. Greek transcriptions {ao, aou} for Latin {au} undermine this assumption (cf. Allen 1978:60).

15 Cf. Niedermann 1953:67.

16 The diphthong remained in *moi̯nia > moe̯nia {moenia} 'city walls' despite the /i/ in the next syllable in order to differentiate the word from mūnia {munia} 'tributes' (cf. Meiser 1998:87). After non-initial /p/, /oi̯/ developed to /ū/ such as in *spoi̯ma > spūma {spuma} 'foam'.

Deep Structure of the Monophthongization Processes

	Diphthong	Lowering of Semivowel	Leveling of Vowels	Contraction	Raising of Long Vowel
11.1	ai̯	ae̯	ẹe̯	ẹ̄	
11.2	ei̯	ee̯	ẹe̯	ẹ̄	ī
11.3	oi̯	oe̯	ọo̯	ọ̄	ū
11.4	oi̯	oe̯	ẹe̯	ẹ̄	ī
11.5	au̯	ao̯	ọo̯	ọ̄	
11.6	ou̯	oo̯	ọo̯	ọ̄	ū

Assimilation of Manner of Articulation

Desonorization: Stop + Stop

SCN	Rule	C [+voiced] > [-voiced] / _[-voiced]	Exercises
12.1	b > p / _p	*sub-pressus > suppressus[17]	15.1B
12.2	b > p / _t	*sub-tīlis > suptīlis {subtilis} > (18.1)	22.3A
12.3	b > p / _k	{subcedo} *sub-kēdō > *sup-kēdō > (18.2)	-
12.4	d > t / _p	*ku̯idpe > *ku̯itpe > (18.3)	24.1E, 26.2A/B
12.5	d > t / _t	adtulī > attulī	13.3A, 19.1E, 26.2F
12.6	d > t / _k	{idcirco} idkirkō > *itkirkō > (18.4)	13.3C, 24.1C/D/F, 26.2C, 29.2E
12.7	g > k / _t	*agtos > (2.3) *āgtos > *āktos > (9.18)	11.3A-D, 22.3B/C

Desonorization: Stop + Fricative

SCN	Rule	C [+voiced] > [-voiced] / _[-voiced]	Exercises
13.1	b > p / _f	ob-ferō > *op-ferō > (16.1)	-
13.2	b > p / _s	*plebs > pleps {plebs}[18]	-
13.3	d > t / _f	adferō > *atferō > (16.3)	24.2A
13.4	d > t / _s	*prōdsum > *prōtsum > (16.4)	17.2E, 24.1A/B/G, 24.2D/E, 26.3A/B, 30.2B
13.5	g > k / _f	No examples for this context.	-
13.6	g > k / _s	> (40.4) *eks-stiŋgsī > eks-stiŋksī {exstinxi}	15.3A, 30.3D, 33.1F, 36.2A

Sonorization: Voiceless Stop + Nasal

SCN	Rule	C [-voiced] > [+voiced] / _[+voiced]	Exercises
14.1	p > b / _m	*supmos > *submos > (17.1)	24.2F, 30.1B2
14.2	p > b / _n	> (40.5) *sopnos > *sobnos > (17.2)	17.2A, 23.2A/C
14.3	t > d / _m	No examples for this context.	-
14.4	t > d / _n	*u̯atnos > *u̯adnos > (17.4)	-

---

17 The prefixes *ab- / ob- / sub-* go back to *ap- / *op- / *sup-, all having a voiceless /p/. The final voiced sound was due to Latin internal sandhi. The spelling {sub} was pronounced [sup] before voiceless sounds.

18 /b/ was pronounced /p/ before /s/. {pleps} is an inscriptional form (cf. Niedermann 1953:139).

14.5	k > g / _n	*urkna > urgna > (35.6b)	16.1A, 23.2D
14.6	k > g / ŋ_d[19]	*ku̯īŋkdekem > *ku̯īŋgdekem > (34.4)	-
14.7	k > g / _m	*sekmentum > segmentum > VL (17.6)	30.1A2

Sonorization: The Voiceless Fricative /s/ next to Voiced Sounds

SCN	Rule	s > [+voiced] / [+voiced] _ [+voiced]	Exercises
15.1	s > z / V_m	OL {cosmis} kosmis > *kozmis > (2.2)	27.4A, 30.3D
15.2	s > z / V_n	> (32.1) *lou̯sna > *lou̯zna > (10.3)	11.2ABC, 13.3E, 27.4BCD, 30.3EF
15.3	s > z / V_l	> (23,11) *preslom > *prezlom > (2.2)	25.2C, 27.4EF, 30.3CG
15.4	s > z / V_r	*fūnesris > *fūnezris > (x7.3a)	-
15.5	s > z / V_D	*dis-gerō > *dizgerō > (2.2)	11.2DEFG
15.6	s > z / V_V[20]	PIT *āsa > OL āza {asa} > (26.1)	17.2C, 36.1A, 36.2BD, 36.3A
15.7	s > z / l_	*u̯else > *u̯elze > (22.1)	22.2AC
15.8	s > z / r_V	*ferse > *ferze > (22.2)	22.2B
15.9	s > z / r_#	(6.2) > *sakers > sakerz > (22.3)	29.2CD, 32.5, 34.3E, 35.3B

Fricativization of Stops Before Fricatives

SCN	Rule	C [+stop, -voiced] > [+fricative] / _[+fricative]	Exercises
16.1	p > f / _f	> (13.1) *opferō > offerō	9.1
16.2	p > s / _s	ipsam > (38.1) VL *ipsa > *issa	9.1
16.3	t > f / _f	> (13.3) *atferō > afferō	24.2A
16.4	t > s / _s	> (13.4) *prōtsum > *prōssum > (39.1)	17.2E, 23.3ABCD, 24.1ABG, 4.2BCDE, 26.3AB, 29.1AB, 34.2B
16.5	k > f / _f	{ecferō} ekferō > efferō	-
16.6	k > s / _s	{vixit} u̯īksit > VL u̯īssit {vixit, visit}	-

Stop + Nasal

SCN	Rule	C [+plosive, +voiced] > [+nasal] / _N	Exercises
17.1	b > m / _m	> (14.1) *submos > *summos > (9.18)	24.2FG, 30.1B2
17.2	b > m / _n	> (14.2) *sobnos > *somnos > (9.18)	17.2A, 23.2ABC
17.3	d > n / _m[21]	admou̯eō > *anmou̯eō > (19.3)	22.1C
17.4	d > n / _n	> (14.4) *u̯adnos > *u̯annos > (9.18)	-
17.5	g > ŋ {g} / _n	> (14.5) *segnom > *seŋnom > (9.6)	23.2D, 16.1ABC
17.6	g > m / _m[22]	*flagma > flamma	30.1A2

---

19 In this case, the context is stop before stop.
20 Already in Proto-Italic times.
21 Or assimilation d > m / _m. Cf. SCN 36.3 for the loss of /d/ in the same context.
22 Maybe via g > γ > u̯ > m. An alternative explanation is g > ŋ / _m followed by ŋ > m / _m.

Assimilation of Place of Articulation

Stop + Stop

SCN	Rule	C > C [+place] / _C [+place]	Exercises
		1. Voiceless Stops	
18.1	p > t / _t	{scriptus} *skriptus* > VL **skrittus* {scrittus}	-
18.2	p > k / _k	> (12.3) **supkēdō* > *sukkēdō* {succedo}	-
18.3	t > p / _p	> (12.4) **ku̯itpe* > *ku̯ippe* {quippe}	24.1E, 26.2AB
18.4	t > k / _k	> (12.6) **itkirkō* > *ikkirkō* {iccirco}	13.3BC, 24.1CDF, 26.2C, 29.2E, 30.2C
18.5	k > t / _t	> (12.7) *au̯ktor* > VL *au̯ttor* > (39.1)	-
		2. Voiced Stops	
18.6	b > d / _d	{subduco} *subdūkō* > VL **suddūkō*	-
18.7	b > g / _g	*subgerō* > *suggerō*	-
18.8	d > g / _g	*adgerō* > *aggerō*	-

Nasal + Consonant

SCN	Rule	N > N [+place] / _C [+place][23]	Exercises
19.1	n > m / _p	*in-potēns* > *impotēns*	-
19.2	n > m / _b	*in-berbis* > *imberbis*	-
19.3	n > m / _m	*in-molō* > *immolō*	22.1C
19.4	n > ŋ / _k	*in-kendō* > *iŋkendō* {incendo}	-
19.5	n > ŋ / _g	**ŋguen* > **enguen* > **eŋguen* > *iŋguen* {inguen}	-
19.6	ŋn > ɲɲ[24]	> (17.5) **seŋnom* > VL **seɲɲom*	-
19.7	m > n / _t	**ku̯am-tus* > *ku̯antus* {quantus}	34.1DF
19.8	m > n / _d	**ku̯am-diū* > *ku̯andiū* {quandiu}	23.1ABC
19.9	m > n / _s	*kom-sūmō* > *konsūmō* > (2.1) *kōnsūmō*	-
19.10	m > n / _n[25]	*damnum* > VL **dannum*	-
19.11	m > ŋ / _k	**klam-kułum* > *klaŋkułum* {clanculum}	23.1D, 15.3B

Assimilation of Manner and Place of Articulation

Stop + Liquid

SCN	Rule	B > R / _R (R=r, l; B=d,g)	Exercises
20.1	b > r / _r	**subrigō* > *surrigō*	-
20.2	b > l / _l	{subleuo} *suble̯uō* > VL **sulle̯uō* {sulleuo}	-
20.3	d > r / _r	*adrīdeō* > *arrīdeō*	-
20.4	d > l / _l	{adloquor} *adloku̯or* > *alloku̯or* {alloquor}	19.1B, 22.1AD, 25.2D

---

23 Before labiodental /f/, the assimilation N > ɱ is expected (cf. Allen 1978:29). This assimilation is disregarded in this book because [ɱ] was not phonologically relevant.

24 Probably via a mutual assimilation such as ŋn > ɲn > ɲɲ or ŋn > ŋɲ > ɲɲ.

25 The assimilation can be avoided by the insertion of an epenthetic transitional consonant: *au̯tumnus* > (29.5) *au̯tumpnus*.

Nasal and Liquid before a Liquid or /s/

SCN	Rule	n > R / _R	Exercises
21.1	n > r / _r	*inruō > irruō*	-
21.2	n > l / _l	> (6.4) *skabinlom > *skabillom > (9.18) *skabillum* {scabillum}	22.1A, 30.3B, 34.3AB
21.3	r > l / _l	> (6.2) *agerlos > agellos*	34.3CD
21.4	r > s / _s[26]	*torstus > *tosstus > (39.2) tostus*	-

Liquid before Consonant

SCN	Rule	(z,d) > R / R_	Exercises
22.1	z > l / l_	> (15.7) *u̯elze > u̯elle*	22.2AC
22.2	z > r / r_	> (15.8) *ferze > ferre*	22.2B
22.3	z > r / r_#	> (15.9) *sakerz > *sakerr > (39.8)	29.2CD, 32.5, 34.3E, 35.3B
22.4	d > l / l_	*sāl* 'salt' :: *saldō > sallō*	-

Dissimilation of Consonants

SCN	Rule	Examples	Exercises
	X...X > Y...X	**Regressive Dissimilation**	
23.1	l...l > r...l	*ka̯eluleus > ka̯eruleus* {caeruleus}	25.1, 25.2
23.2	l...l > n...l	*kultellus > kuntellus* {cuntellus}	-
23.3	r...r > l...r	*peregrīnus > pelegrīnus*	-
23.4	r...r > n...r	{meretrix} *meretrīks > menetrīks* {menetrix}	-
23.5	n...n > r...n	*kanmen > karmen* {carmen}	-
23.6	n...n > l...n	*monimentum* > VL *molimentum*	25.1G
23.7	d...d > r...d	*medīdiēs > merīdiēs*	-
23.8	m...b > n...b	*temesra̯e > (...) *temebra̯e > tenebra̯e*	-
	X...X > X...Y	**Progressive Dissimilation**	
23.9	l...l > l...r	*singulālis > singulāris*	25.1ADEF, 25.2A
23.10	r...r > r...l	*presrom > *preslom > (15.3)	25.2CD

Dissimilatory Deletion of Sounds / Methesis

SCN	Rule	Examples	Exercises
	X...X > 0...X	**Dissimilatory Deletion of Sounds**	
24.1	r...r > 0...r	*traberna > taberna*	-
24.2	r...r > r...0	*pra̯estrīgia̯e* > VL *pra̯estīgia̯e*	-
24.3	l...l > 0...l	{caluor} :: *kalu̯illa* > VL *kau̯illa* {cauilla}	-
24.4	ł...ł > ł...0	*alterułtrum > alterutrum*	-
24.5	n...n > 0...n	*Sabnīnī > Sabīnī*	-

26   This rule is needed for the derivation of the deep-structural assimilation of SCN 33.

24.6	sC...sC > sC...C	*stāre :: *ste-st-ī = *stestī > stetī*	-
24.7	P...P > P...0	{fauilla} *fauilla* > VL *fai̯lla*	-
	X...Y > Y...X	**Metathesis**	-
24.8	au̯rV > aru̯V	{pauci} *pau̯kī :: *pau̯ros > paru̯os > (9.18) > paru̯us* {paruus}	-
24.9	dn > nd	*udna > unda*	-
24.10	ps > sp	*u̯opsa > *u̯ospa > (9.15) u̯espa* {uespa}	-

Various Sound Changes

The Sporadic Changes d > r and d > l

SCN	Rule	d > R	Exercises
25.1	d > r / a_(u̯, f, b)	*bae̯tō :: *ad-bīter > arbīter > (?) arbiter* [27]	-
25.2	d > l	*odor* 'smell' :: *odēre > olēre* 'to smell'	-

The Change z > r

SCN	Rule	z > r	Exercises
26.1	z > r / V_V	(15.6) > *āza* {asa} > *āra*	17.2C, 36.1A, 36.2BD, 36.3A
26.2	z > r / _g	*mezgō > mergō*	-
26.3	z > r / _u̯	*Menezu̯a > Meneru̯a > (9.7)*	-

The Semivowels /i̯/ and /u̯/ Become /i/ and /u/

SCN	Rule	Examples	Exercises
27.1	i̯ > i / C_C [28]	*medʰi̯os > *medʰios > (x6.2) *meδios > *medios > (9.18) medius* {medius}	-
27.2	u̯ > u / C_C [29]	*kón-ku̯atiō > (4.1) *kóŋku̯tiō > kóŋkutiō > (Ac1) koŋkútiō* {concutio}	9.1

Palatal /l/ and Its Positional Velar Allophone [ł]

SCN	Rule	l > ł	Exercises
28.1	l > ł / _C [30]	*kolpa > kołpa* {colpa}	17.1A, 18.2ABC, 18.3GHI
28.2	l > ł / V_#	*konsol > konsoł* {consol}	9.1, 18.2D
28.3	l > ł / _(a,o,u)	> (40.3) > *okłos > *okłos > (9.18) *okłus > (5.2) okulus* {oculus}	17.1BC, 28.3EF, 35.1D, 35.2A
28.4	t > k / _ł	*pōtłom > *pōkłom > (9.18) *pōkłum > (5.2) pōkułum* {poculum}	21.1B, 28.3E

---

27 The vowel shortening in *arbiter* is unexplained.
28 Opposite to SCN 9.13.
29 Opposite to SCN 9.24/25.
30 Only if the following consonant is not /l/.

Epenthetic Consonants

SCN	Rule	0 > C	Exercises
29.1	0 > t / ss_r	{claudo} *klau̯dō* :: **klau̯d-trom* > (12.5) **klau̯ttrom* > (x3) **klau̯ssrom* > **klau̯sstrom* > (39.2) **klau̯strom* > (9.18) *klau̯strum* {claustrum}	-
29.2	0 > p / m_l	**amlus* > *amplus*	-
29.3	0 > p / m_s	*hiems* > VL *hiemps*	-
29.4	0 > p / m_t[31]	*kōmō* {como} :: **kōmtus* > *kōmptus* {comptus}	-
29.5	0 > p / m_n	*au̯tumnus* > VL *au̯tumpnus*	-

Deletion of consonants

Simplification in the Initial Position[32]

SCN	Rule	C > 0 / #_	Exercises
30.1	k > g / #_n	**knīdōs* > **gnīdōs* > (30.2a) > **ŋnīdōs* > (30.2b) **nīdōs* > (…) *nīdor*[33]	28.3I
30.2a	g > ŋ / #_n[34]	> (x2.17) **gnātos* > **ŋnātos* > (30.2b)	28.1ABC, 28.3I
30.2b	ŋ > 0 / #_n	> (30.2a) **ŋnātos* > **nātos* > (9.18) *nātus* {natus}	28.1ABC, 28.3I
30.4	t > d / #_l[35]	> (x2.16) **tlātos* > **dlātos* > (30.5) **lātos* > (9.18) *lātus* 'carried'	-
30.5	d > 0 / #_l	**dloŋgos* > **loŋgos* > (9.18) *loŋgus*[36] {longus}	28.3H
30.6	d > 0 / #_i̯	*Di̯ou̯em* {diouem} > *I̯ou̯em* {iouem}	9.1
30.7	p > 0 / #_s	**psternuō* > *sternuō*	28.3FG
30.8	k > 0 / #_s	**ksentis* > *sentis*	28.3DE
30.9	k > 0 / #_u̯u	> (x7.7) **ku̯ubei̯* > **u̯ubei̯* > (40.10) **ubei̯* > (10.8/9) > *ubī* 'where?'[37]	9.1
30.10	p > 0 / #_t	Greek *ptisanē* > Latin *tisana*	-
30.11	g > 0 / #_u̯	> (x4.1) **gu̯ii̯os* > **u̯ii̯os* > (9.18) *u̯ii̯us* {uiuus}	33.2AB, 34.1F, 36.3D
30.12	s > 0 / #_(n,m,l)[38]	**snō* > *nō* {no} derived from *nāre* 'to swim'	28.1DE, 28.3AEJ

Simplification in the Medial Position

INFO In Latin, all consonant clusters of three or more consonants were simplified. The loss of consonants can be modeled as a deep-structural assimilation followed by a simplification of the newly formed double consonant. In the following, both models are presented. The letter a. stands for loss, the letter b. stands for assimilation with the subsequent simplification of the newly formed double consonant. The rules needed for the deep-structural assimilations are normally considered as vulgar.

---

31 The insertion of an epenthetic transitional consonant can be avoided by the assimilation **kōmtus* > (19.7) **kōntus*.
32 Internal and external reconstruction are grouped together here. For the loss of /u̯/ cf. SCN 40.
33 Weiss 2009:169 cites the attested **knīksos* > **gnīksos* > (9.18) *gnīksus* {gnixus} > (30.2) CL *nīksus* {nixus}.
34 The corresponding development in the medial position (SCN 17.5) corroborates the intermediate step *[ŋ] in the initial position.
35 This rule can be supposed in analogy to SCN 30.5. Otherwise, one must assume a direct loss: t > 0 / #_l.
36 In this word, expected SCN 9.16 was not carried through.
37 In analogy to SCN 30.3 and SCN 30.1, the sonorization k > g is expected. The development k > 0 appears only in words of this pronominal stem and could be due to a wrong separation *k-ubi* in analogy to *alikubi* {alicubi}, which was analysed as *alik-ubi*.
38 An intermediate step of a voiced [z], which disappeared similar to SCN 2.2, can be assumed here.

The Espresso-Rule[39]

SCN	Rule	T > 0 / _sC (T = p, t, k)	Exercises
31.1	p > 0 / _sC	a. *apsportō > asportō b. *apsportō > (16.2) *assportō > (39.2) asportō	30.3A
31.2	t > 0 / _sC	a. adspikio > (13.4) atspikiō > aspikiō {aspicio} b. adspikio > (13.4) atspikiō > (16.4) *asspikiō > (39.2) aspikiō	30.3D
31.3	k > 0 / _sC	a. *sekskentī > seskentī {sescenti} b. *sekskentī > (16.6) *sesskentī > (39.2) seskentī	30.3B

Espresso-Rule before a Nasal (Special Case of the Preceding Sound Change)

SCN	Rule	T > 0 / _sN (N = n, m, l)	Exercises
32.1	k > 0 / _sn	a. *loṷksna > *loṷsna > (15.2) b. *loṷksna > (16.6) *loṷssna > (39.2)	30.3EF
32.2	k > 0 / _sm	a. *traksma > *trasma > (15.1) *trazma > (2.2) b. *traksma > (16.6) *trassma (39.2) > *trasma > (15.1)	-
32.3	k > 0 / _sl	a. *pakslos > *paslos > (15.1) *pazlos > (2.2) b. *pakslos > (16.6) *passlos > (39.2) *paslos > (15.1)	30.3CG
32.4	p > 0 / _sm	a. *aps-mittō > *asmittō > (15.1) *azmittō > (2.2) b. *aps-mittō > (16.2) *assmittō > (39.2) *asmittō > (15.1)	-

Liquid + Fricative /s/ + Stop

SCN	Rule	r > 0 / _s(p,t,k)	Exercises
33.1	r > 0 / _st	a. torreō :: PPP *torstus > tostus b. torreō :: PPP *torstus > (21.4) *tosstus > (39.2) tostus	-
33.2	r > 0 / _sk	a. *Turskus > Tuskus {tuscus} b. *Turskus > (21.4) *Tusskus > (39.2) Tuskus {tuscus}	-
33.3	r > 0 / _sp	a. Mārspiter > Māspiter {maspiter} b. Mārspiter > (21.4) *Māsspiter > (39.2) Māspiter {maspiter}	-

Liquid + /k/ + Consonant /t/ or /s/

SCN	Rule	k > 0 / R_(t,s)	Exercises
34.1	k > 0 / r_t	a. OL {forctis} forktis > fortis b. OL forktis > (18.6) *forttis > (39.3) fortis	9.1
34.2	k > 0 / l_t	a. *ulktus > ultus (PPP of ulkiskī {ulcisci}) b. *ulktus > (18.6) *ulttus > (39.3) ultus	30.2AB
34.3	k > 0 / l_s	a. *fulgsī > (13.6) *fulksī > fulsī b. *fulgsī > (13.6) *fulksī > (16.6) *fulssī > (39.3) fulsī	-
34.4	k > 0 / r_s	a. arks > ars* b. arks > (16.6) arss > (39.3) ars	32.5

39   I would like to thank my espresso machine for supporting my work.

INDEX

Liquid + Stop + Nasal

SCN	Rule	C > 0 / R_N	Exercises
35.1	p > 0 / r_m	a. *sarpmentom > *sarmentom > (9.18) b. *sarpmentom > (14.1) *sarbmentom > (17.1) *sarmmentom > (39.4) > *sarmentom (9.18)	9.1, 30.1B1
35.2	p > 0 / l_m	a. *pulpmentom > *pulmentom b. *pulpmentom > (14.1) *pulbmentom > (17.1) *pulmmentom > (39.5) *pulmentom > (9.18)	-
35.3	k > 0 / l_m	a. *fulkmentom > *fulmentom b. *fulkmentom > (14.7) *fulgmentom > (17.6) *fulmmentom > (39.5) *fulmentom > (9.18)	30.1A1
35.4	d > 0 / r_n	a. *ordnō > *ōrnō b. *ordnō > (17.4) *ornnō > (39.3) ōrnō	-
35.5	g > 0 / l_m	*fulgmen > *fulmen *fulgmen > (17.6) *fulmmen > (39.3) *fulmen	-
35.6	k > 0 / r_n	a. *urkna > urna b. *urkna > (14.5) *urgna > (17.5) *urŋna[40] > (39.4) urna	-
35.7	k > 0 / r_m	a. *torku̯mentom > (40.3) *torkmentom > *tormentom > (9.18) b. *torkmentom > (14.7) *torgmentom > (17.6) *tormmentom > (39.3) *tormentom > (9.18)	-

Medial Voiced Stop + /u̯/ or /m/

SCN	Rule	Examples	Exercises
36.1	g > 0 / V_u̯V	{nix} niks :: gen. sg. *nigu̯is > niu̯is {niuis}	-
36.2	d > 0 / V̄_u̯	{suadeo} su̯ādeō :: *su̯ādu̯is > su̯āu̯is {suauis}	-
36.3	d > 0 / V̄_m[41]	{radix} rādiks :: *u̯rādmos > (40.7) *rādmos > *rāmos > (9.18) rāmus {ramus}	-

Fricative /s/ + /t/ + Nasal or Liquid

SCN	Rule	Examples	Exercises
37.1	t > 0 / s_l	*in-stlokōd > *inslokōd > (…) īliko {ilico}	-
37.2	t > 0 / #s_l	stlokum > *slokum > (30.12) lokum {locum}	28.1DE
37.3	t > 0 / s_(m,n)	*postne > *posne > (15.2) *pozne > (2.2) pōne {pone}	-

Simplification in the Final Position

SCN	Rule	C > 0 / _#	Exercises
38.1	m > 0 / V_#[42]	OL oi̯nom > oi̯no > (…) ūnum	-
38.2	s > 0 / V_#[43]	*Fou̯rios > OL Fou̯rio {fourio} > (…) Fūrius	-
38.3	d > 0 / V̄_#	OL abl. sg. magistrātūd > magistrātū	10.3C, 15.2CD, 28.2C, 29.1
38.4	t > 0 / k_#	gen. sg. laktis :: nom. sg. *lakt > lak {lac}	29.3C

---

40   Cf. 19.6 for a later development of /ŋn/.

41   In this case, the explanation via the assimilation and simplification of the double consonant is possible, too.

42   Probably the weakening of the nasal was accompanied by a slight nasalization of the preceding vowel. In case of a total loss, the analogical restitution would probably not have been possible. The Romance languages do not show any trace of /m/ in this position, which means that in some strata of the population the nasal had been lost very early.

43   No complete loss but only a weakened pronounciation, because of the consistent restitution of the fricative /s/ in CL.

| 38.5 | d > 0 / r_# | gen. sg. *kordis* :: nom. sg. *kord > *kor* {cor} | 29.3B, 34.2A |
| 38.6 | i̯ > 0 / V̄_# | {numasioi} *Numazio̅i̯* > (…) > *Numerio̅* | - |

Simplification of Double Consonants

SCN	Rule	$C_1C_1 > C_1$	Exercises
		In the Medial Position after a Long Vowel or a Diphthong	
39.1	$C_1C_1 > C_1$ / V̄_[44]	(16.4) > **pro̅ssum* > *pro̅sum*	13.3C, 15.2D, 19.1E, 19.2A, 24.2G, 26.2
		In the Medial Position before a Consonant	
39.2	$C_1C_1 > C_1$ / _C_2	*dissto̅* > *disto̅*	13.3D, 26.3
	$C_1C_1 > C_1$ / (R,N)_	**In the Medial Position after a Liquid or a Nasal**	
39.3	$C_1C_1 > C_1$ / (l,r)_	> (x3) **u̯orssos* > **u̯orsos* > (9.15) **u̯ersos* > (9.18)	30.2C
39.4	$C_1C_1 > C_1$ / (n,ŋ)_	*koŋ-kekidī > (4.1) *koŋkkidī > *koŋkidī* {concidi}	-
		The Mamilla-Rule: Simplification of Double Consonants Before a Stressed Syllable.	
39.5	$C_1C_1 > C_1$ / _.V́	*mammílla > *mamílla*	30.1A2B2, 26.4
	$C_1C_1 > C_1$ / _#	**In the Final Position**	
39.6	k > 0 / k_#	*hokk > *hok* {hoc}	24.1C, 29.2E
39.7	s > 0 / s_#	*mīless > *mīles*	17.2E, 23.3, 24.1B, 24.2BCDE, 29.2AB, 34.2B
39.8	r > 0 / r_#	(22.3) > *sakerr > *saker* {sacer}	29.2CD, 32.5, 34.3E, 35.3B
39.9	l > 0 / l_#	gen. sg. *fellis* :: *fell > *fel*	-

The Semivowels /i̯/ and /u̯/[45]

SCN	Rule		Exercises
40.1	i̯ > 0 / V_V[46]	**trei̯es* > *trees* > (3.1) *trēs*	12.2D, 33.2A
40.2	u̯ > 0 / V1_V1[47]	{audiuit} *audi̯u̯īt* > **audi̯īt* > (1.1) **audi̯īt* > (3.1) *audi̯t* {audit}	12.1CFG, 12.2BCF, 32.1
40.3	u̯ > 0 / k_C	> (x4.1) **oku̯los* > *oklos > (28.4)	33.1ABCD
40.4	u̯ > 0 / g_C	**eks-stiŋgu̯sī* > *eks-stiŋgsī > (13.6) *eks-stiŋksī* {exstinxi}	33.1EF
40.5	u̯ > 0 / _(o, ō, u, ū)[48]	> (9.11) **ku̯oku̯ō* > *koku̯ō* {coquo}[49]	17.1B, 17.2, 31.2/ 31.4, 32.4, 33.3A, 34.2C

44 Double /ll/ is not simplified after a long vowel. Examples: *u̯īlla* {uilla} 'country house', *nūllus* {nullus} 'not any', *mīlle* {mille} 'thousand'.

45 For the sake of clarity, the examples for the initial and the medial position, as well as for internal and external reconstruction are grouped together here.

46 Already in Proto-Italic times.

47 /u̯/ was lost only if the syllable after /u̯/ was not stressed (cf. unit 31).

48 As in *nou̯us*, *nou̯ī*, a lost intervocalic /u̯/ was analogically reintroduced into the word.

49 The expected form is *kokō. The second /u̯/, however, remained in analogy to forms such as 2. sg. *koku̯is* {coquis}, 3. sg. *koku̯it* {coquit} or 2. sg. sub. *koku̯ās* {coquas}.

40.6	ų > 0 / a_C(C)u	{augustus} *augustus* > VL *agustus*	-
40.7	ų > 0 / #_R	{uello} *ųellō* :: *ųlāna* > *lāna* {lana} 'wool'	28.3BC
40.8	ų > 0 / (p,b)_	ER *apųeriō* > *aperiō*	-
40.9	ų > 0 / l_	> (x5.4) *mollųis* > *mollis*	-
40.10	ų >0 / #_u[50]	> (30.9) *ųubeį* > *ubeį* > (10.8) ... *ubī* {ubi} 'where?'	-
40.11	dų > b / #_[51]	{duidens} *dųidēns* > *bidēns* {bidens}	28.2A-F

From PIE to Latin

PIE Palatal Stops Merge with PIE Velar Stops

SCN	Rule	Example	Exercises
x1.1	*k̂ > k	*k̂m̥tóm* > *km̥tóm* > (Ac0) *km̥tom* > (x5.7) *kemtom* > (9.18)	34.1DE, 34.2A, 36.3C
x1.2	*ĝ > g	*h₂eĝō* > *h₂egō* > (x2.1)	36.1C, 36.2A
x1.3	*ĝʰ > *gʰ	*ĝʰanser* > *gʰanser* > (x6.3) *ɣanser* > (x6.9a)	35.1D, 35.2D

Laryngeal */h₂/ Colors */e/ to /a/. Laryngeal */h₃/ Colors */e/ to /o/[52]

SCN	Rule	Example	Exercises
x2.1	e > a / *h₂_	> (x1.2) *h₂egō* > *h₂agō* > (x2.6)	36.2A-D
x2.2	e > o / *h₃_	*h₃ekʷlos* > *h₃okʷlos* > (x2.7)	
x2.3	e > a / _*h₂	*bʰeh₂tom* > *bʰah₂tom* > (x2.9)	35.1B, 35.2AC, 36.3ABC
x2.4	e > o / _*h₃	*deh₃nom* > *doh₃nom* > (x2.10)	36.4AB

Loss of Laryngeals before a Vowel

SCN	Rule	Example	Exercises
x2.5	*h₁ > 0 / _V	*h₁edō* > *edō*	36.1AC
x2.6	*h₂ > 0 / _V	> (x2.1) *h₂agō* > *agō* {ago}	36.2A-D
x2.7	*h₃ > 0 / _V	> (x2.2) *h₃okʷlos* > *okʷlos* > (x4.1)	35.1D

Loss of Laryngeals after a Vowel with Compensatory Lengthening

SCN	Rule	Example	Exercises
x2.8	*eh₁ > ē	*seh₁mn̥* > *sēmn̥* > (x5.6) *sēmen* {semen}	36.1BD
x2.9	*ah₂ > ā	> (x2.3) *bʰah₂tom* > *bʰātom* > (x6.1)	35.2AC, 36.3ABC
x2.10	*oh₃ > ō	> (x2.4) *doh₃nom* > *dōnom* > (9.18) *dōnum* {donum}	36.4AB
x2.11	*iH > ī	*gʷih₃ųós* > *gʷīųós* > *gʷī́ųos* > (x4.2)	36.3D
x2.12	*uH > ū	*dʰuh₂mós* > *dʰūmós* > (Ac0) *dʰū́mos* > (x6.2)	-

---

50 An initial /ų/ normally remains before a vowel. This rule is needed for explaining the regular development of *ku > ų according to SCN 30.9.

51 Possible intermediate steps are dų > *db > b or dų > *bų > b.

52 This presentation of PIE reflexes in Latin covers only the most important developments. For a complete presentation cf. Schijver, P. (1991). *The Reflexes of Proto-Indo-European Laryngeals in Latin*. Amsterdam-Atlanta.

Laryngeals are Lost in the Initial Position before a Consonant

SCN	Rule	Example	Exercises
x2.13	*H > 0 / #_C	*h₃miŋghō > *miŋghō > (x6.3) *miŋγō > (x8.9) miŋgō {mingo}	36.4A

Laryngeals are Vocalized to /a/ Between Consonants

SCN	Rule	Example	Exercises
x2.14	*H > a / C_C	*ph₂tḗr > *patḗr > (Ac0) *pátēr > (1.4) páter	-

Laryngeal plus Resonant Results in Resonant plus Long /ā/

SCN	Rule	Example	Exercises
x2.15	*r̥h₂ > rā	*ǵr̥h₂nóm > (x1.2) *gr̥h₂nóm > *grānóm > (Ac1) *gránom > (9.18)	33.1E
x2.16	*l̥h₂ > lā	*tl̥h₂tós > *tlātós > (Ac0) *tlắtos > (30.4)	-
x2.17	*n̥h₁ > nā	*ǵn̥h₁tós > (x1.2) *gn̥h₁tós > *gnātós > (Ac0) *gnắtos > (30.2a)	-

PIE */tt/ Becomes Proto-Italic */ss/ and Latin /ss/

SCN	Rule	Example	Exercises
x3	PIE *tt > PIT *ss	*u̯orttos > *u̯orssos > (39.3)	19.1E, 26.2F

The Monophonematic Labiovelars Become a Sequence of Two Phonemes

SCN	Rule	Example	Exercises
x4.1	*kʷ > ku̯	> (x2.7) *okʷlos > *oku̯los > (40.3)	33.1BD, 33.3A, 34.2C
x4.2	*gʷ > gu̯	> (x2.11) *gʷīu̯os > *gu̯īu̯os > (30.11)	33.1EF, 33.2AB, 34.1F, 36.3D
x4.3	*gʷh > *ghu̯	*gʷhormos > *ghu̯ormos > (x6.4)	-

Anaptyctic Vowels next to the PIE Syllabic Liquids *[r̥] and *[l̥]

SCN	Rule	Example	Exercises
x5.1	*r̥ > or / _C[53]	*mr̥tis > *mortis > (4.2) *morts > (16.4) *morss > (39.7) mors	34.2AB
x5.2	*r̥ > ur / u̯_C	*u̯r̥gei̯ō > *u̯urgei̯ō > (40.1) *u̯urgeō > (40.10) urgeō {urgeo}	34.2C
x5.3	*r̥ > ar / _V	*kr̥-ō(n) > *karō(n) > karō {caro}	-
x5.4	*l̥ > ol / _C	*ml̥du̯is > *moldu̯is > (22.4) *mollu̯is > (40.9) mollis {mollis}	-
x5.5	*l̥ > al / _V	*k̂l̥-eh1-i̯ō > (...) kaleō {caleō}	-

Anaptyctic Vowels next to the PIE Syllabic Nasals *[n̥] and *[m̥]

SCN	Rule	Example	Exercises
x5.6	*n̥ > en	> (x2.8) *sēmn̥ > sēmen {semen}	34.1A, 36.4A
x5.7	*m̥ > em	*dek̂m̥ > (x1.1) > dekm̥ > dekem {decem}	34.1

---

53   The reasons for the divergent developments r̥ > or and r̥ > ur are not clear. Cf. 9.20 for an internal Latin development of or > ur, which could serve as an explanation. Cf. Meiser 1998:63/64 for further sporadic reflexes.

The Mediae Aspiratae Become Voiced Fricatives

SCN	Rule	Example	Exercises
x6.1	*bʰ > *β	> (x2.9) *bʰātom > *βātom > (x6.5a)	35.1AB, 35.2AB, 36.3B, 36.4B
x6.2	*dʰ > *δ	> (x2.12) *dʰūmos > *δūmos > (x6.6)	35.1C, 35.2C, 35.3AB
x6.3	*gʰ > *γ[54]	*gʰladʰros > *γladʰros > (x6.2) *γlaδros > (x6.7)	35.1D, 35.2D
x6.4	*gʰu̯ > *γu̯	*gʰu̯ormos > * γu̯ormos > (x6.10)	-

Voiceless Allophonic Fricatives in the Initial Position. /γ/ Becomes /g/ before R.

SCN	Rule	Example	Exercises
x6.5a	*β > *φ / #_	> (x6.1) *βātom > *φātom > (x6.5b)	35.1AB, 36.3B, 36.4B
x6.5b	*φ > f / #_	> (x6.5a) *φātom > *fātom > (9.18)	
x6.6	*δ > *θ / #_V	> (x6.2) *δūmos > *θūmos > (x7.1)	35.1C
x6.7	*γ > g / #_l[55]	> (x6.3) *γlaδros > *gladros > (x7.3b) *glaβros > ... glaber	-
x6.8	*γ > g / #_r	> (x6.3) *γrasmen > *grasmen > (15.1) *grazmen > (2.2)	-
x6.9a	*γ > *χ / #_V	> (x6.3) *γanser > *χanser > (x6.9b)	35.1D
x6.9b	*χ > h / #_V	> (x6.9a) *χanser > hanser > (x6.9c)	
x6.9c	h > 0 / #_V	> (x6.9b) hanser > anser > (2.1) ānser	-
x6.10	*γu̯ > *χf > *hf > f / #_V	> (x6.4) *γu̯ormos > *χformos > *hformos > *formos > (9.18)	-
x6.11	*χ > f / #_u[56]	*ĝʰundō > (x1.3) *gʰundō > (x6.3) γundō > (x6.9a) χundō > fundō {fundo} 'I pour'	-

MA in the Initial Position: Dental Fricatives Merge with Labial Fricatives

SCN	Rule	Example	Exercises
x7.1	*θ > f / #_(V,r)	(x6.6) > *θūmos > *fūmos > (9.18)	35.1C
x7.2	*s > *θ / #_r	*srīgos > *θrīgos > (x7.1) *frīgos > (9.18)	-

MA in the Medial Position: Dental Fricatives Merge with Labial Fricatives[57]

SCN	Rule	Example	Exercises
x7.3a	*z > *δ / V_r	> (15.4) *fūnezris > *fūneδris > (x7.3b)	-
x7.3b	*δ > *β / _r	> (x7.3a) *fūneδris > *fūneβris > (x8.4)	35.3B
x7.4	*δ > *β / r_	> (x6.2) *u̯erδom > *u̯erβom > (x8.5)	35.3A
x7.5	*δ > *β / _l	> (x6.2) *staδlom > *staβlom > (x8.3)	-
x7.6	*δ > *β / u̯_	> (x6.2) *i̯ou̯δei̯ō > *i̯ou̯βei̯ō > (x8.6) OL iou̯beō > (...) CL i̯ūbeō	-
x7.7	*δ > *β / u_	*kʷudʰei̯ > (x4.1) *ku̯udʰei̯ > (x6.2) *ku̯uδei̯ > *ku̯uβei̯ > (x8.1) *ku̯ubei̯ > (30.9) ... CL ubī {ubi} 'where?'	-

---

54   It is possible that this development did not happen after a nasal. In this case, SCN x8.9 must be omitted.
55   It can also be argued that the groups *gʰr- and *gʰl- give r- and l- as in *ĝʰrāu̯os > rāu̯us {rauus} 'grey', *gʰreu̯dos > rūdus 'broken stones, rubble'. Cf. Weiss 2009:163.
56   Only this example exists.
57   Weiss 2009:75 calls it the RubL-rule, grouping SCN x7.3b to x7.7 together.

MA in the Medial Position: Fricatives Become Stops *β > b, *δ > d, *γ > g. The Development of */γu̯/

SCN	Rule	Example	Exercises
x8.1	*β > b / V_V	*neβeła > *nebeła > (8.8) *neboła > (8.10) nebuła {nebula}	35.2A
x8.2	*β > b / l_V	*albʰos > (x6.1) *alβos > *albos > (9.18) albus	35.2B
x8.3	*β > b / V_l	> (x7.5) staβlom > *stablom > (9.18) *stablum > (5.2)	-
x8.4	*β > b / V_r	> (x7.3b) *fūneβris > fūnebris	35.3B
x8.5	*β > b / r_V	> (x7.4) *u̯erβom > *u̯erbom > (9.18)	35.3A
x8.6	*β > b / (u̯,u)_	> (x7.6) *i̯ou̯βei̯ō > OL i̯ou̯beō > (10.3) iūbeō {iubeo}	-
x8.7	*δ > d / V_V	*medʰi̯os > (27.1) *medʰios > (x6.2) *meδios > *medios > (9.18)	35.2C
x8.8	*γ > g / _C	fiŋgō {fingo} :: *dʰigʰlos > (...) *figlos > (...) figulus	-
x8.9	*γ > g / N_	> (x2.13) *miŋγō > miŋgō {mingo}	-
x8.10	*γu̯ > u̯ / V_V[58]	*dʰogʷʰei̯ō > (...) *θoγu̯ē-ō > (...) fou̯eō {foueo}	-
x8.11	*γu̯ > b / _r	*dʰegʷʰris > (...) > *θeγu̯ris > (...) *feβris > (...) febris	-

MA in the Medial Position: Intervocalic */γ/ is Devoiced and Lost via */χ/ and /h/

SCN	Rule	Example	Exercises
x8.12a	*γ > *χ / V_V	*u̯egʰō > (x1.3) *u̯egʰō > (x6.3) *u̯eγō > *u̯eχō > (x8.12b)	35.2D
x8.12b	*χ > h / V_V	> (x8.12a) *u̯eχō > u̯ehō {ueho}	
x8.12c	h > 0 / V_V	*u̯ehemēns > *u̯eemēns > (3.1) u̯ēmēns {uemens}	12.1D, 12.2AE, 21.3C

Strengthening of /m/ to /b/ Before a Liquid

SCN	Rule	Example	Exercises
x9.1	m > b /#_l	*mlāndus > *blāndus > (1.2) blandus {blandus}	-
x9.2	m > b / #_r	*mregu̯is > *bregu̯is > (36.1) breu̯is {breuis}	9.1
x9.3	m > b / _r	*ĝʰei̯m-rinos > (...) *hīmrinos > *hībrinos > (...) hībernus	-

Nasal Weakening before a Fricative

SCN	Rule	Example
x10.1	n > 0 / _s + ED	OL konsol > kōsol > (A) kōnsol > (9.18) kōnsul[59]
x10.2	ŋ > 0 / _ *χ + ED	*saŋktos > ([60]) *saŋχtos > *sāχtos > (A:saŋkiō) *sāŋktos > (9.18) sāŋktus {sanctus}

I
N
D
E
X

---

58   Or γ > g / _u̯ and then SCN 36.1. g > 0 / _u̯. The same development of /γu̯/ and /gu̯/ are found in this context.
59   Analogical restitution of the nasal after the morpheme boundary in *kom-* and *in-*. Cf. SCN 2.1 and unit 11.
60   In this case, a PIT rule k > χ / n_t is assumed, which is corroborated by Osk. {saahtum} and Umb. {sahatam}. Cf. Meiser 1998:78.

Assimilations

SCN	Rule	Example	Exercises
x11.1	g > i̯ / _i̯	**magi̯ōs* > **mai̯i̯ōs* > (A: *mai̯i̯ōrem*) **mai̯i̯ōr* > (1.4) *mai̯i̯or* {maior}	31.3AB
x11.2	d > i̯ / _i̯	**pedi̯ōs* > **pei̯i̯ōs* > (A: *pei̯i̯ōrem*) **pei̯i̯ōr* > (1.4) *pei̯i̯or* {peior}	31.3C
x11.3	*p > *kʷ / _...*kʷ	**pekʷō* > **kʷekʷō* > (x4.1) **ku̯eku̯ō* > (9.11)	33.3A

Accent rules

Ac0	The morphological free PIE word accent transforms into an initial stress accent.	**ḱm̥tóm* > **km̥tóm* > (Ac0) **km̥tom* > (x5.7) **kemtom* > (9.18)	**Exercises**
Ac1	The initial stress accent transforms into the classic penult accentuation system.	**éks-erkeō* > *eks-érkeō* {exerceo}	Cf. chapters 14 and 15
Ac2	Muta cum liquida closes a preceding syllable.	CL *ín.te.grum* > VL *in.tég.rum*	8.3

A1 Apophony (Ablaut) in Latin

Roots function as the basis of derivation and carry the basic meaning of derived words

By comparing the forms *u̯olō* {uolo} 'I want', *u̯ult* {uult} 'he wants' and *u̯elle* {uelle} 'to want', which come from **u̯elō > u̯olō, *u̯elt > *u̯olt > u̯ult* and **u̯else > *u̯elze > u̯elle*, the lexical root **u̯el-* is identified, which is the derivation base and carries the basic meaning of 'to want'. This meaning is modified by adding the grammatical morphemes *-ō* for the 1. ps. sg., *-t* for the 3. ps. sg and *-se* for the infinitive. By comparing the IE languages, it is possible to reconstruct many lexical roots which consist of two consonants surrounding an ablaut vowel **/e/*. Examples are **bʰer-* 'carry', **men-* 'think', **gʷem-* 'come/go', **deh₃-* 'give'.

The vocalization of a root by the ablaut vowel */e/

The comparison of the PIE languages furthermore shows a systematic interchange of the ablaut vowel **/e/* with the vowels **/o/, */ē/, */ō/* as well as no vowel (which means the absence of a vowel) within the same root. This systematic interchange has been obscured in Latin by numerous sound changes.

	e-grade	o-grade	zero-grade	ē-grade
1	*nek-ō* {neco}	*nok-eō* {noceo}		
2	**fei̯dō > fīdō*	**foi̯dos > foedus*	-	-
3	*teg-ō* {tego}	*tog-a* {toga}	-	*tēg-uła* {tegula}
4	**deu̯kō > dūk-ō* {duco}	-	*duk-s* {dux}	-
5	*gen-uī*	-	*gi-gn-ō*	-
6	**h₁ed-ō > edō*	-	**h₁d-ent-s > dēns*	-
7	**seh₁mn̥ > sēmen*	-	**sh₁tos > satus*	-
8	**dʰeh₁-k-ī > fēkī* {feci}	-	**dʰh₁k-i̯ō > fakiō* {facio}	-
9	*dek-et* {decet}	*dok-eō* {doceo}	**di-dk-skō > diskō* {disco}	-
10	*sed-eō*	**sod-ium > solium*	**si-sd-ō > sīdō*	*sēdēs*

L1: The two verbs continue the e-grade and the o-grade. **L2**: This example shows how sound changes can totally obscure the original ablaut pattern. There is no phonological correlation in Latin which can explain systematically the difference between *fīdō* und *foedus*. **L3**: CL *tēguła* {tegula} is an example for the ē-grade. **L4**: The e-grade has been obscured by the developments SCN 10.2–10.4, by which **/eu̯/* became /ū/. **Z5**: The reduplicated present *gi-gn-ō* continues the zero-grade of the root. **L6**: The initial laryngeal is lost due to SCN x2.5. The word for 'tooth' was originally an aorist participle with the meaning 'the biting one'. **L7/8**: The long vowels of *sēmen* and *fēkī* were caused by compensatory lengthening after laryngeal loss (SCN x2.8). They do not continue ē-grades. The zero-grades in **sh₁tos > satus* and **dʰh₁k-i̯ō > fakiō* {facio} are continued by Latin /a/ because laryngeals were vocalized to /a/ between consonants. The element *-k-* in *fēkī* could correspond to Greek k-perfects like in *étʰē-k-a* 'I did' but the details are not clear. **L9**: The zero-grade is not easily detected here because the complex derivation is: **di-dk-skō > (12.6) *ditskō > (18.4) *dikkskō > (39.2) *dikskō > (31.3) diskō*. **L10**: *solium* has /l/ according to SCN 25.3.

Chronology of Sound Changes

The following table visualizes the chronology of the most important sound changes. The data has been gathered from the literatur given in the bibliography in appendix 6. On a case-by-case basis, the exact absolute and relative chronology of Latin sound changes cannot be determined with safety because many inscriptions, which are used for dating the sound changes, cannot be dated exactly. Furthermore, archaic forms are used in many inscriptions to give the language a more official or formal sound. Some sound changes such as Osthoff's law SCN 1.2, syncope and apocope SCN 4, or the assimilations SCN 12–22 occurred more than once during the evolution of Latin and cannot be attributed to a specific era. Sometimes, they can also be distributed to different strata of the language. Another difficulty is the distinction between Proto-Italic and common Italic changes. Common Italic changes are those processes which can be found in several Italic languages, but which do not go back to a common origin but are due to mutual interference between the languages.

	From PIE to Proto-Italic. Ca. 3000 BC until 1500 BC. **= Features in which the Italic languages differ from other IE languages.**
3000	SCN x1 PIE palatal and velar stops merge in all centum-languages.
	SCN x2 Coloring and loss of the laryngeals, with or without compensatory lengthening.
	SCN x3 The cluster */tt/ becomes /ss/.
	SCN Ac0 The PIE morphological free accent is changed to an initial accent.
	SCN x5 Anaptyctic vowels next to the syllabic resonants *[r̥] and *[l̥].
	SCN 40.1 Loss of intervocalic */i̯/.
	SCN x6.1-x6.11 The mediae aspiratae become voiced and voiceless fricatives.
	SCN x7 Partial merger of the fricatives which originated from SCN x6 and SCN x7.2/x7.3a.
	SCN x7.2/x7.3a The sibilants */s/ and *[z] become interdental before /r/.
	SCN 15.6 Sonorization of intervocalic */s/ to *[z] (prestage of rhotazism SCN 26.1).
	SCN x11.3 Assimilation of */p/ to a non-adjacent */kʷ/.
	SCN 10.2 The PIE diphthong */eu̯/ becomes Proto-Italic */ou̯/ (maybe common Italic).
	SCN 1.2 Shortening of long vowels before a resonant (rule remains active).
1500	SCN 9.31 The pius-rule: Assimilation of PIT */ū/ to following */i̯/.
	From Proto-Italic until the start of Early Latin. Ca. 1500 BC until 700 BC. **=Features in which Latin differs from the other Italic languages.**
1500	SCN x4 The monophonematic labiovelars become a sequence of two phonemes.
	SCN x5 Anaptyctic vowels next to the PIE syllabic resonants *[n̥] and *[m̥].
	SCN x8 Fricatives stemming from SCN x6/x7 become stops in the medial position
	SCN x9 Strengthening of */m/ to /b/ before a resonant.
	SCN x10 Loss of a nasal before a fricative (common Italic).
	SCN x11.1/2 Assimilations g > i̯ / V_i̯V and d > i̯ / V_i̯V.
	SCN 28 Emergence of velar [ł] (common Italic).
	SCN 28.4 The cluster */tło/ becomes */kło/ (common Italic).
	SCN 30.1/2 Loss of initial */k/ before /n/.
	SCN 30.11 Loss of initial /g/ before /u̯/.
	SCN 30.12 Loss of */s/ before an initial liquid or nasal.
	SCN 30.7/8 Loss of an initial stop before /s/ (common Italic).
	SCN 40.7 */u̯/ is lost before a liquid in the initial position.
	SCN 1.2 Shortening of a long vowel before a resonant (rule remains active).
	SCN 1.6 Shortening of final long */ā/.
700	SCN 3 Contractions of vowels in hiatus after the loss of intervocalic */i̯/ (SCN 40.1.).

	From the start of Early Latin until Old Latin. Ca. 700 BC until 240 BC.
	SCN 4.1/2 Syncope.
	SCN 6 Anaptyctic vowels next to the syllabic resonants stemming from SCN 4.
	SCN 9.11 o-umlaut.
	SCN x6.9c/x8.12c Loss of /h/ in the initial and medial position.
	SCN x10.1/2 Weakening of /n/ before a fricative (CL restitutes the nasal).
	SCN 1.1 The vowels /ā/, /ē/, /ō/ are shortened before a vowel.
400	SCN Ac1 The initial accent transforms into the rule of the penult.
	SCN 4.1/2 Syncope.
	SCN 6 Anaptyctic vowels next to syllabic resonants stemming from SCN 4.
	SCN 1.3 Correptio iambica.
	SCN 8 Vowel weakening in medial syllables.
	SCN 26.1 Rhotazism.
	SCN 1.1 The vowels /ā/, /ē/, /ō/ are shortened before a vowel.
	SCN x10.1/2 Weakening of /n/ before a fricative (restitution of the nasal in CL).
	SCN 40.2 Loss of /u̯/ between similar vowels.
	SCN 30.6 Loss of initial /d/ before /i̯/ (rule remains active in VL).
300	SCN 1.1 The vowels (/ā/, /ē/, /ō/) are shortened before a vowel.
	SCN 1.3 Correptio iambica.
	SCN 40.5 Loss of /u̯/ before /o/, /ō/, /u/, /ū/.
	SCN 1.4 Vowel shortening in final closed syllables.
	SCN 38.2 Tendency to drop final /s/.
	SCN 9.9 /e/ is backed to /o/ next to velar /ł/.
	SCN 9.18 /o/ is raised to /u/ in final syllables.
	SCN 10.6/10.10 Lowering of the second element of diphthongs as a prestage of monophthongization.
	SCN 10.3/10.8 Monophthongization of ou̯ > ǭ and ei̯ > ē (/ẹ̄/ preserved as {ei, i} in Plautus).
	From Old Latin to Classical Latin. Ca. 240 BC until 14 AD.
250	SCN 9.18 /o/ is raised to /u/ in final syllables.
	SCN 9.16 /o/ is raised to /u/ next to velar [ŋ].
	SCN 40.11 The initial cluster /du̯/ is simplified to /b/.
200	SCN 1.1 The vowels /ū/, /ī/ are shortened before a vowel.
	SCN 10.4/9 Raising of ǭ > ū and ẹ̄ > ī after monophthongization.
	SCN 10.1/7 Monophthongization of ae̯ > ẹ̄ and au̯ > ǭ in common speech.
	SCN 9.8 Raising of e > i in closed final syllables.
	SCN 38.3 Loss of final /d/ after a long final vowel.
	SCN 30.2 Loss of initial /g/ before /n/.
	SCN 39.6/7 Simplification of final double consonants (in Plautus still *mīless).
150	SCN 9.21 /o/ is raised to /u/ before [ł] plus consonant.
	SCN 9.15 Dissimilation of /o/ to /e/ next to /u̯/.
50	SCN 9.19 Raising of o > u after /u̯/.

PIE

	Labial	Inter-dental	Dental	Alveolar	Palatal	Velar	Labio-velar	Glottal
Plosive	*p *(b) *bʰ		*t *d *dʰ		*k̂ *ĝ *ĝʰ	*k *g *gʰ	*kʷ *gʷ *gʷʰ	? *h₁ = ?
Fricative		*[θ]	*s ~ *[z]			? *h₂ = χ ? *h₃ = γ	? *h₃ = γʷ	
Nasal	*m ~ *[m̥]		*n ~ *[n̥]		*[ɲ]	*[ŋ]		
Lateral				*l ~ *[l̥]				
? Trill				*r ~ *[r̥]				
Approximant	*u̯				*i̯			

SCN x1, SCN x2, SCN x5.1–5.5, SCN x6.1–6.4, SCN x7, SCN x11.3

Proto-Italic

	Labial	Inter-dental	Dental	Alveolar	Palatal	Velar	Labio-velar
Plosive	*p *b		*t *d			*k *g	*kʷ *gʷ
Fricative	*[φ] ~*β	*[θ] ~ *δ	*s ~ *[z]			*[χ] ~ *γ	*[χʷ] ~ *γʷ
Nasal	*m ~ *[m̥]		*n ~ *[n̥]			*[ŋ]	
Lateral				*l		*[ɫ]	
Trill				*r			
Approximant	*u̯ ~ *[u̯ᵞ]				*i̯		

SCN x4, SCN x5.6–5.7, SCN x6.5a–6.11, SCN x7, SCN 8

Latin

	Labial	Labiodental	Dental	Alveolar	Palatal	Velar	Glottal
Plosive	p b		t d			k g	
Fricative		f	s ~ [z]				h
Nasal	m	[ɱ]	n			[ŋ]	
Lateral				l		[ɫ]	
Trill				r			
Approximant	u̯ᵞ				i̯		

EARLY LATIN	
{iouesat} EL i̯ou̯ezat > CL i̯ūrat {iurat}	No syncope of unstressed vowels (SCN 4)
{deiuos} EL dei̯u̯ōs > CL deōs {deos}	No monophthongization (SCN 10)
{cosmis} EL kozmis > CL kōmis {comis}	[z] is preserved as {s} before /m/ (SCN 2.2)
{numasioi} EL Numazi̯ōi̯ > CL Numeriō {numerio}	No rhotazism (SCN 26.1)
{iouxmenta} EL i̯ou̯ksmenta > CL i̯ūmenta {iumenta}	/k/ is preserved before /sm/ (SCN 32)
{suodales} EL su̯odālēs > sodālēs {sodales}	/u̯/ is preserved before /o/ (SCN 40.5)
{duenos} EL du̯enos > CL bonus {bonus}	No o-umlaut (SCN 9.11)

OLD LATIN	
OL tinnīt > CL tinnit	Long vowels in final syllables (SCN 1.4)
OL fūimus > CL fuimus	Long /ī/ and /ū/ before a vowel (SCN 1.1)
OL mihī > CL mihi	Final long vowels often preserved (SCN 1.3
{consol} OL kōnsoł > CL kōnsuł {consul}	/o/ instead of CL /u/ in final syllables (SCN 9.18)
OL sententiād > CL sententiā	Final /d/ after a long vowel is preserved (SCN 38.3)
{moltai} OL mołtai̯ > CL mułtae̯ {multae}	/o/ is preserved before [ł] (SCN 9.21)

CLASSICAL LATIN	
{scriptus} skriptus 'written'	
{mensa} mēnsa 'table'	
{homo} homō 'human'	
{capio} kapiō 'I grasp'	
{calidus} kalidus 'warm'	
{lautus} lau̯tus 'washed'	
{caelum} kae̯lum 'sky'	

VULGAR LATIN	
skrittus	Assimilation of /pt/ to /tt/ (SCN 18.1)
mēsa	Complete loss of /n/ before /s/ (SCN x10.1)
omō	Complete loss of /h/ (SCN x6.9c)
kapi̯ō	Consonantification of /i/ to /i̯/ (SCN 9.13)
kaldus	Frequent syncopes (SCN 4.1)
lǭtus	Monophthongization of /ae̯/ to /ǭ/ (SCN 10.1)
kḗlum	Monophthongization of /ae̯/ to /ḗ/ (SCN 10.7)

A
P
P
E
N
D
I
X

The Indo-European Languages[61]

Anato-lian	Centum-Languages					Satem-Languages				
	Tochar-ian	Greek	Celtic	Ger-manic	**Italic**	Indo-Iranian	Baltic	Slavic	Alba-nian	Arme-nian

The Italic Languages[62]

Sabellic Languages			Latino-Faliscan Languages		Venetic
Umbrian Aequian Marsian Volscian	South Picene Pre-Samnite	Oscan Paelignian Marrucinian Vestinian ? Hernican	**Latin**	Faliscan	**Venetic**

The Romance Languages[63]

Western Romance	Eastern Romance	Sardinian
Upper Italian		
Iberian-Romance Catalan Spanish Galician-Portuguese	Southern Italian Central Italian Romanian Dalmatian	Sardinian
Gallo-Romance French Arpitan Occitan		
Rhaeto-Romance Friulian Ladin Romansh		

---

61 Cf. Meiser 1998:25 and Meier-Brügger 2000:18ff. The division of the IE languages in centum-languages and satem-languages is dealt with in paragraph 7 of unit 37. For the special status of Anatolian cf. paragraph 7.3 of unit 37.
62 According to Wallace 2007:1. Cf. also Baldi 1999:167ff.
63 According to Kümmel 2007:39.

Allen, W. Sidney. (1978). *Vox Latina*. Cambridge.

Baldi, P. (1998). *The Foundations of Latin*. Berlin.

Bammesberger, A. (1984). *Lateinische Sprachwissenschaft*. Regensburg.

Blümel, W. (1972). *Untersuchungen zu Lautsystem and Morphologie des vorklassischen Lateins*. München.

Eichner, H. (1992). *Indogermanisches Phonemsystem und lateinische Lautgeschichte*. In Panagel, O./ Krisch, T. *Latein und Indogermanisch*. Innsbruck.

Kent, R. (1932). *The Sounds of Latin. A Descriptive and Historical Phonology*. Baltimore.

Kieckers, E. (1930/1931). *Historische lateinische Grammatik*. 2 Bde. München.

Kümmel, M.J. (2007). *Konsonantenwandel*. Wiesbaden.

Leumann, M. (1977). *Lateinische Laut- und Formenlehre*. München.

Lindsey, W. (1948). *Brief historical grammar of the Latin language*. Moscow.

Meier-Brügger, M. (2000). *Indogermanische Sprachwissenschaft*. Berlin.

Meillet, A. (2004). *Esquisse d'une histoire de la langue latine*. Paris.

Meiser, G. (1986). *Lautgeschichte der umbrischen Sprache*. Innsbruck.

Meiser, G. (1998). *Historische Laut- und Formenlehre der lateinischen Sprache*. Darmstadt.

Müller-Lancé, J. (2006). *Latein für Romanisten*. Tübingen.

Niedermann, M. (1953). *Historische Lautlehre des Lateinischen*. Heidelberg.

Palmer, L.R. (1954). *The Latin Language*. London.

Pulgram, E. (1958). *The Tongues of Italy, Prehistory and History*. Harvard.

Ramat, A./ Ramat, P. (1998). *The Indo-European Languages*. London/New York.

Safarewicz, J. (1969). *Historische lateinische Grammatik*. Halle.

Sihler, A.L. (1995). *New comparative grammar of Greek and Latin*. New York.

Sommer, F. (1977). *Handbuch der lateinischen Laut- und Formenlehre*. Heidelberg.

Sturtevant, E. (1940). *The Pronunciation of Greek and Latin*. Philadelphia.

Väänänen, V. (1963). *Introduction au latin vulgaire*. Paris.

Wallace, R.E. (2007). *The Sabellic Languages of Ancient Italy*. Lincom Europa.

Weiss, M. (2009). *Outline of the historical and comparative Grammar of Latin*. Ann Arbor.

Etymological dictionaries:

Ernout, A./ Meillet, A. (2001). *Dictionnaire étymologique de la langue latine*. Paris.

Walde, A./ Hofmann, J.B. (1982). *Lateinisches Etymologisches Wörterbuch*. Heidelberg.

De Vaan, M. (2008). *Etymological dictionary of Latin and the other Italic languages*. Leiden.

Reading Tips: Niedermann 1953 and Bammesberger 1984 are very suitable for beginners. Allen 1978, Kent 1932 and Sturtevant 1940 analyze the statements of Latin grammarians. Pulgram 1958, Wallace 2007 and Baldi 1998 give more information about the other Italic languages. Meiser 1998 and Weiss 2009 are the most up-to-date historical grammars of Latin. Meier-Brügger 2000 and Ramat 1998 present the material in a more Indo-European perspective.

Definitions of sound symbols (the upper of two sounds represents the voiceless sound).

	Labial	Labio-dental	Inter-dental	Dental	Alveo-lar	Retro-flex	Palatal	Velar	Uvular	Glottal
Plosive	p b			t d		ṭ ḍ	k̂ ĝ	k g		ʔ
Affricate							ʧ ʤ			
Fricative	φ β	f v	θ δ	s z	ṣ		ʃ	χ γ	ʁ	h
Nasal	m	ɱ		n		ṇ	ɲ	ŋ		
Lateral					l			ɫ		
Flap					ɾ					
Trill					r				R	
Approx-imant	u̯	ʋ			ɹ	ɻ	i̯	u̯		

e̯, i̯, u̯   A vowel with a semi-circle at the bottom is a consonantal semivowel.
n̥   Syllabic resonants are written with a circle at the bottom.
[ŋ]   Allophones are put into square brackets.
/n/   Phonemes are put into slashes.
a^h Aspiration a^w Labialization
a^n Weak articulation of /n/ a^γ Velarization
ã   Nasalization / Circumflex in Greek words

Miscellaneous		**Languages**		**Symbols**	
A	Analogy	Skr.	Sanskrit	*word	Reconstructed preform
OL	Old Latin	Eng.	Englisch	word*	Expected regular form
ER	External reconstruction	Gr.	Greek	ˣword	Non-existent word
EL	Early Latin	Hit.	Hittite	>	Derivational operator
IE	Indo-European	It.	Italian	::	Comparing operator
IPA	International Phonetic	Ital.	Italic	#	Word boundary
	Alphabet	Lat.	Latin	{...}	Graphematic notation
inf.	infinitive	Rom.	Romance	.	Syllable boundary
CL	Classical Latin	Sab.	Sabellic	(4.9)	Sound change number
SC	Sound change	Sp.	Spanish	?	Unsure form/derivation/rule
SCN	Sound change number	Umb.	Umbrian	/	SCN - environment
MA	Mediae Aspiratae	PIE	Proto-Indo-	_	Position of a sound in the SC
PIT	Proto-Italic		European		environment
perf.	perfect tense	PSab.	Proto-Sabellic	-	Morphological separation
PPP	Perfect passive			e...i	The sounds /e/ and /i/ are
	participle				separated by further sounds.
prs.	present tense			~	corresponds not exactly to
L	Line				

Beiträge zur Iranistik

Ed. by Georges Redard, ab Band 15 von Nicholas Sims-Williams

Vol. 38 From Old to New Persian
Collected Essays

By Bo Utas
Ed. by Carina Jahani and Mehrdad Fallahzadeh

2013. 8°. 304 pp., 1 s/w-Abb., cl. (978-3-89500-970-9)

In a long series of essays, written during almost half a century, Bo Utas analyses the development of West Irani-an languages, particularly Old, Middle, and New Persian, from various perspectives. The focus is placed on the transition from Middle to New Persian and the final essays (hitherto partly unpublished) especially elucidate this process in the light of an interaction between oral and written language.

Vol. 37 The Gorani language of Zarda, a village of West Iran
Texts, grammar, and lexicon

By Parvin Mahmoudveysi and Denise Bailey

2013. 8°. 240 pp., cl. (978-3-89500-952-5)

This volume presents the documentation and description of an endangered variety of the Gorani language as spoken in Zarda, a village located near Sar Pol-e Zahab and Kerend in Kermanshah province, western Iran. The volume contains background information about the village and society, eight texts with English translations, an interlinear morphemic glossed text, and a grammatical description and lexicon based on the material in the texts. Audio recordings of the texts are included on a CD.

Vol. 36 Grammaire juhuri, ou judéo-tat, langue iranienne des Juifs du Caucase de l'est

By Gilles Authier

2012. 8°. 336 pp., cl. (978-3-89500-935-8)

Juhuri (Judeo-Tat), the language of the so-called "Mountain Jews" of Daghestan and Azerbaijan, belongs to the Caucasian Tat group of South-Western Iranian. Its Iranian heritage, reflected by noteworthy archaisms, constitutes an important component of the language, but Juhuri has also been under the influence of Turkic and indigenous Caucasian languages since it arrived in the Caucasus more than a millenium ago. Owing to its unique history as the language of an Iranian Jewish community in the Caucasus, Juhuri exhibits many unusual and typologically rather remarkable characteristics. The book, based on written sources complemented by the author's fieldwork, offers a comprehensive description of the language, each feature illustrated by numerous example sentences, and concludes with sample texts and a full glossary.

Vol. 35 The Gorani language of Gawrajū, a village of West Iran
Texts, grammar, and lexicon

By Parvin Mahmoudvsi, Denise Bailey, Ludwig Paul, Geoffrey Haig

2012. 8°. 270 pp., cl., incl. Audio-CD (978-3-89500-855-9)

This book describes an endangered variety of Gorani spoken by an Ahl-i Haqq (Yaresan) community in a village of western Iran, Kermanshah province. It contains a grammatical sketch, transcribed and analysed texts that were recorded in the village, and a lexicon with all words occurring in the text. The book is accompanied by an audio CD with the recordings of all texts.